THE IRON CURTAIN OVER AMERICA

Also read:

THE IRON CURTAIN
OVER AMERICA

By John Beaty

THE DOT CONNECTOR LIBRARY, BOOK 5

CONTENTS

To the mighty company of American soldiers,
sailors, airmen, and marines
whose graves are marked by white crosses
far from home this book is dedicated
with the solemn pledge
that the Christian civilization
of which they were the finest flower
shall not die.

TO THE READER

Many authors of books on the current world scene have been White House confidants, commanders of armies, and others whose authority is indicated by their official or military titles. Such authors need no introduction to the public. A prospective reader is entitled, however, to know something of the background and experience of an unknown or little-known writer who is offering a comprehensive volume on a great and important subject.

In the spring of 1926, the author was selected by the Albert Kahn Foundation to investigate and report on world affairs. Introduced by preliminary correspondence and provided with numerous letters of introduction to persons prominent in government, politics, and education, he gained something more than a tourist's reaction to the culture and institutions, the movements and the pressures in the twenty-nine countries which he visited. In several countries, including great powers, he found conditions and attitudes significantly different from the conception of them which prevailed in the United States. Though previously successful in disposing of his writings, he was unable, however, to get his observations on the world situation published, except as the Annual Report of the Foundation and in his friendly home state of Texas – in the *Dallas Morning News*, of which he was a special foreign correspondent, and in the *Southwest Review*, in whose files his "Race and Population, Their Relation to World Peace" can still be seen as a virtual prognosis of the oncoming war.

After his return to America in the autumn of 1927, the author kept abreast of world attitudes by correspondence with many of the friends he had made in his travels and by reading French, German, and Italian news periodicals, as well as certain English language periodicals emanating from Asia. World trends continued to run counter to what the American people were allowed to know, and a form of virtual censorship blacked out efforts at imparting information. For instance, though the author's textbooks continued to sell well and though his novel *Swords in the Dawn* (1937) was favorably received, his book *Image of Life* (Thomas Nelson and Sons, 1940), which attempted to show Americans the grave world-wide significance of the degradation of their cultural standards, was granted, as far as he knows, not a single comment in a book review or a book column in New York. Indeed, the book review periodical with the best reputation for full coverage failed to list *Image of Life* even under "Books Received."

In 1940 – as our President was feverishly and secretly preparing to enter World War II and publicly denying any such purpose – the author, a reserve captain, was "alerted," and in 1941 was called to active duty in the Military Intelligence Service of the War Department General Staff. His first assignment was to write, or help write, short pamphlets on military subjects, studies of several campaigns including those in Western Europe and Norway, and three bulletins on the frustration of an enemy's attempts at sabotage and subversion.

In 1942, the author became a major and Chief of the Historical Section (not the later Historical Branch of the War Department Special Staff). In his new capacity, he supervised a group of experts who prepared a current history of events in the various strategically important areas of the world. Also, he was one of the two editors of the daily secret "G-2 Report," which was issued each noon to give persons in high places, including the White House, the world picture as it existed four hours earlier. While Chief of the Historical Section, the author wrote three widely circulated studies of certain phases of the German-Russian campaign.

In 1943 – during which year he was also detailed to the General Staff Corps and promoted to lieutenant colonel – the author was made Chief of the Interview Section. In the next three years he interviewed more than two thousand persons, most of whom were returning from some high mission, some delicate assignment, or some deed of valor – often in a little-known region of the world. Those interviewed included military personnel in rank from private first class to four stars, diplomatic officials from vice-consuls to ambassadors and special representatives of the President, senators and congressmen returning from overseas investigations, missionaries, explorers, businessmen, refugees, and journalists – among the latter, Raymond Clapper and Ernie Pyle, who were interviewed between their next to the last and their last and fatal voyages. These significant people were presented sometimes individually, but usually to assembled groups of officers and other experts from the various branches of G-2, from other General Staff divisions, from each of the technical services, and from other components interested in vital information which could be had by interview perhaps six weeks before being received in channelled reports. In some cases the author increased his knowledge of a given area or topic by consulting documents suggested during an interview. Thus, from those he interviewed, from those specialists for whom he arranged the interviews, and from study in which he had expert guidance, he had a unique opportunity for learning the history, resources, ideologies, capabilities, and intentions of the great foreign powers. In its most essential aspects, the picture was terrifyingly different from the picture presented by our government to the American people!

After the active phase of the war was over, the author was offered three separate opportunities of further service with the army – all of them interesting, all of them flattering. He wished, however, to return to his home and his university and to prepare himself for trying again to give the American people the world story as he had come to know it; consequently, after being advanced to the rank of colonel, he reverted to inactive status, upon his own request, in December, 1946. Twice thereafter he was recalled for a summer of active duty: in 1947 he wrote a short history of the Military Intelligence Service, and in 1949 he prepared for the Army Field Forces an annotated reading list for officers in the Military Intelligence Reserve.

From 1946 to 1951 the author devoted himself to extending his knowledge of the apparently diverse but actually interrelated events in the various strategic areas of the present-day world. The goal he set for himself was not merely to uncover the facts but to present them with such a body of documented proof that their validity could not be questioned. Sustaining quotations for significant truths have thus been taken from standard works of reference; from accepted historical writings; from government documents; from periodicals of wide public acceptance or of known accuracy in fields related to America's foreign policy; and from contemporary writers and speakers of unquestioned standing.

The final product of a long period of travel, army service, and study is *The Iron Curtain Over America*. The book is neither memoirs nor apology, but an objective presentation of "things as they are." It differs from many other pro-American books principally in that it not only exhibits the external and internal dangers which threaten the survival of our country, but shows how they developed and why they continue to plague us.

The roads we "travel so briskly lead out of dim antiquity," said General James G. Harbord, and we must study the past "because of its bearing on the living present" and because it is our only guide for the future. The author has thus turned on the light in certain darkened or dimmed out yet tremendously significant phases of the history of medieval and modern Europe. Since much compression was obligatory, and since many of the facts will to most readers be wholly new and disturbing, Chapters I and II may be described as "hard reading." Even a rapid perusal of them, however, will prepare the reader for understanding better the problems of our country as they are revealed in succeeding chapters.

In *The Iron Curtain Over America* authorities are cited not in a bibliography or in notes but along with the text to which they are pertinent. The documentary matter is enclosed by parentheses, and many readers will pass over it. It is there, however, for those who wish its assurance of validity, for those who wish to locate and examine the context of quoted material, and especially for those who wish to use this book as a springboard for further study.

In assembling and documenting his material, the author followed Shakespeare's injunction, "nothing extenuate, nor set down aught in malice" [*Othello*, Act 5, Scene 2. – *Ed.*]. Writing with no goal except to serve his country by telling the truth, fully substantiated, he has humbly and reverently taken as his motto, or text, a promise of Christ the Saviour as recorded in the *Gospel According to Saint John* (VIII, 32):

AND YE SHALL KNOW THE TRUTH,
AND THE TRUTH SHALL MAKE YOU FREE.

Only an informed American people can save America – and *they can save it only if all those, to whom it is given to know, will share their knowledge with others.*

CHAPTER I

THE TEUTONIC KNIGHTS AND GERMANY

For more than a thousand years a fundamental problem of Europe – the source, seat, and historic guardian of Western civilization – has been to save itself and its ideals from destruction by some temporary master of the men and resources of Asia. This statement implies no criticism of the peoples of Asia, for Europe and America have likewise produced leaders whose armies have invaded other continents.

Since the fall of the Roman Empire of the West in 476 A.D., a principal weakness of Western Europe has been a continuing lack of unity. Charlemagne (742-814) – who was crowned Emperor of the West in Rome in 800 – gave the post-Roman European world a generation of unity, and exerted influence even as far as Jerusalem, where he secured the protection of Christian pilgrims to the shrines associated with the birth, the ministry, and the crucifixion of Christ. Unfortunately, Charlemagne's empire was divided shortly after his death into three parts (Treaty of Verdun, 843). From two of these France and Germany derived historic boundaries – and a millennium of wars fought largely to change them!

After Charlemagne's time, the first significant power efforts with a continent-wide common purpose were the Crusades (1096-1291). In medieval Europe the Church of Rome, the only existing international organization, had some of the characteristics of a league of nations, and it sponsored these mass movements of Western Europeans toward the East. In fact, it was Pope Urban II, whose great speech at Clermont, France, on November 26, 1095, initiated the surge of feeling which inspired the people of France, and of Europe in general, for the amazing adventure. The late medieval setting of the epochal speech is recreated with brilliant detail by Harold Lamb in his book, *The Crusades: Iron Men and Saints* (Doubleday, Doran & Co., Inc., Garden City, New York, 1930, Chapters VI and VII).

The Pope crossed the Alps from schism-torn Italy and, Frenchman himself, stirred the people of France as he rode among them. In the chapel at Clermont, he first swayed the men of the church who had answered his summons to the meeting; then, surrounded by cardinals and mail-clad knights on a golden-canopied platform in a field by the church, he addressed the multitude:

> You are girded knights, but you are arrogant with pride. You turn upon your brothers with fury, cutting down one the other. Is this the service of Christ?... Come forward to the defense of Christ.

The great Pope gave his eager audience some pertinent and inspiring texts from the recorded words of Jesus Christ:

> For where two or three are gathered together in my name, there am I in the midst of them (*The Gospel According to Saint Matthew*, Chapter XVIII, Verse 20).
>
> And every one that hath forsaken houses, or brethren, or sisters, or father, or mother, or wife, or children, or lands, for my name's sake, shall receive a hundredfold, and shall inherit everlasting life (*Saint Matthew*, Chapter XIX, Verse 29).

To the words of the Saviour, the Pope added his own specific promise:

> Set forth then upon the way to the Holy Sepulcher ... and fear not. Your possessions here will be safeguarded, and you will despoil the enemy of greater treasures. Do not fear death, where Christ laid down His life for you. If any should lose their lives, even on the way thither, by sea or land, or in strife with the pagans, their sins will be requited them. I grant this to all who go, by the power vested in me by God (Harold Lamb, *op. cit.*, p. 42).

Through the long winter, men scanned their supplies, hammered out weapons and armor, and dreamed dreams of their holy mission. In the summer that followed, they "started out on what they called the voyage of God" (Harold Lamb, *op. cit.,* p. vii). As they faced East they shouted on plains and in mountain valleys, "God wills it!"

Back of the Crusades there was a "mixture of motives" (*Encyclopædia Britannica*, Fourteenth Edition, Vol. VI, p. 773). The immediate goal of those who made the journey was the rescue of the tomb of Christ from the non-Christian power which then dominated Palestine. Each knight wore a cross on his outer garment, and they called themselves by a Latin name *Cruciati* (from *crux*, cross), or soldiers of the cross, which is translated into English as Crusaders. A probable ecclesiastical objective of the great international effort was to purify the Church of Rome from the dissension which plagued it and to extend its influence not only in the Moslem world but in areas dominated by the Byzantine Empire with its Orthodox church. Other objectives were the containment of Mohammedan power and the protection of pilgrims to the Holy Land (*Encyc. Brit.,* Vol. VI, p. 722).

Inspired by the promise of an eternal home in heaven, alike for those who might perish on the way and those who might reach the Holy Sepulcher, the Crusaders could not fail. Some of them survived the multiple perils of the journey and reached Palestine, where they captured the Holy City and founded the Latin Kingdom of Jerusalem (1099). In this land, which they popularly called Outremer, or Beyond The Sea, they established the means of livelihood, built churches, and saw children and grandchildren born. The Latin Kingdom's weaknesses, vicissitudes, and final destruction by the warriors of Islam, who had been driven back but not destroyed, constitute a vivid chapter of history – alien, however, to the subject matter of *The Iron Curtain Over America.*

Many of the Crusaders became members of three military-religious orders. Unlike the Latin Kingdom, these orders have survived, in one form or another, the epoch of the great adventure, and are of significant interest in the middle of the twentieth century. The Knights Hospitalers – or by their longer title, the Knights of the Order of the Hospital of St. John of Jerusalem – were "instituted" upon an older charitable foundation by Pope Paschal II in 1113 (*Encyc. Brit.,* Vol. XIX, pp. 836-838). The fraternity of the Knights Templars (Poor Knights of Christ and of the Temple of Solomon) was founded not as a Hospital but directly as a military order about 1119, and was installed by Baldwin I, King of Jerusalem, in a building known as the "Temple of Solomon" – hence the name Templars (*Encyc. Brit.,* Vol. XXI, pp. 920-924). Both Hospitalers and Templars are fairly well known to those who have read such historical novels as *The Talisman* by Sir Walter Scott.

The Latin Kingdom of Jerusalem maintained its rule for nearly a hundred years, 1099-1187 (see Lamb, *op. cit.,* and *The Crusade: The World's Debate,* by Hilaire Belloc, Cassell and Company, Ltd., London, 1937). Still longer the Crusaders held Acre on the coast of Palestine.

When their position on the mainland became untenable, the Templars moved to the island of Cyprus, which was the seat of its Grand Master at the time of its dissolution (1306-1312) as an international military brotherhood. The Hospitalers moved to the island of Rhodes, where their headquarters buildings – visited and studied by the author – still stand in superb preservation facing the waters of the Inland Sea. From Rhodes, the Knights of the Hospital moved to Malta – hence their later name, Knights of Malta –and held sovereignty on that famous island until 1798. The two principal Mediterranean orders and their history, including the assumption of some of their defense functions by Venice and then by Britain, do not further concern us. It is interesting to note, however, as we take leave of the Templars and the Hospitalers, that the three Chivalric Orders of Crusaders are in some cases the direct ancestors and in other cases have afforded the inspiration, including the terminology of knighthood, for many of the important present-day social, fraternal, and philanthropic orders of Europe and America. Among these are the Knights Templar, which is "claimed to be a lineal descendant" of the Crusade order of similar name; the Knights of Pythias, founded in 1864; and the Knights of Columbus, founded in 1882 (quotation and dates from Webster's *New International Dictionary,* Second Edition, 1934, p. 1370).

The third body of medieval military-religious Crusaders was the Knighthood of the Teutonic Order. This organization was founded as a hospital in the winter of 1190-91 – according to tradition, on a small ship which had been pulled ashore near Acre. Its services came to be so highly regarded that in March, 1198, "the great men of the army and the [Latin] Kingdom raised the brethren of the German Hospital of St. Mary to the rank of an Order of Knights" (*Encyc. Brit.,* Vol. XXI, pp. 983-984). Soon, however, the Order found that "its true work lay on the Eastern frontiers of Germany" (*Encyc. Brit.,* Vol. XXI, p. 984).

Invited by a Christian Polish Prince (1226) to help against the still unconverted Prussians, a body of knights sailed down the Vistula establishing blockhouses and pushed eastward to found Koenigsburg in 1255. In 1274, a castle was established at Marienburg and in 1309 the headquarters of the Grand Master was transferred (*Encyc. Brit.,* Vol. XIV, p. 886) from Venice to this remote border city on the Nojat River, an eastern outlet of the Vistula (*The Rise of Brandenburg-Prussia to 1786,* by Sidney Bradshaw Fay, Henry Holt and Company, New York, 1937).

It was to the Teutonic Order that the Knight of Chaucer's famous *Canterbury Tales* belonged (*Selections from Chaucer,* edited by Clarence Griffin Child, D. C. Heath & Co., Boston, 1912, p. 150). Chaucer's lines (*Prologue to the Canterbury Tales,* ll., 52-53):

> Ful ofte tyme he hadde the bord bigonne
> Aboven alle naciouns in Pruce

tell us that this Knight occupied the seat of Grand Master, presumably at the capital, Marienburg, and presided over Knights from the various nations assembled in "Pruce" (Prussia) to hold the pagan East at bay. In his military-religious capacity, Chaucer's Knight "fought for our faith" in fifteen battles, including those in Lithuania and in Russia (*Prologue,* ll., 54-63).

The Teutonic Knights soon drove eastward, or converted to Christianity, the sparsely settled native Prussian people, and assumed sovereignty over East Prussia. They encouraged the immigration of German families of farmers and artisans, and their domain on the south shore of the Baltic became a self-contained German state, outside the Holy Roman Empire. The boundaries varied, at one time reaching the Gulf of Finland (see *Historical Atlas,* by William R. Shepherd, Henry Holt and Company, New York, 1911, maps 77, 79, 87, 99, 119). "The hundred years from 1309 to 1409 were the Golden Age of the Teutonic Knights. Young nobles from all over Europe found no greater honor than to come out and fight under their banner and be knighted by their Grand Master" (Fay, *op. cit.,* pp. 32-33). As the years passed, the function of the Teutonic Knights as defenders, or potential defenders, of the Christian West remained unchanged.

Those who founded the Teutonic Order on the hospital ship in Palestine spoke German and from the beginning most of the members were from the various small states into which in medieval times the German people were divided. As the Crusading spirit waned in Europe, fewer Knights were drawn from far-off lands and a correspondingly larger number were recruited from nearby German kingdoms, duchies, and other autonomies.

Meanwhile, to Brandenburg, a neighbor state to the west of the Teutonic Order domain, the Emperor Sigismund sent as ruler Frederick of Hohenzollern and five years later made him hereditary elector. "A new era of prosperity, good government, and princely power began with the arrival of the Hohenzollerns in Brandenburg in the summer of 1412" (Fay, *op. cit.*, pp. 7-9).

After its Golden Age, the Teutonic Order suffered from a lack of religious motivation, since all nearby peoples including the Lithuanians had been converted. It suffered, too, from poor administration and from military reverses. To strengthen their position, especially against Poland, the Knights elected Albert of Hohenzollern, a cousin of the contemporary elector Joachim I (rule, 1499-1535), as Grand Master in 1511. Unlike Chaucer's Knight, a lay member who was the father of a promising son, Albert was a clerical member of the Teutonic Order. He and his elector cousin were both great grandsons of Frederick, the first Hohenzollern elector (Fay, *op. cit., passim*).

In most German states in the first quarter of the sixteenth century, "things were not right," "there was discontent deep in men's hearts," and "existing powers," ecclesiastical as well as lay, "abused their trust." The quoted phrases are from an essay, "Luther and the Modern Mind" (*The Catholic World*, October, 1946) by Dr. Thomas P. Neill, who continues: "This was the stage on which Luther appeared when he nailed his ninety-five theses to the church door at Wittenberg on Hallowe'en of 1517. The Catholic Church had come on sorry days, and had there been no Luther there would likely have been a successful revolt anyway. But there was a Luther."

The posting of the famous "ninety-five theses" by Martin Luther foreshadowed his break, complete and final by the spring of 1522, with the Church of Rome. Since the church in Germany was temporarily at a low ebb, as shown by Dr. Neill, Luther's controversy with its authorities won him "the sympathy and support of a large proportion of his countrymen" (*Encyc. Brit.*, Vol. XIV, p. 944).

The outcome was a new form of Christianity, known later as Protestantism, which made quick headway among North Germans and East Germans. Its adherents included many Teutonic Knights, and their German chief was interested. Still nominally a follower of the Church of Rome, Albert visited Luther at Wittenberg in 1523. "Luther advised: 'Give up your vow as a monk; take a wife; abolish the order; and make yourself hereditary Duke of Prussia'" (Fay, *op. cit.*, p. 38). The advice was taken.

Thus since a large proportion of its members and its chief had embraced Protestantism, the Knighthood severed its slender tie with the Church of Rome. In the words of the *Encyclopædia Britannica* (Vol. I, p. 522), "Albert of Hohenzollern, last Grand Master of the Teutonic Order" became "first Duke of Prussia."

In this manner the honorable and historic heritage of extending Christianity in the lands south of the Baltic passed from a military-religious order to a Germany duchy. Prussia and not the Teutonic Order now governed the strategically vital shoreland of the southeast Baltic, between the Niemen and Vital shore land of the southeast Baltic, between the Niemen and Vistula rivers.

Proud of their origin as a charitable organization and proud of being a bulwark of Christianity, first Catholic and then Protestant, the people of Prussia, many of them descended from the lay knights, developed a "strong sense of duty and loyalty." From them came also "many of the generals and statesmen who helped to make Prussia great..." (Fay, *op. cit.*, p. 2).

This duchy of Prussia was united with Brandenburg in 1618 by the marriage of Anna, daughter and heiress of the second Duke of

Prussia, to the elector, John Sigismund (Hohenzollern). Under the latter's grandson, Frederick William, the "Great Elector" (reign, 1640-1688), Brandenburg-Prussia became second only to Austria among the member states of the Holy Roman Empire – some of its territory, acquired from the Teutonic Order, extending even beyond the loose confederation – and it was "regarded as the head of German protestantism" (*Encyc. Brit.*, Vol. IV, p. 33 and *passim*).

By an edict of the Holy Roman Emperor, the state of Brandenburg-Prussia became the kingdom of Prussia in 1701; the royal capital was Berlin, which was in the heart of the old province of Brandenburg. Under Frederick the Great (reign, 1740-1786), Prussia became one of the most highly developed nations of Europe. A century later, it was the principal component of the German Empire which the Minister-President of Prussia, Otto von Bismarck, caused to be proclaimed in the Hall of Mirrors at Versailles (January 18, 1871).

Prussia's historic function, inherited from the Teutonic Order, of standing as a bastion on the Baltic approach to Europe, was never fully forgotten by the West. The Hohenzollern monarchy was the strongest Protestant power on the continent and its relations with the governments of both England and America were intimate and friendly. The royal family of England several times married into the Prussian dynasty. Frederick William II of Brandenburg-Prussia, later to be Frederick, first king of Prussia (see preceding paragraph) helped William of Orange, the archenemy of Louis XIV of France, to land in England, where he became (1688) co-sovereign with his wife, Mary Stuart, and a friend and helper of the American colonies. It was a Prussian Baron, Frederick William von Steuben, whom General George Washington made Inspector General (May, 1778), responsible for the training and discipline of the green American troops. In 1815 Prussian troops under Field Marshal von Bluecher helped save Wellington's England from Napoleon. In 1902 Prince Henry of Prussia, brother of the German Emperor, paid a state visit to the United States and received at West Point, Annapolis, Washington, and elsewhere, as royal a welcome as was ever accorded to a foreign visitor by the government of the United States. The statue of Frederick the Great, presented in appreciation, stood in front of the main building of the Army War College in Washington during two wars between the countrymen of Frederick of Hohenzollern and the countrymen of George Washington, an evidence in bronze of the old Western view that fundamental relationships between peoples should survive the temporary disturbances occasioned by wars.

The friendly relationships between the United States and Germany existed not only on the governmental level but were cemented by close racial kinship. Not only is the basic blood stream of persons of English descent very nearly identical with that of Germans; in addition, nearly a fourth of the Americans of the early twentieth century were actually of German descent (Chapter IV, below).

Thus, in the early years of the twentieth century the American people admired Germany. It was a strong nation, closely akin; and it was a Christian land, part Protestant and part Catholic, as America had been part Catholic since Lord Baltimore founded Maryland and part Protestant since the Cavaliers came to Virginia and the Puritans to New England. Moreover, the old land of the Teutonic Knights led the world in music, in medicine, and in scholarship. The terms *Prussia* and *Prussian*, *Germany* and *German* had a most favorable connotation.

Then came World War I (1914), in which Britain and France and their allies were opposed to Germany and her allies. Since the citizens of the United States admired all three nations they were stunned at the calamity of such a conflict and were slow in taking sides. Finally (1917), and to some extent because of the pressure of American Zionists (Chapter III, below), we joined the Entente group, which included Britain and France. The burden of a great war was accepted by the people, even with some enthusiasm on the Atlantic seaboard, for according to our propagandists it was a war to end all wars. It was pointed out, too, that Britain among the world's great nations was closest to us in language and culture, and that France had been traditionally a friend since the Marquis of Lafayette and the Count of Rochambeau aided General Washington.

With a courage fanned by the newly perfected science of propaganda, the American people threw themselves heart and soul into defeating Germany in the great "war to end all wars." The blood-spilling – the greatest in all history and between men of kindred race – was ended by an armistice on November 11, 1918, and the American people entertained high hopes for lasting peace. Their hopes, however, were soon to fade away. With differing viewpoints, national and personal, and with the shackles of suddenly revealed secret agreements between co-belligerents, President Woodrow Wilson, Prime Minister David Lloyd George, Premier Georges Clemenceau of France, and Prime Minister Vittorio Orlando of Italy had much difficulty in agreeing on the terms of peace treaties (1919), the merits or shortcomings of which cannot in consequence be fully chalked up to any one of them.

It remains indisputable, however, that in what they agreed to in the treaty made with Germany at Versailles (June 28, 1919) and in the treaty made with Austria at St. Germain (September 10, 1919) the four American delegates, dominated by President Wilson, departed at least to some extent from our tradition of humane treatment of a defeated enemy. The heavily populated German nation was deprived of much territory, including vital mineral areas and a "Polish Corridor" which, under the terms of the treaty, separated the original duchy of Prussia from the rest of the country. Germany was deprived also of its merchant fleet and was saddled with an impossible load of reparations. As a consequence, the defeated country was left in a precarious position which soon produced an economic collapse. The Austro-Hungarian Empire, ancient outpost of the Teutonic peoples and of Western Christian civilization on the Danube Valley invasion route from Asia, was destroyed at St. Germain. The result was the serious general economic dislocation to be expected from the collapse of an imperial government, and the inevitable dire distress to the people, especially in the capital city of Vienna (population over 2,000,000), which was left with little sustaining territory, except scenic and historic mountains. Moreover, although Austro-Hungary was broken up under the theory that its people should be put into small pigeon-hole nations on racial and linguistic considerations, the new Czechoslovak state was given 3,500,000 persons of German blood and speech.

In this treatment of Germany and Austria our leaders not merely set up conditions conducive to the extreme distress of millions of people; they also by those same conditions flouted the recognized principles of sound military and national policy, for the strategic use of victory demands that the late enemy be drawn into the victor's orbit as friend and ally. As one example of the strategic use of victory, our War of 1812, with Britain, was followed by an earnest bilateral effort at the solution of mutual problems by the Monroe Doctrine (1823) in the field of international relations, and by the crumbling of unused forts on the U.S.-Canadian border. As a second example, Britain's war with South Africa, which ended in 1902, was followed by such humanity and fairness that a defeated people, different in speech and culture, became an ally instead of an enemy in the great war which began only twelve years later in 1914.

The crash in Germany came in 1923, when German money lost its value. There was terrible suffering among the people everywhere and especially in the cities and industrial areas. As the mark's purchasing power approached zero, a widow would realize from her husband's life insurance "just enough to buy a meal" ("Inflation Concerns Everyone," by Samuel B. Pettengill, *Readers Digest*, October, 1951). "Berlin in 1923 was a city of despair. People waited in the alley behind the Hotel Adlon ready to pounce on garbage cans immediately they were placed outside the hotel's kitchen." A cup of coffee "cost one million marks one day, a million and a half the next and two million the day following" (Drew Pearson, March 22, 1951).

In hunger and desperation, many Germans blamed their troubles on Jews, whom they identified with Communism. "The fact that certain Jews, such as Kurt Eisner, Toller, and Levine, had been leaders of Communist Movements [1918, 1919] ... gave the conservatives the opportunity of proclaiming that the Jews were responsible for the national misfortunes and disorders" (*Universal Jewish Encyclopedia*, Vol. I, pp. 366, 367). The German attitude was intensified by the new power German Jews acquired in the terrible year 1923 from using funds derived from rich race-conscious Jews in other countries and by an inrush of Jews from the destroyed Austro-Hungarian Empire and from the East. "Some of those Eastern European Jews took an active part in the speculation, which was rampant in Germany because of the unstable currency and the shortage of commodities" (*America's Second Crusade*, by William Henry Chamberlin, Henry Regnery Company, 1950, pp. 30, 31). The influx from the East had also the effect of reviving the viewpoint of certain earlier Germans that Jews were not assimilable but were really invaders. "In 1880 the learned but fanatical Professor Treitschke's phrase, 'Die Juden sind unser Unglueck' ['The Jews are our misfortune'], gained currency all through the German empire" (H. Graetz, *Popular History of the Jews*, Vol. VI, by Max Raisin, The Jordan Publishing Co., New York, 1935, p. 162). Also, "according to Grattenauer's *Wider die Juden* (1803), the Jews of Germany were, as early as that period, regarded as 'Asiatic Immigrants' " (*Univ. Jew. Encyc.*, Vol. I, p. 341).

This fateful German-Jewish tension was destined to have a major role in the history of the United States, and will be dealt with further in subsequent chapters.

The immediate result of the events of 1923 was an increase of Jewish power in the Reich. "Bled white" in World War I, like Britain and France, Germany bent to its economic tragedy without significant resistance, but the resentment of the people at being starved and humiliated (as they believed) by a minority of less than one percent smoldered like live coals awaiting almost any fanning into flame. Our usual helping hand – so generously extended in the Japanese earthquake tragedy of 1923 and in other calamities – was withheld, while this small group increased its control (for some idea of the extent of the control by Jews in the city of Berlin five years after Hitler assumed power, see the *Reader's Digest* for May, 1938, p. 126).

After 1919, anti-German propaganda in the United States did not cease, as was strategically desirable, but was continued unremittingly in the press and by the new opinion-controlling medium, the radio. Americans were taught to hate Germany and Germans and to loathe Prussia and Prussians, not any longer as a war-time "psychological" attack, but as a permanent attitude.

The task of the propagandists was made easier by the appearance on the world's stage (1933) of the demagogue Adolf Hitler, whose assumption of the combined offices of Chancellor and President of Germany (Chapter IV, below), under the alien and repugnant title of "Fuehrer," shocked the sensibilities of the American people who were accustomed to a Republican form of government with the still effective checks and balances of the Legislative, Executive, and Judicial branches.

In 1936, Britain was making efforts to establish workable arrangements with Germany. Symbolically, and with much publicity, a thousand German war veterans were entertained in England by a thousand British war veterans. A naval ratio, most favorable to Britain, had been agreed upon. The President of the United States, Franklin D. Roosevelt, had in his first year of office (1933) recognized the Communist government of Russia (Chapter III, below), but was otherwise "isolationist" in his general attitude toward Europe. Then on October 5, 1937, in Chicago, he made an about-face (Chapter IV, below) in his famous "Quarantine" speech against Germany. Though his sudden "fears" had no foundation in facts – as known then or as discovered later – our policy was charted, and England, forced to a decision, became a partner in our anti-German action. With no enthusiasm, such as was generated in 1919, the American people soon found themselves (December, 1941) involved in a second and even more frightful World War against two of our former allies, Japan and Italy, and against our World War I opponent, Germany (see Chapters IV and V, below).

The propagandists against Germany and the German people did not cease, however, with Hitler's defeat and death (1945) and the resultant effacement of his government and his policies. After Hitler, as before Hitler, these propagandists did not allow the American public to realize the strategic fact that a country like an individual needs friends and that a permanent destructive attitude toward a nation because of a former ruler is as stupid, for instance, as a hatred for the people of an American state because of an unpopular ex-governor.

Thus, instead of correcting our error of 1919 and making certain at the end of World War II to draw a properly safeguarded but humanely treated Germany definitely into our orbit, we adopted in 1945 an intensified policy of hate, denied the Germans a peace treaty more than six years after the suspension of active warfare, and took additional steps (Chapters IV, VI, and VII, below) which could have had no other purpose – concealed, of course, even from some of those who furthered it – than the final destruction of Germany.

Woodrow Wilson, despite the terrible and still largely undocumented pressures upon him, had at least preserved Prussia at the close of World War I. Franklin Roosevelt, however, tossed it from his failing hands to the minority (see Chapter II) who, with converts to their Marxist concept of statism, had succeeded the Romanov Czars as masters of Russia. With Malta lost in 1798 and Prussia destroyed in 1945, the temporal state-structures of the Crusaders and their successors ceased to exist.

Under the preaching of Urban II, most of the Western World had developed a frenzy of unity; under Roosevelt II, or rather under those who manipulated him, it did so again. The goal this time, however, was not the defense of Europe or the rescue of the tomb of Christ; the goal, on the contrary, was a monstrous surrender of the Western heritage of Christian civilization. Yes, it was actually the United States of America which was mainly responsible for destroying the successor state to the Teutonic Knights and for delivering the ruins, with the hegemony of Europe, to the Soviet Union, the new Communist power of our creation.

The facts outlined in this chapter have – as will be shown in following chapters – a significant bearing on the present mid-century world struggle between Communism and Western Christian civilization.

RUSSIA AND THE KHAZARS

Having traced the Knighthood of the Teutonic Order from its origin to its dissolution as a military-religious brotherhood, and having noted the development of successor sovereignties down to the obliteration of Prussia in 1945, we must turn back more than a thousand years, to examine another thread – a scarlet one – in the tangled skein of European history.

In the later years of the dimly recorded first millennium of the Christian era, Slavic people of several kindred tribes occupied the land which became known later as the north central portion of European Russia. South of them, between the Don and Volga rivers and north of the lofty Caucasus Mountains lived a people known to history as Khazars (*Ancient Russia,* by George Vernadsky, Yale University Press, 1943, p. 214).

These people had been driven westward from Central Asia and entered Europe by the corridor between the Ural Mountains and the Caspian Sea. They found a land occupied by primitive pastoral people of a score or more of tribes, a land which lay beyond the boundaries of the Roman Empire at its greatest extent under Trajan (ruled, 98-117 A.D.), and also beyond the boundaries of the Byzantine Empire (395-1453). By slow stages the Khazars extended their territory eventually to the Sea of Azov and the adjacent littoral of the Black Sea. The Khazars were apparently a people of mixed stock with Mongol and Turkic affinities. "Around the year 600, a belligerent tribe of half-Mongolian people, similar to the modern Turks, conquered the territory of what is now Southern Russia. Before long the kingdom [khanate] of the Khazars, as this tribe was known, stretched from the Caspian to the Black Sea. Its capital, Ityl, was at the mouth of the Volga River" (*A History of the Jews*, by Solomon Grayzel, Philadelphia, The Jewish Publication Society of America, 1947).

In the eighth or ninth century of our era, a khakan (or chagan, roughly equivalent to tribal chief or primitive king) of the Khazars wanted a religion for his pagan people. Partly, perhaps, because of incipient tension between Christians and the adherents of the new Mohammedan faith (Mohammed died in 632), and partly because of fear of becoming subject to the power of the Byzantine emperor or the Islamic caliph (*Ancient Russia*, p. 291), he adopted a form of the Jewish religion at a date generally placed at c. 741 A.D., but believed by Vernadsky to be as late as 865. According to the *Universal Jewish Encyclopedia* (Vol. VI, pp. 375-377), this chieftain, probably Bulan, "called upon the representatives of Judaism, Christianity and Mohammedanism to expound their doctrines before him. This discussion convinced him that the Jewish faith was the most preferable, and he decided to embrace it. Thereupon he and about 4,000 Khazars were circumcised; it was only by degrees that the Jewish teachings gained a foothold among the population."

In his *History of the Jews* (The Jewish Publication Society of America, Vol. III, 1894, pp. 140-141), Professor H. Graetz gives further details:

> A successor of Bulan, who bore the Hebrew name of Obadiah, was the first to make serious efforts to further the Jewish religion. He invited Jewish sages to settle in his dominions, rewarded them royally, founded synagogues and schools ... caused instruction to

be given to himself and his people in the Bible and the Talmud, and introduced a divine service modeled on the ancient communities. After Obadiah came a long series of Jewish chagans, for according to a fundamental law of the state only Jewish rulers were permitted to ascend the throne.

The significance of the term "ancient communities" cannot be here explained. For a suggestion of the "incorrect exposition" and the "tasteless misrepresentations" with which the Bible, i.e., the Old Testament, was presented through the Talmud, see below, in this chapter, the extensive quotation from Professor Graetz.

Also in the Middle Ages, Viking warriors, according to Russian tradition by invitation, pushed from the Baltic area into the low hills west of Moscow. Archaeological discoveries show that at one time or another these Northmen penetrated almost all areas south of Lake Ladoga and West of the Kama and Lower Volga rivers. Their earliest, and permanent, settlements were north and east of the West Dwina River, in the Lake Ilmen area, and between the Upper Volga and Oka rivers, at whose junction they soon held the famous trading-post of Nizhni-Novgorod (*Ancient Russia*, p. 267).

These immigrants from the North and West were principally "the 'Russ' – a Varangian tribe in ancient annals considered as related to the Swedes, Angles, and Northmen" (*Encyclopædia Britannica*, Vol. XIX, p. 712). From the local Slavic tribes, they organized (c. 862) a state, known subsequently from their name as Russia, which embraced the territory of the upper Volga and Dnieper rivers and reached down the latter river to the Black Sea (*An Introduction to Old Norse*, by E. V. Gordon, Oxford University Press, 1927, map between pp. xxiv-xxv) and to the Crimea. Russ and Slav were of related stock, and their languages, though quite different, had common Indo-Germanic origin. They accepted Christianity as their religion. "Greek Orthodox missionaries, sent to Rus [i.e., "Russia"] in the 860's baptized so many people that

Rus vs. Slavs (handwritten)

shortly after this a special bishop was sent to care for their needs"
(*A History of the Ukraine,* by Michael Hrushevsky, Yale University
Press, 1941, p. 65).

The "Rus" (or "Russ") were absorbed into the Slav population
which they organized into statehood. The people of the new state
devoted themselves energetically to consolidating their territory
and extending its boundaries. From the Khazars, who had extended
their power up the Dnieper Valley, they took Kiev, which "was
an important trading center even before becoming, in the 10th
cent., the capital of a large recently Christianized state" (*Universal
Jewish Encyclopedia,* Vol. VI, p. 381). Many Varangians (Rus) had
settled among the Slavs in this area (the Ukraine), and Christian
Kiev became the seat of an enlightened Westward-looking dynasty,
whose members married into several European royal houses,
including that of France. *Seat of Enlightenment* (handwritten)

The Slavs, especially those in the area now known as the Ukraine,
were engaged in almost constant warfare with the Khazars and
finally, by 1016 A.D., destroyed the Khazar government and took a
large portion of Khazar territory. For the gradual shrinking of the
Khazar territory and the development of Poland, Lithuania, the
Grand Duchy of Moscow, and other Slavic states, see the pertinent
maps in *Historical Atlas,* by William R. Shepherd (Henry Holt
and Company, New York, 1911). Some of the subjugated Khazars
remained in the Slav-held lands their khakans had long ruled, and
others "migrated to Kiev and other parts of Russia" (*Universal
Jewish Encyclopedia,* Vol. VI, p. 377), probably to a considerable
extent because of the dislocations wrought by the Mongols under
Genghis Khan (1162-1227), who founded in and beyond the old
Khazar khanate the short-lived khanate of the Golden Horde. The
Judaized Khazars underwent further dispersion both northwest-
ward into Lithuanian and Polish areas, and also within Russia
proper and the Ukraine. In 1240 in Kiev "the Jewish community
was uprooted, its surviving members finding refuge in towns

34

further west" (*Univ. Jew. Encyc.,* Vol. VI, p. 382) along with the fleeing Russians, when the capital fell to the Mongol soldiers of Batu, the nephew of Genghis Khan. A short time later many of these expelled Jews returned to Kiev. Migrating thus, as some local power impelled them, the Khazar Jews became widely distributed in Western Russia. Into the Khazar khanate there had been a few Jewish immigrants – rabbis, traders, refugees – but the people of the Kievan Russian state did not facilitate the entry of additional Jews into their territory. The rulers of the Grand Duchy of Moscow also sought to exclude Jews from areas under its control. "From its earliest times the policy of the Russian government was that of complete exclusion of the Jews from its territories" (*Univ. Jew. Encyc.,* Vol. I, p. 384). For instance, "Ivan IV [reign, 1533-1584] refused to allow Jewish merchants to travel in Russia" (*op. cit.,* Vol. I, p. 384).

Relations between Slavs and the Judaized Khazars in their midst were never happy. The reasons were not racial – for the Slavs had absorbed many minorities – but ideological. The rabbis sent for by Khakan Obadiah were educated in and were zealots for the Babylonian Talmud, which after long labors by many hands had been completed on December 2, 499. In the thousands of synagogues which were built in the Khazar khanate, the imported rabbis and their successors were in complete control of the political, social, and religious thought of their people. So significant was the Babylonian Talmud as the principal cause of Khazar resistance to Russian efforts to end their political and religious separatism, and so significant also are the modern sequels, including those in the United States, that an extensive quotation on the subject from the great *History of the Jews,* by Professor H. Graetz (Vol. II, 1893, pp. 631 ff.), is here presented:

> The Talmud must not be regarded as an ordinary work, composed of twelve volumes; it possesses absolutely no similarity to any

other literary production, but forms, without any figure of speech, a world of its own, which must be judged by its peculiar laws...

The Talmud contains much that is frivolous of which it treats with great gravity and seriousness; it further reflects the various superstitious practices and views of its Persian birthplace which presume the efficacy of demonical medicines, of magic, incantations, miraculous cures, and interpretations of dreams... It also contains isolated instances of uncharitable judgments and decrees against the members of other nations and religions, and finally it favors an incorrect exposition of the scriptures, accepting, as it does, tasteless misrepresentations.

More than six centuries lie petrified in the Talmud... Small wonder then, that ... the sublime and the common, the great and the small, the grave and the ridiculous, the altar and the ashes, the Jewish and the heathenish, be discovered side by side...

The Babylonian Talmud is especially distinguished from the Jerusalem or Palestine Talmud by the flights of thought, the penetration of mind, the flashes of genius, which rise and vanish again... It was for this reason that the Babylonian rather than the Jerusalem Talmud became the fundamental possession of the Jewish race, its life breath, its very soul ... nature and mankind, powers and events, were for the Jewish nation insignificant, non-essential, a mere phantom; the only true reality was the Talmud.

Not merely educated by the Talmud but actually living the life of its Babylonian background, which they may have regarded with increased devotion because most of the Jews of Mesopotamia had embraced Islam, the rabbi-governed Khazars had no intention whatever of losing their identity by becoming Russianized or Christian. The intransigent attitude of the rabbis was increased by their realization that their power would be lost if their people accepted controls other than Talmudic. These controls by rabbis were responsible not only for basic mores, but for such externals as the peculiarities of dress and hair. It has been frequently stated by writers on the subject that the "ghetto" was the work not of Russians or other Slavs but of rabbis.

As time passed, it came about that these Khazar people of mixed non-Russian stock, who hated the Russians and lived under Babylonian Talmudic law, became known in the western world, from their place of residence and their legal-religious code, as Russian Jews.

In Russian lands after the fall of Kiev in 1240, there was a period of dissension and disunity. The struggle with the Mongols and other Asiatic khanates continued and from them the Russians learned much about effective military organization. Also, as the Mongols had not overrun Northern and Western Russia (Shepherd, *op. cit.,* Map 77), there was a background for the resistance and counter-offensive which gradually eliminated the invaders. The capital of reorganized Russia was no longer Kiev but Moscow (hence the terms Muscovy and Muscovite). In 1613, the Russian nobles (boyars) desired a more stable government than they had had and elected as their czar a boy named Michael Romanov, whose veins carried the blood of the grand dukes of Kiev and the grand dukes of Moscow.

Under the Romanovs of the seventeenth and eighteenth centuries, there was no change in attitude toward the Judaized Khazars, who scorned Russian civilization and stubbornly refused to enter the fold of Christianity. "Peter the Great [reign, 1682-1725] spoke of the Jews as 'rogues and cheats' " (*Popular History of the Jews,* by H. Graetz, New York, The Jordan Publishing Co., 1919, 1935, Vol. VI, by Max Raisin, p. 89). "Elizabeth [reign, 1741-1762] expressed her attitude in the sentence: 'From the enemies of Christ, I desire neither gain nor profit' " (*Univ. Jew. Encyc.,* Vol. I, p. 384). With the expansion of Russia in the last half of the eighteenth century, many additional Jews were acquired with the new territory, especially in Russia's portion of divided Poland (1772, 1793, 1795).

The Empress, Catherine II [reign, 1762-1796] had no choice but to receive the Jews along with the other inhabitants of the land, but she created out of the provinces taken from Poland a "Pale of Settlement" from which the newly acquired Jews could not move (Graetz-Raisin, *op. cit.*, p. 90). As before, "from that time on the attitude of the government was to hem in the Jews as much as possible" (*Univ. Jew. Encyc.*, Vol. I, p. 384).

Under the Romanov dynasty (1613-1917) many members of the Russian upper classes were educated in Germany, and the Russian nobility, already partly Scandinavian by blood, frequently married Germans or other Western Europeans. Likewise many of the Romanovs themselves – in fact all of them who ruled in the later years of the dynasty – married into Western families. Prior to the nineteenth century, the two occupants of the Russian throne best known in world history were Peter I, the Great, and Catherine II, the Great. The former – who in 1703 gave Russia its "West window," St. Petersburg, later known as Petrograd, and recently as Leningrad – chose as his consort and successor on the throne as Catherine I [reign, 1725-1727], a captured Marienburg (Germany) servant girl whose mother and father were respectively a Lithuanian peasant woman and a Swedish dragoon. Catherine II, the Great, was a German princess who was proclaimed reigning Empress of Russia after her husband, the ineffective Czar Peter III, "subnormal in mind and physique (*Encyc. Brit.*, Vol. V, p. 37), left St. Petersburg. During her thirty-four years as Empress, Catherine, by studying such works as Blackstone's *Commentaries,* and by correspondence with such illustrious persons as Voltaire, F. M. Grimm, Frederick the Great, Diderot, and Maria Theresa of Austria, kept herself in contact with the West (*Encyc. Brit.*, Vol. XIX, p. 718 and *passim*). She chose for her son, weak like his father and later the "madman" Czar Paul I [reign, 1796-1801], a German wife.

The nineteenth century Czars were Catherine the Great's grandson, Alexander I [reign, 1801-1825 – German wife]; his brother, Nicholas I [reign, 1825-1855 – German wife, a Hohenzollern]; his son, Alexander II [reign, 1855-1881 – German wife]; his son Alexander III [reign, 1881-1894 – Danish wife]; and his son, Nicholas II [reign, 1894-1917 – German wife], who was murdered with his family (1918) after the Communists seized power (1917) in Russia.

Though many of the Romanovs, including Peter I and Catherine II, had far from admirable characters – a fact well advertised in American books on the subject – and though some of them including Nicholas II were not able rulers, a general purpose of the dynasty was to give their land certain of the advantages of Western Europe. In the West they characteristically sought alliances with one country or another, rather than ideological penetration.

Like their Slavic overlords, the Judaized Khazars of Russia had various relationships with Germany. Their numbers from time to time, as during the Crusades, received accretions from the Jewish communities in Germany – principally into Poland and other areas not yet Russian; many of the ancestors of these people, however, had previously entered Germany from Slavic lands. More interesting than these migrations was the importation from Germany of an idea conceived by a prominent Jew of solving century-old tension between native majority population and the Jews in their midst. In Germany, while Catherine the Great was Empress of Russia, a Jewish scholar and philosopher named Moses Mendelssohn (1729-1786) attracted wide and favorable attention among non-Jews and a certain following among Jews. His conception of the barrier between Jew and non-Jew, as analyzed by Grayzel (*op. cit.*, p. 543), was that the "Jews had erected about themselves a mental ghetto to balance the physical ghetto around them." Mendelssohn's objective was to lead the Jews "out of this mental ghetto into the wide world of general culture – without, however, doing harm to their specifically Jewish culture." The movement received the name Haskalah, which may be rendered as "enlightenment." Among other things, Mendelssohn wished Jews in Germany to learn the German language.

The Jews of Eastern Europe had from early days used corrupted versions of local vernaculars, written in the Hebrew alphabet (see "How Yiddish Came to Be," Grayzel, *op. cit., p.* 456), just as the various vernaculars of Western Europe were written in the Latin alphabet, and to further his purpose Mendelssohn translated the Pentateuch – *Genesis, Exodus, Leviticus, Numbers, Deuteronomy* – into standard German, using however, the accepted Hebrew alphabet (Grayzel, *op. cit.,* p. 543). Thus in one stroke he led his readers a step toward Westernization by the use of the German language and by offering them, instead of the Babylonian Talmud, a portion of scripture recognized by both Jew and Christian.

The Mendelssohn views were developed in Russia in the nineteenth century, notably by Isaac Baer Levinsohn (1788-1860), the "Russian Mendelssohn." Levinsohn was a scholar who, with Abraham Harkavy, delved into a field of Jewish history little known in the West, namely "the settlement of Jews in Russia and their vicissitudes during the dark ages... Levinsohn was the first to express the opinion that the Russian Jews hailed not from Germany, as is commonly supposed, but from the banks of the Volga. This hypothesis, corroborated by tradition, Harkavy established as a fact" (*The Haskalah Movement in Russia,* by Jacob S. Raisin, Philadelphia, The Jewish Publication Society of America, 1913, 1914, p. 17).

The reigns of the nineteenth century Czars showed a fluctuation of attitudes toward the Jewish "state within a state" (*The Haskalah Movement,* p. 43). In general, Nicholas I had been less lenient than Alexander I toward his intractable non-Christian minority, but he took an immediate interest in the movement endorsed by the highly respected Levinsohn, for he saw in "Haskalah" an opportunity for possibly breaking down the separatism of the Judaized Khazars. He put in charge of the project of opening hundreds of

Jewish schools a brilliant young Jew, Dr. Max Lilienthal. From its beginning, however, the Haskalah movement had had bitter opposition among Jews in Germany – many of whom, including the famous Moses Hess (Graetz-Raisin, *op. cit.*, Vol. VI, pp. 371 ff.), became ardent Jewish nationalists – and in Russia the opposition was fanatical. "The great mass of Russian Jewry was devoid of all secular learning, steeped in fanaticism, and given to superstitious practices" (Graetz-Raisin, *op. cit.*, Vol. VI, p. 112), and their leaders, for the most part, had no notion of tolerating a project which would lessen or destroy their control. These leaders believed correctly that the new education was designed to lessen the authority of the Talmud, which was the cause, as the Russians saw it, "of the fanaticism and corrupt morals of the Jews." The leaders of the Jews also saw that the new schools were a way "to bring the Jews closer to the Russian people and the Greek church" (Graetz-Raisin, *op. cit.*, Vol. VI, p. 116). According to Raisin, "the millions of Russian Jews were averse to having the government interfere with their inner and spiritual life" by "foisting upon them its educational measures. The soul of Russian Jewry sensed the danger lurking in the imperial scheme" (*op. cit.*, p. 117). Lilienthal was in their eyes "a traitor and informer," and in 1845, to recover a modicum of prestige with his people, he "shook the dust of bloody Russia from his feet" (Graetz-Raisin, *op. cit.*, Vol. VI, p. 117). Thus the Haskalah movement failed in Russia to break down the separatism of the Judaized Khazars.

When Nicholas I died, his son Alexander II [reign, 1855-1881] decided to try a new way of winning the Khazar minority to willing citizenship in Russia. He granted his people, including the Khazars, so many liberties that he was called the "Czar Liberator."

By irony, or nemesis, however, his "liberal régime" contributed substantially to the downfall of Christian Russia. Despite the ill-success of his Uncle Alexander's "measures to effect the 'betterment' of the 'obnoxious' Jewish element" (*Univ. Jew. Encyc.,*

Vol. I, p. 384), he ordered a wholesale relaxation of oppressive and restraining regulations (Graetz-Raisin, *op. cit.,* p. 124) and Jews were free to attend all schools and universities and to travel without restrictions. The new freedom led, however, to results the "Liberator" had not anticipated.

Educated, and free at last to organize nationally, the Judaized Khazars in Russia became not merely an indigestible mass in the body politic, the characteristic "state within a state," but a formidable anti-government force. With non-Jews of nihilistic or other radical tendencies – the so-called Russian "intelligentsia" – they sought in the first instance to further their aims by assassinations (*Modern European History,* by Charles Downer Hazen, Holt, New York, p. 565). Alexander tried to abate the hostility of the "terrorists" by granting more and more concessions, but on the day the last concessions were announced "a bomb was thrown at his carriage. The carriage was wrecked, and many of his escorts were injured. Alexander escaped as by a miracle, but a second bomb exploded near him as he was going to aid the injured. He was horribly mangled, and died within an hour. Thus perished the Czar Liberator" (*Modern European History,* p. 567).

Some of those involved in earlier attempts to assassinate Alexander II were of Jewish Khazar background (see *The Anarchists* by Ernest Alfred Vizetelly, John Lane, London and New York, 1911, p. 66). According to the *Universal Jewish Encyclopedia,* the "assassination of Alexander II in which a Jewess had played a part" revived a latent "anti-Semitism." Resentful of precautions taken by the murdered Czar's son and successor, Alexander III, and also possessing a new world plan, hordes of Jews, some of them highly educated in Russian universities, migrated to other European countries and to America. The emigration continued (see below) under Nicholas II. Many Jews remained in Russia, however, for "in 1913 the Jewish population of Russia amounted to 6,946,000" (*Univ. Jew. Encyc.,* Vol. IX, p. 285).

Various elements of this restless aggressive minority nurtured the amazing quadruple aims of international Communism, the seizure of power in Russia, Zionism, and continued migration to America, with a fixed purpose to retain their nationalistic separatism. In many instances, the same individuals were participants in two or more phases of the four-fold objective. Among the Jews who remained in Russia, which then included Lithuania, the Ukraine (*A History of the Ukraine*, Michael Hrushevsky, Yale University Press, 1941, *passim*), and much of Poland, were the founders of the Russian Bolshevik party:

> In 1897 was founded the Bund, the union of Jewish workers in Poland and Lithuania... They engaged in revolutionary activity upon a large scale, and their energy made them the spearhead of the Party. (Article on "Communism" by Harold J. Laski, *Encyc. Brit.*, Vol. III, pp 824-827).

The name *Bolsheviki* means majority (from Russian *bolshe*, the larger) and commemorates the fact that at the Brussels-London conference of the party in late 1902 and early 1903, the violent Marxist program of Lenin was adopted by a 25 to 23 vote, the less violent minority or "Mensheviki" Marxists fading finally from the picture after Stalin's triumph in October, 1917. It has been also stated that the term *Bolshevik* refers to the "larger" or more violent program of the majority faction. After 1918 the Bolsheviki called their organization the Communist Party.

The Zionist Jews were another group that laid its plan in Russia as a part of the new reorientation of Russian Jewry after the collapse of Haskalah and the assassination (1881) of Alexander II, "On November 6, 1884, for the first time in history, a Jewish international assembly was held at Kattowitz, near the Russian frontier, where representatives from all classes and different countries met and decided to colonize Palestine..." (*The Haskalah Movement*

43

in Russia, p. 285). For a suggestion of the solidarity of purpose between the Jewish Bund, which was the core of the Communist Party, and early Zionism, see Grayzel (*op. cit.,* p. 662). "Henceforth a heightened sense of race-consciousness takes the place formerly held by religion and is soon to develop into a concrete nationalism with Zion as its goal" (Graetz-Raisin, Vol. VI, p. 168).

In Russia and abroad in the late nineteenth century, not only Bundists but other Khazar Jews had been attracted to the writings of Karl Marx (1818-1883), partly, it seems, because he was Jewish in origin. "On both paternal and maternal sides Karl Marx was descended from rabbinical families" (*Univ. Jew. Encyc.,* Vol. VII, p. 289).

The Marxian program of drastic controls, so repugnant to the free western mind, was no obstacle to the acceptance of Marxism by many Khazar Jews, for the Babylonian Talmud under which they lived had taught them to accept authoritarian dictation on everything from their immorality to their trade practices. Since the Talmud contained more than 12,000 controls, the regimentation of Marxism was acceptable – provided the Khazar politician, like the Talmudic rabbi, exercised the power of the dictatorship.

Under Nicholas II, there was no abatement of the regulations designed, after the murder of Alexander II, to curb the anti-government activities of Jews; consequently, the "reaction to those excesses was Jewish support of the Bolsheviks..." (*Univ. Jew. Encyc.,* Vol. I, p. 286). The way to such support was easy, since the predecessor organization of Russian Communism was the Jewish "Bund." Thus Marxian Communism, modified for expediency, became an instrument for the violent seizure of power. The Communist Jews, together with revolutionaries of Russian stock, were sufficiently numerous to give the venture a promise of success, if attempted at the right time. After the rout of the less violent faction in 1903, Lenin remained the leader.

The blow fell in the fateful year, 1917, when Russia was staggering under defeat by Germany – a year before Germany, in turn, staggered to defeat under the triple blows of Britain, France, and the United States. "The great hour of freedom struck on the 15th of March, 1917," when "Czar Nicholas's train was stopped" and he was told "that his rule was at an end... Israel, in Russia, suddenly found itself lifted out of its oppression and degradation" (Graetz-Raisin, *op. cit.*, Vol. VI, p. 209).

At this moment Lenin appeared on the scene, after an absence of nine years (*Encyc. Brit.*, Vol. XIII, p. 912). The Germans, not realizing that he would be anything more than a trouble-maker for their World War I enemy, Russia, passed him and his party (exact number disputed – about 200?) in a sealed train from Switzerland to the Russian border. In Lenin's sealed train, "Out of a list of 165 names published, 23 are Russian, 3 Georgian, 4 Armenian, 1 German, and 128 Jewish" (*The Surrender of an Empire*, Nesta H. Webster, Boswell Printing and Publishing Company, Ltd., 10 Essex St., London, W.C. 2, 1931, p. 77). "At about the same time, Trotsky arrived from the United States, followed by over 300 Jews from the East End of New York and joined up with the Bolshevik Party" (*op. cit.*, p. 73).

Thus under Lenin, whose birth name was Ulianov and whose racial antecedents are uncertain, and under Leon Trotsky, a Jew, whose birth-name was Bronstein, a small number of highly-trained Jews from abroad, along with Russian Judaized Khazars and non-Jewish captives to the Marxian ideology, were able to make themselves masters of Russia. "Individual revolutionary leaders of Jewish origin – such as Trotsky, Zinoviev, Kamenev, and Sverdlov – played a conspicuous part in the revolution of November, 1917, which enabled the Bolshevists to take possession of the state apparatus" (*Univ. Jew. Encyc.*, Vol. IX, p. 668). Here and there in the *Universal Jewish Encyclopedia* other Jews are named as co-founders of Russian Communism, but not Lenin and Stalin. Both of these, however, are said by some writers to be half-Jewish. Whatever the racial antecedents of their top man, the first Soviet commissariats were largely staffed with Jews. The Jewish position in the Communist movement was well understood in Russia. "The White Armies which opposed the Bolshevik government linked Jews and Bolsheviks as common enemies" (*Univ. Jew Encyc.,* Vol. I, p. 336).

Those interested in the ratio of Jews to others in the government in the early days of Communist rule in Russia should, if possible, see *Les derniers jours des Romanov* (The Last Days of the Romanovs) by Robert Wilton, long the Russian correspondent of the London *Times*. A summary of its vital passages is included in the "foreword to Third Edition" of *The Mystical Body of Christ in the Modern World* (Brown and Nolan, Limited, Waterford, Dublin, Belfast, Cork, London, 1939, 1947) by Rev. Denis Fahey, a well-known Irish professor of philosophy and Church history. Professor Fahey gives *names* and *nationality* of the members of the Council of Peoples Commissars, the Central Executive Committee, and the Extraordinary Commissions, and in summary quotes from Wilton as follows:

> According to the data furnished by the Soviet press, out of 556 important functionaries of the Bolshevik State … there were, in 1918-1919, 17 Russians, 2 Ukrainians, 11 Armenians, 35 Letts, 15 Germans, 1 Hungarian, 10 Georgians, 3 Poles, 3 Finns, 1 Karaïm, 457 Jews.

As the decades passed by – after the fateful year 1917 – Judaized Khazars kept a firm hand on the helm of the government in the occupied land of Russia. In due time they built a bureaucracy to their hearts' desire. The government-controlled Communist press "issued numerous and violent denunciations of anti-semitic episodes, either violence or discriminations." Also, "in 1935 a court ruled that anti-semitism in Russia was a penal offense" (*Univ. Jew Encyc.,* Vol. I, p. 386). Among top-flight leaders prominent in the middle of the twentieth century, Stalin, Kaganovich, Beria, Molotov, and Litvinov all have Jewish blood, or are married to Jewesses. The latter circumstance should not be overlooked, because from Nero's Poppæa (*Enciclopedia Italiana*, Vol. XXVII, p. 932; also, *The Works of Flavius Josephus*, translated by William Whiston, David McKay, Philadelphia, n.d., pp. 8, 612, 616) to the Montreal chemist's woman friend in the Canadian atomic espionage trials (*Report of the Royal Commission*, Government Printing Office, Ottawa, Canada, 1946, $1.00) the influence of a certain type of wife – or other closely associated woman – has been of utmost significance. Nero and Poppæa may be allowed to sleep – if their crimes permit – but Section III, 11, entitled "RAYMOND BOYER, Montreal," in the *Report of the Canadian Royal Commission* should be read in full by all who want facts on the subject of the corruption of scientists, and others working on government projects. In the Soviet Embassy records, turned over to Canadian authorities by Igor Gouzenko, was Col. Zabotin's notebook which contained the following entries (pp. 375 and 397 respectively):

Professor
Frenchman. Noted chemist, about 40 years of age. Works in McGill University, Montreal. Is the best of the specialists on VV on the American Continent. Gives full information on explosives and chemical plants. Very rich. He is afraid to work. (Gave the formula of RDX, up to the present there was no evaluation from the boss.)
Contact
1. Freda. Jewess – works as a co-worker in the International Bureau of Labour. A lady friend of the Professor.

In view of the facts furnished above as to the racial composition of the early Communist bureaucracy, it is perhaps not surprising that a large portion of the important foreign efforts of the present government of Russia are entrusted to Jews.

This is especially notable in the list of current or recent exercisers of Soviet power in the satellite lands of Eastern Europe. Ana Rabinsohn Pauker, Dictator of Rumania; Matyas Rakosi, Dictator of Hungary; Jacob Berman, Dictator of Poland; D. M. Manuilsky, Dictator of the Ukraine; and many other persons highly placed in the governments of the several Eastern European countries are all said to be members of this new Royal Race of Russia.

Of Eastern European origin are the leaders of late nineteenth century and twentieth century political Zionism which flowered from the already recorded beginnings at Kattowitz in 1884. Born at Budapest, Hungary, was Theodor Herzl (1860-1904), author (1896) of *Der Judenstatt* (The Jews' State), who presided over the "Zionist Congress," which "took place at Basel, Switzerland, on August 29, 30, and 31, 1897" (*Univ. Jew. Encyc.*, Vol. II, p. 102). Dr. Chaim Weizmann, the head of political Zionism at the moment of its recourse to violence, was born in Plonsk, Poland. Since these top leaders are Eastern Europeans, it is not surprising that most of the recent immigrants into Palestine are of Soviet and satellite origin and that their weapons have been largely from the Soviet Union and from Soviet-controlled Czechoslovakia (see below, Chapter VI).

As a number of writers have pointed out, political Zionism entered its violent phase *after* the discovery of the incredibly vast mineral wealth of Palestine. According to "Zionists Misleading World with Untruths for Palestine Conquest," a full-page article inserted as an advertisement in the New York *Herald-Tribune* (January 14, 1947), "an independent Jewish state in Palestine was the only certain method by which Zionists could acquire complete control and outright ownership of the proven Five Trillion Dollar ($5,000,000,000,000) chemical and mineral wealth of the Dead Sea." The long documented article is signed by R. M. Schoendorf, "Representative of Cooperating Americans of the Christian Faiths"; by Habib I. Katibah, "Representative of Cooperating Americans of

Arab Ancestry"; and by Benjamin H. Freedman, "Representative of Cooperating Americans of the Jewish Faith," and is convincing. Irrespective, however, of the value of the Dead Sea minerals, the oil flow of Middle Eastern wells is something unbelievable to those familiar with slow-flowing American wells. Also in 1951, oil was "discovered" in the Negeb Desert, an area for which "Israeli" authorities had so much fervor that they seized it (see Chapter VI, b, below).

The dominance of the motive of self-aggrandizement in political Zionism has been affirmed and denied; but it is difficult for an observer to see any possible objective apart from mineral wealth or long range grand strategy, including aggression (see Chapters VI and IX, below), in a proposal to make a nation out of an agriculturally poor, already overpopulated territory the size of Vermont. The intention of aggression at the expense of Moslem peoples, particularly in the direction of Iraq and Iran, is suggested also by the fact that the Eastern European Jews, adherents to the Babylonian Talmud, had long turned their thoughts to the lands where their sages lived and where most of the native Jewish population had embraced the Moslem faith. Any possible Zionist religious motive such as the hope of heaven, which fired the zeal of the Crusaders, is apparently ruled out by the nature of Judaism, as it is generally understood. "The Jewish religion is a way of life and has no formulated creed, or articles of faith, the acceptance of which brings redemption or salvation to the believer..." (opening words, p. 763, of the section on "Doctrines," in *Religious Bodies*, 1936, Vol. II, Part I, Denominations A to J, U.S. Department of Commerce, Jesse H. Jones, Secretary, Bureau of Census, Superintendent of Documents, Government Printing Office, Washington, D.C.).

The secret or underground overseas efforts of Khazar-dominated Russia apparently have been entrusted principally to Jews. This is especially true of atomic espionage. *The Report of the*

49

Royal Commission of Canada, already referred to, shows that Sam Carr (Cohen), organizer for all Canada; Fred Rose (Rosenberg), organizer for French Canada, and member of the Canadian Parliament from a Montreal constituency; and Germina (or Hermina) Rabinowich, in charge of liaison with U.S. Communists, were all born in Russia or satellite lands. In this connection, it is important to stress the fact that the possession of a Western name does not necessarily imply Western European stock. In fact, the maneuver of name-changing frequently disguises an individual's stock or origin. Thus the birth-name of John Gates, editor of the Communist *Daily Worker,* was Israel Regenstreif. Other name changers among the eleven Communists found guilty by a New York jury in October, 1949, included Gil Green – born Greenberg; Gus Hall – born Halberg; and Carl Winter – born Weissberg. (For details on these men and the others, see the article, "The Trial of the Eleven Communists," by Sidney Shalett, *Reader's Digest,* August, 1950, pp. 59-72.) Other examples of name-changing can be cited among political writers, army officers, and prominent officials in the executive agencies and departments in Washington. Parenthetically, the maneuver of acquiring a name easily acceptable to the majority was very widely practiced by the aliens prominent in the seizure of Russia for Communism, among the name-changers being Lenin (Ulianov), Trotsky (Bronstein), and Stalin (Dzugashvili), the principal founders of state Communism.

The United States Government refused Canada's invitation early in 1946 to cooperate in Canada's investigation of atomic spies, but in 1950, when (despite "red herring" talk of the Chief Executive) our atomic spy suspects began to be apprehended, the first was Harry Gold, then Abraham Brothman, and Miriam Moskowitz. Others were M. Sobell, David Greenglass, Julius Rosenberg, and Mrs. Ethel Rosenberg (not to be confused with Mrs. Anna Rosenberg). Various sentences were given. Mr. and Mrs. Rosenberg received the death penalty (see *Atom Treason,* by Frank Britton, Box 15745, Crenshaw Station, Los Angeles 8, California). As of early May 1952, however, the sentence had not been carried out, and a significant portion of the Jewish press was campaigning to save the Rosenbergs. Referring to Julius and Ethel Rosenberg, Samuel B. Gach, Editor-in-Chief and Publisher of the *California Jewish Voice* ("Largest Jewish Circulation in the West") wrote as follows in his issue of April 25, 1952: "We deplore the sentence against the two Jews and despise the cowardly Jewish judge who passed same..." In March, 1951, Dr. William Perl of the Columbia University Physics Department was arrested "on four counts of perjury in connection with the crumbling Soviet atomic spy ring... Perl, whose father was born in Russia, ... had his name changed from Utterperl [Mutterperl?] to Perl" in 1945 (Washington *Times-Herald*, March 15, 1951). For further details on these persons and others, see "Atomic Traitors," by Congressman Fred Busbey of Illinois, in the June, 1951, number of *National Republic*. Finally, the true head of Communism in America was found not to be the publicly announced head, but the Jew, Gerhardt Eisler, who, upon detection, "escaped" from America on the Polish S. S. "Batory," to a high position in the Soviet Government of East Germany (*Communist Activities Among Aliens and National Groups,* part III, Government Printing Office, Washington, D.C., 1950, p. A121).

Very pertinent to the subject under consideration is a statement entitled "Displaced Persons: Facts vs. Fiction," made in the Senate of the United States on January 6, 1950, by Senator Pat McCarran, Democrat of Nevada, Chairman of the Judiciary Committee. Senator McCarran said in part: "Let it be remembered that the Attorney General of the United States recently testified that an analysis of 4,984 of the more militant members of the Communist Party in the United States showed that 91.4 percent of the total were of foreign stock or were married to persons of foreign stock."

With more than *nine-tenths* of our "more militant" Communists thus recruited from or allied to "foreign stock" and with that "stock" totaling perhaps not more than 10,000,000 or *one-fifteenth* of our nation's population, a little recourse to mathematics will suggest that the employment of an Eastern European or other person of recent alien extraction or connection is *one hundred and fifty times* more likely to yield a traitor than is the employment of a person of native stock!

An "authoritative" Jewish point of view toward Soviet Russia is explained in the *Universal Jewish Encyclopedia* in the concluding paragraphs on Karl Marx. According to this source, Jews "recognize the experience of the Soviet Union, home of 6,000,000 Jews, as testimony of the Marxist position on the question of national and racial equality." The *Encyclopedia* comments further on the "striking fact that the one country which professes official allegiance to Marxian teachings is the one where anti-Semitism has been outlawed and its resurgence rendered impossible by the removal of social and economic inequalities" (Vol. VIII, p. 390). In *The Jewish People Face the Post-War World* by Alexander Bittelman (Morning Freiheit Association, 35 East 12th Street, New York 3, N.Y., 1945, p. 19) the affection of a considerable body of American Jews for the Soviet Union is expressed dramatically:

> If not for the Red Army, there would be no Jews in Europe today, nor in Palestine, nor in Africa; and in the United States, the length of our existence would be counted in days... THE SOVIET UNION HAS SAVED THE JEWISH PEOPLE. Therefore, let the American Jewish masses never forget our historic debt to the Saviour of the Jewish people – the Soviet Union.

Be it noted, however, that Mr. Bittelman admits indirectly that he is not speaking for *all* American Jews, particularly when he assails as "reactionary" the "non-democratic forces in Jewish life ... such as the Sulzbergers, Rosenwalds, and Lazarons" (p. 9). In addition to ideology, another factor in the devotion to their old homelands of so many of the newer American Jews of Eastern European source is kinship. According to *The American Zionist Handbook*, 68 to 70% of United States Jews have relations in Poland and the Soviet Union.

Quite in harmony with the Bittelman attitude toward the Soviet was the finding of the Canadian Royal Commission that Soviet Russia exploits fully the predilection of Jews toward Communism: "It is significant that a number of documents from the Russian Embassy specifically note 'Jew' or 'Jewess' in entries on their relevant Canadian agents or prospective agents, showing that the Russian Fifth Column leaders attached particular significance to this matter" (*The Report of the Royal Commission*, p. 82).

In view of the above-quoted statement of a writer for the great New York publication, the *Universal Jewish Encyclopedia*, which is described on its title-page as "authoritative," and in view of the findings of the Canadian Royal Commission, not to mention other facts and testimonies, it would seem that no one should be surprised that certain United States Jews of Eastern European origin or influence have transmitted atomic or other secrets to the Soviet Union. Those who are caught, of course, must suffer the fate of spies, as would happen to American espionage agents abroad; but, in the opinion of the author, the really guilty parties in the United States are those Americans of native stock who, for their own evil purposes, placed the pro-Soviet individuals in positions where they could steal or connive at the stealing of American secrets of atomic warfare. This guilt, which in view of the terrible likely results of atomic espionage is really blood-guilt, cannot be sidestepped and should not be overlooked by the American people.

The presence of so many high-placed spies in the United States prompts a brief reference to our national habit (a more accurate term than policy) in regard to immigration. On December 2, 1823, President Monroe proclaimed, in the famous Doctrine

Doctrine

which bears his name, that the American government would not allow continental European powers to "extend their system" in the United States. At that time and until the last two decades of the nineteenth century, immigration brought us almost exclusively European people whose ideals were those of Western Christian civilization; these people became helpers in subduing and settling our vast frontier area; they wished to conform to rather than modify or supplant the body of traditions and ideals summed up in the word "America."

After 1880, however, our immigration shifted sharply to include millions of persons from Southern and Eastern Europe. Almost all of these people were less sympathetic than predecessor immigrants to the government and the ideals of the United States and a very large portion of them were non-Christians who had no intention whatever of accepting the ideals of Western Christian civilization, but had purposes of their own. These purposes were accomplished not by direct military invasion, as President Monroe feared, but covertly by infiltration, propaganda, and electoral and financial pressure (Chapters I, III, IV, V, VI, VII). The average American remained unaware and unperturbed.

Among those who early foresaw the problems to be created by our new immigrants was General Eisenhower's immediate predecessor as President of Columbia University. In a small but extremely valuable book, *The American As He Is*, President Nicholas Murray Butler in 1908 called attention to "the fact that Christianity in some one of its many forms is a dominant part of the American nature." Butler, then at the zenith of his intellectual power, expressed fear that our "capacity to subdue and assimilate the alien elements brought ... by immigration may soon be exhausted." He concluded accordingly that "The dangers which confront America will come, if at all, from within."

Statistics afford ample reasons for President Butler's fears. "The new immigration was comprised preponderantly of three elements: the Italians, the Slavs, and the Jews" (*The Immigration and Naturalization Systems of the United States,* Government Printing office, Washington, D.C., p. 236). The Italians and the Slavs were less assimilable than immigrants from Northern and Western Europe, and tended to congregate instead of distributing themselves over the whole country as the earlier Northern European immigrants had usually done.

The assimilation of Italians and Slavs was helped, however, by their belonging to the same parent Indo-Germanic racial stock as the English-German-Irish majority, and above all by their being Christians – mostly Roman Catholics – and therefore finding numerous co-religionists not only among fully Americanized second and third generation Irish Catholics but among old stock Anglo-American Catholics descending from Colonial days. Quite a few persons of Italian and Slavic stock were or became Protestants, chiefly Baptists – among them being ex-Governor Charles Poletti of New York and ex-Governor Harold Stassen of Minnesota. The new Italian and Slavic immigrants and their children soon began to marry among the old stock. In a protracted reading of an Italian language American newspaper, the author noted that approximately half of all recorded marriages of Italians were to persons with non-Italian names.

Thus in one way or another the new Italian and Slavic immigrants began to merge into the general American pattern. This happened to some extent everywhere and was notable in areas where the newcomers were not congregated – as in certain urban and mining areas – but were dispersed among people of native stock. With eventual complete assimilation by no means impossible, there was no need of a national conference of Americans and Italians or of Americans and Slavs to further the interests of those minorities.

With the new Jewish immigrants, however, the developments were strikingly different – and quite in line with the fears of

President Butler. The handful of Jews, mostly Sephardic (Webster's *New International Dictionary*, 1934, p. 2281) and German, already in this country (about 280,000 in 1877, *Religious Bodies, op. cit.,* above), were not numerous enough to contribute cultural guidance to the newcomers (see Graetz-Raisin, Vol. VI, Chapter IV, "American Continent," A "The Sephardic and German Periods," B "The Russian Period"). These newcomers arrived in vast hordes – especially from territory under the sovereignty of Russia, the total number of legally recorded immigrants from that country between 1881 and 1920 being 3,237,079 (*The Immigration and Naturalization Systems of the United States,* p. 817), most of them Jews. Many of those Jews are now referred to as Polish Jews because they came from that portion of Russia which had been the kingdom of Poland prior to the "partitions" of 1772-1795 (*Modern History,* by Carl L. Becker, Silver Burdett Company, New York, p. 138) and was the Republic of Poland between World War I and World War II. Accordingly New York City's 2,500,000 or more Jews (*op. cit.,* p. 242) are sometimes said to be largely Polish Jews (*op. cit.,* p. 240).

Thus by sheer weight of numbers, as well as by aggressiveness, the newcomer Jews from Eastern Europe pushed into the background the more or less Westernized Jews, who had migrated or whose ancestors had migrated to America prior to 1880 and had become for the most part popular and successful merchants with no inordinate interest in politics. In striking contrast, the Eastern European Jew made himself "a power to be reckoned with in the professions, the industries, and the political parties" (Graetz-Raisin, *op. cit.,* Vol. VI, p. 344).

The overwhelming of the older Americanized Jews is well portrayed in *The Jewish Dilemma* by Elmer Berger (The Devin-Adair Company, New York, 1945). Of the early American Jews, Berger writes: "Most of these first 200,000 came from Germany. They integrated themselves completely" (*op. cit.,* p. 232). This integration was not difficult; for many persons of Jewish religion in Western Europe in the nineteenth century not only had no racial or ethnic connection with the Khazars, but were not separatists or Jewish nationalists. The old contentions of their ancestors with their Christian neighbors in Western Europe had been largely overlooked on both sides by the beginning of the nineteenth century, and nothing stood in the way of their full integration into national life. The American kinsmen of these Westernized Jews were similar in outlook.

But after 1880 and "particularly in the first two decades of the twentieth century, immigration to the United States from Eastern Europe increased rapidly." The Eastern European immigrant Jews "brought with them the worn-out concept of 'a Jewish people' " (*op. cit.*, p. 233). Soon these newcomers of nationalist persuasion actually exerted influence over the old and once anti-nationalist organization of American Reform Judaism. "In the winter of 1941-'42, the Central Conference of American Rabbis had endorsed the campaign to organize a Jewish Army. The event indicated the capitulation of the leadership of Reform Judaism to Jewish Nationalism." Many American-minded Jews protested, but "the voices were disorganized and therefore could by safely ignored" (*op. cit.*, p. 242). American Jewry "had succumbed to the relentless pressure of the Zionists."

With the domination of American Jewry by Judaized Khazars and those who travel with them, the position of American Jews who wished to be Americans became most unhappy. The small but significant group which met at Atlantic City in June, 1942, to lay the foundations for an organization of "Americans whose religion is Judaism," were at once pilloried. "Charges" of being " 'traitors', 'Quislings', 'betrayers' were thundered" from the synagogues of America and "filled the columns of the Jewish press" (*op. cit.*, p. 244). Many were silenced or won over by the pressure and the abuse – but not all. Those brave Jews who are persecuted because they are not hostile to the American way of life should not be confused with those Jews who persecute them, as Mr. Berger shows, but should on the other hand receive the sympathy of all persons who are trying to save Christian civilization in America.

Since the predominant new Jews consider themselves a superior people (*Race and Nationality as Factors in American Life,* by Henry Pratt Fairchild, The Ronald Press Company, New York, 1947, p. 145), and a separate nationality (*op. cit.,* p. 140), assimilation appears now to be out of the question. America now has virtually a nation within the nation, and an aggressive culture-conscious nation at that.

The stream of Eastern Europeans was diminished in volume during World War I, but was at flood level again in 1920. At last the Congress became sufficiently alarmed to initiate action. The House Committee on Immigration, in its report on the bill that later became the quota law of 1921, reported:

> There is a limit to our power of assimilation ... the processes of assimilation and amalgamation are slow and difficult. With the population of the broken parts of Europe headed this way in ever-increasing numbers, why not peremptorily check the stream with this temporary measure, and in the meantime try the unique and novel experiment of enforcing all of the immigration laws on our statutes?...

Accordingly, the 67th Congress "passed the first quota law, which was approved on May 19, 1921, limiting the number of any nationality entering the United States to 3 percent of the foreign-born of that nationality who lived here in 1910. Under this law, approximately 350,000 aliens were permitted to enter each year, mostly from Northern and Western Europe" (*The Immigration and Naturalization Systems of the United States,* p. 56).

The worry of the Congress over unassimilated aliens continued and the House Committee on Immigration and Naturalization of the Sixty-eighth Congress reported that it was "necessary to the successful future of our nation to preserve the basic strain of our population" and continued (*op. cit.*, p. 60) as follows:

> Since it is the axiom of political science that a government not imposed by external force is the visible expression of the ideals, standards, and social viewpoint of the people over which it rules, it is obvious that a change in the character or composition of the population must inevitably result in the evolution of a form of government consonant with the base upon which it rests. If, therefore, the principle of individual liberty, guarded by a constitutional government created on this continent nearly a century and a half ago, is to endure, the basic strain of our population must be maintained and our economic standards preserved.
>
> ... the American people do not concede the right of any foreign group in the United States, or government abroad, to demand a participation in our possessions, tangible or intangible, or to dictate the character of our legislation.

The new law "changed the quota basis from 1910 to 1890, reduced the quotas from 3 to 2 percent, provided for the establishment of permanent quotas on the basis of national origin, and placed the burden of proof on the alien with regard to his admissibility and the legality of his residence in the United States." It was passed by the Congress on May 15, and signed by President Calvin Coolidge on May 26, 1924.

The new quota system was still more favorable relatively to the British Isles and Germany and other countries of Northern and Western Europe and excluded "persons who believe in or advocate the overthrow by force or violence of the government of the United States."

Unfortunately, within ten years, this salutary law was to be largely nullified (see Chapters VI and VII, below) by misinterpretation of its intent and by continued scandalous maladministration, a principal worry of the Congress (as shown above) in 1921 and continuously since (*op. cit.,* p. 65 and *passim*).

By birth and by immigration either clandestine or in violation of the intent of the "national origins" law of 1924, the Jewish population of the U.S. increased rapidly. The following official Census Bureau statement is of interest: "In 1887 there were at least 277 congregations in the country and 230,000 Jews; in 1890, 533 congregations and probably 475,000 Jews; in 1906, 1700 congregations and about 1,775,000 Jews; in 1916, 1900 congregations and about 3,300,000 Jews; in 1926, 3,118 permanent congregations and 4,081,000 Jews; and in 1936, 3,728 congregations and 4,641,184 Jews residing in the cities, towns and villages in which the congregations were located" (*Religious Bodies,* p. 763). On other religions, the latest government statistics are mostly for the year 1947, but for Jews the 1936 figure remains (*The Immigration and Naturalization Systems of the United States,* p. 849). As to the total number of Jews in the United States the government has no exact figures, any precise figures beyond a vague "over five million" being impossible because of incomplete records and illegal immigration. The Committee on the Judiciary of the Senate (*op. cit.,* p. 842), however, accepts the *World Almanac* figure of 15,713,638 Jews of religious affiliation in the world and summarizes thus: "statistics indicate that over 50 percent of the World Jewish population is now residing in the Western Hemisphere" (*op. cit.,* p. 21), i.e., at least 8,000,000. Since some three-fourths of a million Jews live in other North and South American countries besides the United States, the number of Jews *known* to be in the United States may be placed at a minimum of about 7,250,000. Jews unaffiliated with organizations whose members are counted, illegal entrants, etc., may place the total number in the neighborhood of 10,000,000. This likely figure would justify the frequently heard statement that more than half of the Jews of the world are in the United States.

Percentage-wise this is the government summary (*op. cit.,* p. 241) of Jewish population in the United States:

> In 1937, Jews constituted less than 4 percent of the American people, but during the 7-year period following (1937-43), net Jewish immigration to the United States ranged between 25 and 77 percent of total net immigration to this country. For the 36-year period, 1908-43, net Jewish immigration constituted 14 percent of the total. The population of the United States has increased three-fold since 1877, while the Jewish population has increased twenty-one-fold during the same period.

The above government figures require elucidation. The figures include only those Jews connected with an organized Jewish congregation and, as a corollary, exclude the vast number of Jews, illegal entrants and others, who are not so connected, and hence not officially listed as Jews. *The stated increase of Jews by 2100 percent since 1877 is thus far too small* because non-Congregational Jews are not counted. Moreover, since the increase of 300 per cent in the total population includes known Jews, who increased at the rate of 2100 percent, *the increase in population of non-Jews is far less than the 300 percent increase* of the total population.

This powerful and rapidly growing minority – closely knit and obsessed with its own objectives which are not those of Western Christian civilization – will in subsequent chapters be discussed along with other principal occupants of the stage of public affairs in America during the early 1950's. Details will come as a surprise to many readers, who are the unwitting victims of censorship (Chapter V, below). Valuable for its light on the global projects of political Zionism, with especial reference to Africa, is Douglas Reed's *Somewhere South of Suez* (Devin-Adair Company, New York, 1951). After mentioning that the "secret ban" against publishing the truth on "Zionist Nationalism," which he holds "to be allied in its roots to Soviet Communism," has grown in his adult lifetime "from nothing into something approaching a law of lèse majesté at some absolute court of the dark past," Mr. Reed states further that "the Zionist Nationalists are powerful enough to govern governments in the great countries of the remaining West!" He concludes further that "American Presidents and British Prime Ministers, and all their colleagues," bow to Zionism as if venerating a shrine.

The subject-matter of a book can be best determined not by its preface but by its index. It is believed that an examination of the index of *The Iron Curtain Over America* will show a unique completeness in the listing of names and subjects bearing upon the present peril of our country. In brief, *The Iron Curtain Over America* presents in complete detail – along with other matters – the problems created in the United States by a powerful minority possessed of an ideology alien to our traditions and fired by an ambition which threatens to involve us in the ruin of a third world-wide war. The next chapter deals with the above-board infiltration of Judaized Khazars, and other persons of the same ideology, into the United States Democratic Party.

CHAPTER III

THE KHAZARS JOIN
THE DEMOCRATIC PARTY

The triumphant Khazars, aided by other "converts" to Communism, strengthened their grasp on prostrate Russia by a succession of "purges" in which many millions of Russians lost their lives, either by immediate murder or in the slow terror of slave labor camps. These purges do not concern us here except as a sample of what Soviet rule would bring to America, namely, the slaying of 15,000,000 persons on a list already prepared by name and category (statement to the author by a former high-ranking international Communist who has deserted "Stalinism"). The lecturer, Matt Cvetic, a former F.B.I. undercover agent, gives, more recently, a much higher figure; he states that almost all men and women over thirty, having been found too old for "re-education," would be slaughtered. For details, write to Borger *News-Herald*, Borger, Texas, asking reprint of "We Owe a Debt" (April 16, 1952) by J. C. Phillips.

Even as they subjected the Russian people to a rule of terror, the new rulers of Russia promptly and effectively penetrated the countries of Western Europe and also Canada and (as shown in Chapter II) the United States. For their fateful choice of our country as a goal of their major though not yet completely and finally successful endeavor, there were several reasons.

In the first place, with its mutually advantageous capital-labor relations, its enormous productivity, and its high standard of living, the United States of America was an existing visible refutation of the black Soviet lie that their Communist dictatorship did more than our Republic for the workingman. The idea that the "capitalistic" democracies (Britain and America) were formidable obstacles to the spread of Communism and had to be destroyed was expressed many times by Soviet leaders and notably by Stalin in his great address (Moscow, March 10, 1939) to the 18th Congress of the Communist Party.

This elaborate official statement of Soviet policy was made *before the outbreak of World War II, and nearly three years before our involvement, and was trumpeted rather than hidden under a bushel.* It can therefore be safely predicated that our State Department, with its numerous staffs, offices, bureaus, and divisions, was promptly aware of the contents of this speech and of the Soviet goal of overthrowing our "capitalist democracy."

The second reason for large scale Communist exploitation of the United States was our traditional lack of any laws prohibiting or regulating immigration into the United States and our negligence or politics in enforcing immigration laws when they had been passed (Chapter II, above). "The illegal entry of aliens into the United States is one of the most serious and difficult problems confronting the Immigration and Naturalization Service... Since the end of World War II, the problem of illegal entry has increased tremendously... There is ample evidence that there is an alarmingly large number of aliens in the United States in an illegal status. Under the alien registration act of 1940, some 5,000,000 aliens were registered" (*The Immigration and Naturalization Systems of the United States,* pp. 629, 630).

The third principal reason for the Communist exploitation of the United States was the absence of any effective policy regarding resident foreigners even when their activities are directed toward the overthrow of the government. Thus in 1950 several hundreds of thousands of foreigners, among the millions illegally in this country, were arrested and released for want of adequate provisions for deporting them.

As shown in Chapter II, above, persons of Khazar background or traditions had entered the United States in large numbers in the waves of immigration between 1880 and the outbreak of World War I in 1914. The Soviet seizure of Russia took place in 1917, however, and the hey-day for Communist-inclined immigrants from Eastern Europe was the five-year period between the end of World War I (1919) and the passage of the 1924 law restricting immigration. Recorded immigrants to this country in that brief span of time amounted to approximately three million and large numbers of the newcomers were from Eastern Europe. Most significantly, with Communism in power in Russia, many of the new immigrants were not only ideologically hostile to the Western Christian civilization of which America was the finest development, but were actual agents of the new Rulers of Russia. Conspicuous among these was Sidney Hillman, who had turned from his "Rabbinical education" (*Who Was Who in America,* Vol. II, p. 254) to political activities of international scope. Twenty-two years before Franklin Roosevelt gave orders to "clear everything with Sidney," similar orders were given American Communists by Lenin himself, Hillman being at that time President of the Russian-American Industrial Corporation at 103 E. Fourteenth St., New York (article by Walter Trohan and photostat in Washington *Times-Herald,* October 29, 1944).

Surely a relatively small number of Khazar immigrants from Russia came as actual Soviet agents; not all of them came as confirmed Marxists; and some of them have doubtless conformed to the traditional American mores. The contrary is neither stated nor implied as a general proposition. The fact remains, however, that the newer immigrants, to an even greater degree than their predecessors of the same stock, were determined to resist absorption into Western Christian civilization and were determined also to further their aims by political alignment and pressure.

In the first three decades of the twentieth century, few of the several million non-Christian immigrants from Eastern Europe were attracted to the Republican Party, which was a majority party with no need to bargain for recruits. The Democratic Party, on the contrary, was in bad need of additional voters. It had elected Woodrow Wilson by a huge electoral majority in 1912 when the Republican Party was split between the followers of William Howard Taft and those of Theodore Roosevelt, but the Democratic popular vote was 1,413,708 less than the combined Taft and Roosevelt votes. In fact, between 1892 (Cleveland's election over Harrison) and 1932 (F. D. Roosevelt's election over Hoover), the Democratic candidate had pooled more presidential popular votes than the Republican candidate (9,129,606 to 8,538,221) only once, when Woodrow Wilson was elected (1916) to a second term on the slogan, "He kept us out of war." In all the other elections, Republican majorities were substantial. Applying arithmetic to the popular vote of the seven presidential elections from 1904 to 1928 inclusive (*World Almanac*, 1949, p. 91), it is seen that *on the average*, the Democrats, except under extraordinary circumstances, could not in the first three decades of the twentieth century count on as much as 45% of the votes.

In addition to its need for more votes, the Democratic Party had another characteristic which appealed to the politically-minded Eastern European newcomers and drew to its ranks all but a handful of those who did not join a leftist splinter party. Unlike the Republican Party, which still had a fairly homogeneous membership, the Democratic Party was a collection of several groups. "The Democratic Party is not a political party at all; it's a marriage of convenience among assorted bedfellows, each of whom hates most of the others" (William Bradford Huie in an article, "Truman's Plan to Make Eisenhower President," *Cosmopolitan*, July, 1951, p. 31).

In the early part of the twentieth century the two largest components of the Democratic Party were the rural Protestant Southerners and the urban Catholic Northerners, who stood as a matter of course for the cardinal principles of Western Christian civilization, but otherwise had little in common politically except an opposition, chiefly because of vanished issues, to the Republican Party. The third group, which had been increasing rapidly after 1880, consisted of Eastern Europeans and other "liberals," best exemplified perhaps by the distinguished Harvard Jew, of Prague stock, Louis Dembitz Brandeis, whom President Woodrow Wilson, for reasons not yet fully known by the people, named to the United States Supreme Court. This man, at once so able, and in his legal and other attitudes so far to the left for the America of 1916, deserves attention as a symbol of the future for the Democratic Party, and through that party, for America.

According to the *Universal Jewish Encyclopedia*, there was an "historical battle" in the Senate in regard to "Brandeis' 'radicalism,'" and "his alleged 'lack of judicial temperament.'" These alleged qualities provoked opposition to the nomination by seven former presidents of the American Bar Association, including ex-Secretary of State Elihu Root and ex-President William Howard Taft.

Despite the opposition, the nomination was confirmed by the Senate in a close vote on June 5, 1916. This was one of the most significant days in American history, for we had, for the first time since the first decade of the nineteenth century, an official of the highest status whose heart's interest was in something besides the United States – an official, moreover, who interpreted the Law not as the outgrowth of precedent, but according to certain results desired by the interpreter.

The entire article on Justice Brandeis in the *Universal Jewish Encyclopedia* (Vol. II, pp. 495-499) should be read in full, if possible. Here are a few significant quotations:

During the World War, Brandeis occupied himself with a close study of the political phases of Jewish affairs in every country. Since that time his active interest in Jewish affairs has been centered in Zionism... In 1919, he visited Palestine for political and organizational reasons ... he has financed various social and economic efforts in Palestine.

As a justice, Mr. Brandeis:

Never worried about such academic perplexities as the compatibility of Americanism with a minority culture or a Jewish homeland in Palestine... Breaking away from the accepted legal catechisms, he thoroughly and exhaustively probed the economics of each and every problem presented. ... The truth of his conviction that our individualistic philosophy could no longer furnish an adequate basis for dealing with the problems of modern economic life, is now generally recognized ... he envisages a co-operative order... Brandeis feels that the Constitution must be given liberal construction.

This may be taken as the beginning of the tendency of our courts to assume by judicial decisions the function of legislative bodies.

There is testimony, also, to the influence of Brandeis over Wilson as a factor in America's entry into World War I and its consequent prolongation with terrible blood losses to all participants, especially among boys and young men of British, French, and German stock. Although Britain had promised self-rule to the Palestine Arabs in several official statements by Sir Henry MacMahon, the High Commissioner for Egypt, by Field Marshal Lord Allenby, Commander in Chief of British Military forces in the area, and by others (*The Surrender of An Empire*, by Nesta H. Webster, Boswell Printing and Publishing Co., Ltd., 10 Essex St., London, W.C.2, 1931, pp. 351-356), President Wilson was readily won over to a scheme concocted later in another compartment of the British government. This scheme, Zionism, attracted the favor of the Prime Minister, Mr. David Lloyd George, who, like Wilson, had with prominent Jews certain close relations, one of which is suggested in the *Encyclopædia Britannica* article (Vol. XIX, p. 4) on the first Marquess of Reading (previously Sir Rufus Daniel Isaacs). Thus, according to S. Landman, in his paper "Secret History of the Balfour Declaration" (*World Jewry*, March 1, 1935), after an "understanding had been arrived at between Sir Mark Sykes and Weizmann and Sokolow, it was resolved to send a secret message to Justice Brandeis that the British Cabinet would help the Jews to gain Palestine in return for active Jewish sympathy and support in U.S.A. for the allied cause so as to bring about a radical pro-ally tendency in the United States." An article, "The Origin of the Balfour Declaration" (*The Jewish Chronicle*, February 7, 1936), is more specific. According to this source, certain "representatives of the British and French Governments" had been convinced that "the best and perhaps the only way to induce the American President to come into the war was to secure the co-operation of Zionist Jewry by promising them Palestine." In so doing "the Allies would enlist and mobilize the hitherto unsuspectedly powerful force of Zionist Jewry in America and elsewhere." Since President Wilson at that time "attached the greatest possible importance to the advice of Mr. Justice Brandeis," the Zionists worked through him and "helped to bring America in."

The strange power of Brandeis over President Wilson is indicated several times in the book, *Challenging Years: The Autobiography of Stephen Wise* (G. P. Putnam's Sons, New York, 1949), Rabbi Wise, for instance, spoke of Wilson's "leaning heavily, as I well know he chose to do, on Brandeis" (p. 187), and records a surprising remark by the supposedly independent-minded World War I President. To Rabbi Wise, who spoke of Zionism and the plans for convening "the first session of the American Jewish Congress," Wilson said

(p. 189): "Whenever the time comes, and you and Justice Brandeis feel that the time is ripe for me to speak and act, I shall be ready."

The authenticity of these statements, which are well documented in the sources from which they are quoted, cannot be doubted. Full evaluation of President Wilson will have to wait until the secret archives of World War I are opened to the public. Meanwhile, however, the management of the war in such a way as to bleed Europe to death casts persistent reflections upon the judgment if not the motives of President Wilson and Prime Minister David Lloyd George of Great Britain. Their bloody victory and their failure in peace stand in strong contrast to Theodore Roosevelt's dramatic success in ending, rather than joining, the great conflict (1904-1905) between Russia and Japan.

After the eight-year rule of President Wilson, the Democratic Party was retired from office in the election of 1920. For the next twelve years (March 4, 1921-March 4, 1933), the three diverse groups in the Party – Southern Protestants, Northern Catholics, and Brandeis-type "liberals," – were held loosely together by leaders who helped each other toward the day of victory and the resultant power and patronage. Tactfully accustomed to ask no questions of each other, these leaders, still mostly Southern Protestants and Northern Catholics, did not ask any questions of the Party's rapidly increasing contingent of Eastern Europeans.

Thus the astute twentieth century immigrants of Eastern European origin continued to join the Democratic Party, in which everybody was accustomed to strange bedfellows, and in which a largely non-Christian third force was already well entrenched. Parenthetically, the best description of the National Democratic party as it existed from the time of Franklin Roosevelt's first term and on into the early 1950's is probably that of Senator Byrd of Virginia. Speaking at Selma, Alabama, on November 1, 1951 (AP dispatch), he described the party as a "heterogeneous crowd of Trumanites" and added that the group, "if it could be called a party, is one of questionable ancestry, irresponsible direction and predatory purposes."

Woodrow Wilson, who was definitely the candidate of a minority party, was elected in the first instance by a serious split in the Republican Party. By constant reenforcement from abroad, however, the "third force" of Eastern Europeans and associates of similar ideology was instrumental in raising the Democratic Party from a minority to a majority status. Some daring leaders of the alien or alien-minded wing conceived the idea of being paid in a special way for their contributions to victory.

Their price, carefully concealed from the American people, including of course many lesser figures among the Eastern Europeans, was the control of the foreign policy of the United States. At a glance, the achievement of such an objective might seem impossible. In fact, however, it was easy, because it happens under our practice that the entire electoral vote of a state goes to the candidate whose electors poll a majority of the popular votes of the state. With the population of older stock somewhat evenly divided between the Republican and Democratic parties, a well-organized minority can throw enough votes to determine the recipient of the electoral vote of a state. "The states having the largest numbers of Jews are New York, Pennsylvania, Illinois, New Jersey, Massachusetts, Ohio, California, and Michigan" (*The Immigration and Naturalization Systems of the United States*, p. 154). These, of course, are the "doubtful" states with a large electoral vote.

Thus, when the ship of patronage came in with the election of Franklin Delano Roosevelt in 1932, the Democrats of the old tradition, whether Southern Protestants or Northern Catholics, wanted dams, bridges, government buildings, and other government-financed projects in their districts; wanted contracts for themselves and their friends; and wanted also a quota of safe-tenure positions, such as federal judgeships. Neither group of old-time Democrats had many leaders who specialized in languages or in the complex subject matter of "foreign affairs," and neither group objected to the seemingly modest interest of certain of the party's Eastern European recruits for jobs of sub-cabinet rank in Washington.

The first spectacular triumph of the non-Christian Eastern European Democrats was Roosevelt's recognition, less than nine months after his inauguration, of the Soviet government of Russia. A lengthy factual article, "Moscow's RED LETTER DAY in American History," by William La Varre in the *American Legion Magazine* (August, 1951), gives many details on our strange diplomatic move which was arranged by "Litvinov, of deceitful smiles," and by "Henry Morgenthau and Dean Acheson, both protegés of Felix Frankfurter." Incidentally, Litvinov's birth name was Wallach and he also used the name Finkelstein. Three of the four persons thus named by Mr. La Varre as influential in this deal were of the same non-Christian stock or association – and the fourth was Dean Acheson, "who served as law clerk of Justice Louis D. Brandeis" (*U.S. News and World Report*, November 9, 1951) before becoming famous as a "Frankfurter boy" (see below, this chapter). The principal "Frankfurter boy" is the subject of a most important article in the *American Mercury* magazine (11 East 36th Street, New York 16, N.Y., 10 copies for $1.00) for April 1952. The author, Felix Wittner, says in part:

> Acheson's record of disservice to the cause of freedom begins at least nineteen years ago when he became one of Stalin's *paid* American lawyers. Acheson was on Stalin's payroll even before the Soviet Union was recognized by the United States.

Mr. La Varre's article should be read in full, among other things for its analysis of F. D. Roosevelt's betrayal of Latin America to penetration by Communism. Bearing on the basic question of the recognition of the Soviet, here are significant quotations:

The very special agent from Moscow, Commissar of all the Red Square's nefarious international machinations, chief of the Kremlin's schemes for communizing the American hemisphere, sat victoriously at the White House desk at midnight, smiling at the President of the United States.

For fifteen deceitful years the corrupt Kremlin had tried to obtain a communist base, protected by diplomatic immunities, within the United States; four Presidents – Wilson, Harding, Coolidge, and Hoover – had refused to countenance Moscow's pagan ideology or its carriers. But here, at last, was a President the communists could deal with.

Many patriotic, well-informed Americans, in the old Department of State, in the American Legion, and in the American Federation of Labor, had begged Franklin Roosevelt not to use his new leadership of the United States for the aggrandizement of an evil, dangerous and pagan guest – but to send him back to Moscow, red with the blood of the Commissar's own countrymen, without a handshake.

But Franklin Roosevelt, piqued with the power of his new office, stimulated by the clique of Marxian and Fabian socialists posing as intellectuals and liberals – and by radicals in labor unions, universities, and his own sycophant bureaucracy – had signed his name to the Kremlin's franchise. Without the approval of Congress, he made an actual treaty with the Soviets, giving them the right to establish a communist embassy and consulates in the United States, with full diplomatic hospitalities and immunities to Stalin's agents, the bloody bolsheviki...

November 16, 1933 – at midnight! That is a date in American history our children will long have tragic cause to remember. That was the day Soviet Foreign Commissar Maxim Litvinov, plunderer of Estonia and the Kremlin's first agent for socializing England, sat down with Franklin Roosevelt, after Dean Acheson and Henry Morgenthau had done the spadework of propaganda, and made the deal that has led the American people, and our once vast resources, into a social and economic calamity to the very brink, now, of national and international disaster...

One of the greatest concentrations of factual information, wise analyses, police records and military intelligence ever to pile up spontaneously on one subject in Washington, all documenting the liabilities of dealing with the Kremlin, had no effect on Franklin Roosevelt. He had appointed Henry Morgenthau and Dean Acheson, both protegés of Felix Frankfurter, to "study" trade opportunities between the U.S.S.R. and the United States, and he praised their report of the benefits to come to all U.S. citizens from Soviet "friendship."

The record shows that Cordell Hull, upon the receipt of this authentic document disclosing the Soviet's continuing duplicity, sent a note of protest to Moscow, but President Roosevelt could not be persuaded to withdraw his diplomatic recognition. He began, instead, the "reorganization" of the State Department in Washington and the dispatching – to far, isolated posts – of its anti-communist career officers.

The Roosevelt-Stalin deal, of November, 1933, has been so costly to us, as a nation and as a hemisphere, that the full appraisal of our losses and liabilities will not be known for several generations. The Kremlin's gains within the United States and communism's cost to us is only now, in 1951 – after eighteen years of suffering a Soviet embassy in our Capital, and its agents to roam the States – coming to public consciousness.

It has truly been a costly era of mysterious friendship for an appeasement of the devil, of un-American compromises with deceit and pagan ideologies. Some of its protagonists are now dead, their graves monuments to our present predicament, but others, again mysteriously, have been allowed to step into their strategic places.

Under the sort of government described by Mr. La Varre in his *Legion* article, large numbers of recently arrived and recently naturalized "citizens" and their ideological associates were infiltrated by appointment, or by civil service, into the State Department, the presidential coterie, and other sensitive spots in the government. Among those who feathered their Washington nests in this period were not only leftist East Europeans, but actual Communist converts or "sell-outs" to the Communist Party among native Americans. The solicitude of President F. D. Roosevelt for America's Communists was constant, as was shown in his steady opposition to proposed curbs upon them. Ex-Congressman Martin Dies, former Chairman of the House of Representatives Committee on Un-American Activities, bears witness in lectures (one of them heard by the author, 1950) that he was several times summoned to the White House by President Roosevelt and told – with suggestions of great favors to come – that he must stop annoying Communists (see Chapter IV). To the unyielding Dies, Roosevelt's climactic argument was "We need those votes!" A speech (May 17, 1951) on a similar theme by Mr. Dies has been published by the American Heritage Protective Committee (601 Bedell Building, San Antonio, Texas, 25¢). Another speech by Mr. Dies, "White House Protects Communists in Government," was inserted (September 22, 1950) in the Congressional Record by Congressman Harold H. Velde of Illinois.

The government was infiltrated with "risks" from the above described groups of Eastern Europeans and with contaminated native Americans, but those were not all. After the beginning of World War II, so-called "refugees" immediately upon arrival in this country were by executive order introduced into sensitive government positions without the formality of having them wait for citizenship, and without any investigation of their reasons for leaving Europe. The way for this infiltration was paved by an executive order providing specifically that employment could not be denied on the grounds of race, creed, or *national origin.*

Since *no form of investigation could be made by the Unites States in the distant and hostile areas from which these refugees came*, and since their number contained persons sympathetic to the Soviet Union, this executive order was a potential and in many instances a realized death-blow to security.

Almost as if for a *double-check against security*, the control of security measures in the new atom projects was not entrusted to the expert F.B.I., but to the atomic officials themselves. In view of their relative inexperience in such matters and in view of the amazing executive order so favorable to alien employees, the atomic officials were probably less to blame for the theft of atomic secrets than the "left-of-center" administrations which appointed them. Among those admitted to a proper spot for learning atomic secrets was the celebrated alien, the British subject – but not British-born – Klaus Fuchs. Other atomic spies, all aliens or of alien associations, were named in Chapter II.

Next to the atomic energy employees, the United Public Workers of America offered perhaps the best opportunity for the theft of secrets vital to the U.S. defense. This union included a generous number of people of Eastern European stock or connections, among them Leonard Goldsmith and Robert Weinstein, organizers of Panama Canal workers, and both of them said to have definite Communist affiliations (*Liberty*, May, 1948). This union – whose chief bloc of members was in Washington – was later expelled (March 1, 1950) by the C.I.O. on charges of being Communist-dominated ("Directory of Labor Unions in the United States," Bulletin No. 980, U.S. Dept. of Labor, 1950. 25¢). However, *if the U.S. Government has shown any signs of being as particular about its employees* (see Tydings Committee Report, U.S. Senate, 1950) *as the C.I.O. is about its members, the fact has escaped the attention of the author.*

As the years passed, the infiltration of Eastern Europeans into the government had swelled to a torrent. Many of these persons, of course, were not Communists and were not sympathetic with

Communist aims. As repeated elsewhere in this book, the contrary is neither stated nor implied. The author's purpose is simply to show that persons of Eastern European stock, or of an ideology not influential in the days of the founding and formative period of our country, have in recent years risen to many of the most strategic spots in the Roosevelt-Truman Democratic Party and thereby to positions of great and often decisive power in shaping the policy of the United States. The subject was broached by W. M. Kiplinger in a book, *Washington Is Like That* (Harper and Brothers, 1942). According to a *Reader's Digest* condensation (September, 1942), entitled "The Facts About Jews in Washington," Jews were by 1942 conspicuously "numerous" in government agencies and departments concerned with money, labor, and justice. The situation stemmed from the fact that "non-Jewish officials within government, acting under the direction of the President," were "trying to get various agencies to employ more Jews..."

The influence of persons of Eastern European origin, or of related origin or ideology, reached its peak (thus far) with Mr. Milton Katz at the helm of U.S. policy in Europe (to mid-1951); with Mrs. Anna Rosenberg in charge of the manpower of the U.S. Army, Navy, and Air Corps; with Mr. Manly Fleischman as Administrator of the Defense Production Administration; and with Mr. Nathan P. Feinsinger (*New York Times*, August 30, 1951) as Chairman of the Wage Stabilization Board. Likewise, in October, 1948, when President Truman appointed a "committee on religious and moral welfare and character guidance in the armed forces," he named as Chairman "Frank L. Weil, of New York, a lawyer, and President of the National Jewish Welfare Board" (*New York Times*, October 28, 1948).

It is interesting to note the prominence of persons of Khazar or similar background or association in the Socialist minority government of the United Kingdom, and in French politics, beginning with Leon Blum. Among them are the Rt. Hon. Emanuel

Shinwell and Minister Jules Moch – archfoe of Marshal Pétain – who have recently held defense portfolios in the British and French cabinets respectively. Just as in America the non-Christian characteristically joins the Democratic Party, so in Britain he joins the leftist Labor Party. Thus the British House of Commons, sitting in the summer of 1951, had 21 Jews among its Labor members and none among its Conservative members. Whatever his racial antecedents, Mr. Clement Attlee, long leader of the British "Labor" Party and Socialist Prime Minister (1945-1951) has for many years received international notoriety as a Communist sympathizer. For instance, he visited and praised the "English company" in the international Communist force in the Spanish Civil War (see photograph and facsimile in *The International Brigades,* Spanish Office of Information, Madrid, 1948, p. 134).

A few persons of Eastern European origin or background – or associated with persons of such background – in positions high or strategic, or both, have already been named by the author, and others, when their prominence demands it, will be named in the pages which follow. The author hereby assures the reader – again – that no reflection of any kind is intended and that he has no reason for believing that any of these people are other than true to their convictions.

First on any list of Americans of Eastern European origin should be the Vienna-born Felix Frankfurter, who in the middle twentieth century appears to have replaced "the stock of the Puritans" as the shining light and symbol of Harvard University. After leaving his professorship in the Harvard Law School, Dr. Frankfurter became a Supreme Court Justice and President Franklin Roosevelt's top-flight adviser on legal and other matters. In the formation of our national policies his influence is almost universally rated as supreme. "I suppose that Felix Frankfurter … has more influence in Washington than any other American," wrote Rev. John P. Sheerin, Editor of *The Catholic World* (March, 1951, p. 405), and the *Chicago Tribune*, owned by the Presbyterian Colonel Robert R. McCormick, has voiced a similar opinion. In fact, Mr. Justice Frankfurter is frequently referred to by those who know their way around Washington as the "President" of the United States. In a recent "gag," the question "Do you want to see a new picture of the President of the United States?" is followed up by showing a likeness of Frankfurter.

Mr. Justice Frankfurter is influential not only in counsel but in furthering the appointment of favored individuals to strategic positions. The so-called "Frankfurter's boys" include Mr. Acheson, with whom the justice takes daily walks, weather permitting (*New York Times*, January 19, 1949); Alger Hiss; Lee Pressman; David Niles, long a senior assistant to President Truman; Benjamin V. Cohen, long Counsellor of the Department of State; David Lilienthal, long Chairman of the Atomic Energy Commission; John J. McCloy, Joe Rauh, Nathan Margold, Donald Hiss, brother to Alger, and "now a member of the Acheson law firm"; Milton Katz; and former Secretary of War Robert Patterson, "a hundred per cent Frankfurter employee" (all names and quotes in this paragraph are from Drew Pearson's syndicated column, February 1, 1950).

A powerful government figure, the Russian-born Isador Lubin, was frequently summoned by President F. D. Roosevelt for the interpreting of statistics ("send for Lube"); and was subsequently a United States representative to the UN (article in *New York Times*, August 8, 1951). Leo Pasvolsky, Russian-born, was long a power in the Department of State, being, among other things, "executive director Committee on Postwar Program, 1944" and "in charge of international organization and security affairs," 1945-1946 (*Who's Who in America*, Vol. 26, 1950-51, p. 2117). Among others very close to Roosevelt II were Samuel Rosenman, who as "special counsel" was said to write many of the President's speeches; Henry Morgenthau, Secretary of the Treasury and sponsor of the vicious Morgenthau Plan; and Herbert Lehman, Director General (1943 to 1946) of the United Nations Relief and Rehabilitation Administration (UNRRA), most of whose funds – principally derived from the U.S. – were diverted to countries which were soon to become Soviet satellites as a result of the Yalta and Potsdam surrenders.

Strategic positions currently or recently held by persons of Eastern European origin, or ideological association with such people, include a number of Assistant Secretaryships to members of the Cabinet, among them incumbents in such sensitive spots as Defense, Justice (Customs and Solicitor General's Office) and Labor; the governorships of vital outposts such as Alaska (three miles from Russia) and the Virgin Islands (near the Panama Canal); appointments in the Executive Office of the President of the United States; positions in organizations devoted to international trade and assistance; membership on the Atomic Energy Commission; and membership, which may best be described as wholesale, in the U.S. delegation to the United Nations.

The number of persons of Eastern European origin or connection in appointive positions of strategic significance in our national government is strikingly high in proportion to the total number of such persons in America. On the contrary, in elective positions, the proportion of such persons is strikingly below their numerical proportion to the total population. The question arises: Does the high ratio of *appointed* persons of Eastern European origin or contacts in United States *strategic positions* reflect the will of the U.S. people? If not, what controlling *will* does it reflect?

"THE UNNECESSARY WAR"

In a speech before the Dallas, Texas, Alumni Club of Columbia University on Armistice Day, 1950, General of the Army Dwight D. Eisenhower stated that as Supreme Commander in Europe he made a habit of asking American soldiers why they were fighting the Germans and 90% of the boys said they had no idea. Very significantly, General Eisenhower did not offer members of his Alumni Group any precise answer to his own question. The high point of his speech was a statement of his hope that Columbia might become the fountain-head for widely disseminated simple and accurate information which will prevent our country from ever again "stumbling into war" at "the whim of the man who happens to be president" (notes taken by the author, who attended the Alumni Club meeting, and checked immediately with another Columbian who was also present).

The American soldier is not the only one who wondered and is still wondering about the purposes of World War II. Winston Churchill has called it "The Unnecessary War." In view of our legacy of deaths, debt, and danger, Churchill's term may be considered an understatement.

Before a discussion of any war, whether necessary or unnecessary, a definition of the term *war* is desirable. For the purposes of this book, war may be defined, simply and without elaboration, as the ultimate and violent action taken by a nation to implement its foreign policy. The results, even of a successful war, are so horrible to contemplate that a government concerned for the welfare of its people will enter the combat phase of its diplomacy only as a last resort. Every government makes strategic decisions, and no such decision is so fruitful of bitter sequels as a policy of drift or a policy of placating a faction – which has money or votes or both – and it is on just such a hybrid policy of drift and catering that our foreign policy has been built.

A commonly made and thoroughly sound observation about our foreign policy beginning with 1919 is that it creates vacuums – for a hostile power to fill. The collapsed Germany of 1923 created a power vacuum in the heart of Europe, but Britain and France made no move to fill it, perhaps because each of them was more watchful of the other than fearful of fallen Germany. The United States was far-off; its people of native stock, disillusioned by the bursting of Woodrow Wilson's dream bubbles, were disposed to revert to their old policy of avoiding foreign entanglements; and its numerous new Eastern European citizens, hostile to Germany, were watchfully awaiting a second and final collapse of the feeble republic born of the peace treaty of 1919. The new Soviet dictatorship, finding Marxism unworkable and slowly making it over into its later phases of Leninism and Stalinism, was as yet too precariously established for a westward venture across Poland.

As a result, Germany moved along stumblingly with more than a dozen political parties and a resultant near-paralysis of government under the Socialist President Friedrich Ebert to 1925 and then, with conditions improving slightly, under the popular old Prussian Field Marshal Paul von Hindenburg, who was President from 1925 to 1933.

Meanwhile, two of Germany's numerous political parties emerged into definite power – the Communists, many of whose leaders were of Khazar stock, and the National Socialist German

Workers Party, which was popularly called Nazi from the first two syllables of the German word for "National." Faced with harsh alternatives (testimony of many Germans to the author in Germany), the Germans chose the native party, and Adolf Hitler was elected Chancellor.

The date was January 30, 1933, five weeks before Franklin Roosevelt's first inauguration as President of the United States; but it was only after the aged President von Hindenburg's death (on August 2) that Hitler was made both President and Chancellor (August 19). Differences between the rulers of the United States and Germany developed quickly. Hitler issued a series of tirades against Communism, which he considered a world menace, whereas Roosevelt injected life into the sinking body of world Communism (Chapter III, above) by giving full diplomatic recognition to Soviet Russia on November 16, 1933, a day destined to be known as "American-Soviet Friendship Day" by official proclamation of the State of New York.

Sharing the world spotlight with his anti-Communist words and acts, was Hitler's domestic policy, which in its early stages may be epitomized as "Germany for the Germans," of whom in 1933 there were some 62,000,000. Hitler's opponents, more especially those of non-German stock (510,000 in 1933, according to the *World Almanac*, 1939), were unwilling to lose by compromise any of their position of financial and other power acquired in large degree during the economic collapse of 1923, and appealed for help to persons of prominence in the city of New York and elsewhere. Their appeal was not in vain.

In late July, 1933, an International Jewish Boycott Conference (*New York Times*, August 7, 1933) was held in Amsterdam to devise means of bringing Germany to terms. Samuel Untermeyer of New York presided over the Boycott Conference and was elected President of the World Jewish Economic Federation. Returning to America, Mr. Untermeyer described the planned Jewish move against Germany as a "holy war ... a war that must be waged un-remittingly" (speech over WABC, as printed in *New York Times* of August 7, 1933). The immediately feasible tactic of the "economic boycott" was described by Mr. Untermeyer as "nothing new," for "President Roosevelt, whose wise statesmanship and vision are the wonder of the civilized world, is invoking it in furtherance of his noble conception of the relations between capital and labor." Mr. Untermeyer gave his hearers and readers specific instructions:

> It is not sufficient that you buy no goods made in Germany. You must refuse to deal with any merchant or shopkeeper who sells any German-made goods or who patronizes German ships and shipping
>
> .

Before the Boycott Conference adjourned at Amsterdam, ar-rangement was made to extend the boycott to "include France, Holland, Belgium, Britain, Poland and Czechoslovakia and other lands as far flung as Finland and Egypt" (*New York Times*, August 1, 1933). In connection with the boycott, the steady anti-German campaign, which had never died down in America after World War I, became suddenly violent. Germany was denounced in several influential New York papers and by radio.

The public became dazed by the propaganda, and the U.S. Gov-ernment soon placed on German imports the so-called "general" tariff rates as against the "most favored" status for all other nations. This slowed down but did not stop the German manufacture of export goods, and the U.S. took a further step, described as follows in the *New York Times* (June 5, 1936): "Already Germany is paying general tariff rates because she has been removed by Secretary of State Cordell Hull from the most favored nation list... Now she will be required to pay additional duties... It was decided that they would range from about 22 to 56 per cent." There were protests. According to the *New York Times* (July 12, 1936): "importers and others interested in trade with Germany insisted yesterday that commerce between the two countries will dwindle to the vanishing point within the next six months." The prediction was correct. An effort of certain anti-German international financial interests was also made to "call" sufficient German treasury notes to "break" Germany. The German government replied successfully to this maneuver by giving a substantial bonus above the current exchange rate for foreigners who would come to Germany, exchange their currency for marks, and spend the marks in Germany. Great preparations were made for welcoming strangers to such gatherings as the "World Conference on Recreation and Leisure Time" (Hamburg, August, 1936), one of whose programmes, a historic pageant on the Auszen-Alster, was attended by the author (who was visiting northern European museums and coastal areas in the interest of his historical novel, *Swords in the Dawn*). Special trains brought in school children from as far as northern Norway. Whether from sincerity or from a desire to create a good impression, visitors were shown every courtesy. As a result of the German effort and the money bonus afforded by the favorable exchange, retired people, pensioners, and tourists spent enough funds in the Reich to keep the mark stable.

But this German financial victory in 1936, though it prevented an immediate currency collapse, did not solve the problem of 62,000,000 people (69,000,000 by 1939) in an area approximately the size of Texas being effectively denied export trade.

Through Secretary of State Cordell Hull and other officials President Roosevelt sponsored Mr. Untermeyer's economic war against Germany, but he still adhered, in his public utterances, to a policy of non-intervention in the internal affairs of foreign nations. In two speeches in the summer of 1937 he voiced "our national determination to keep free from foreign wars and foreign entanglements" (*American Foreign Policy in the Making, 1932-1940*, by Charles A. Beard, Yale University Press, 1946, p. 183).

Some sinister underground deal must have been consummated within two months, however, for in a speech in Chicago on October 5 the President made an about-face, which was probably the most complete in the whole history of American foreign policy. Here are two excerpts from the famous "Quarantine" speech:

> ... let no one imagine that America will escape, that America may expect mercy, that this Western Hemisphere will not be attacked! ...

When an epidemic of physical disease starts to spread, the community approves and joins in a quarantine of the patients in order to protect the health of the community against the spread of the disease.

This pronouncement, so inflammatory, so provocative of war, caused unprecedented consternation in the United States (see Beard, *op. cit.*, pp. 186 ff.). Most outspoken in opposition to the "quarantine" policy was the *Chicago Tribune*. Violently enthusiastic was the *New Masses*, and Mr. Earl Browder promised the administration the "100 per cent unconditional support of the Communist party," provided Roosevelt adopted a hands-off policy toward Communism. Incidentally, this Democratic-Communist collaboration was openly or covertly to be a factor in subsequent United States foreign and domestic policy to and beyond the middle of the twentieth century. "I welcome the support of Earl Browder or any one else who will help keep President Roosevelt in office," said Harry S. Truman, candidate for Vice President, on October 17, 1944 (*National Republic*, May, 1951, p. 8).

Far more numerous than denouncers or endorsers of the "quarantine" speech of 1937 were those who called for clarification. This, however, was not vouchsafed – nor was it, apart from possible details of method and time, really necessary. It was perfectly obvious that the President referred to Japan and Germany. With the latter country we had already declared that "no quarter" economic war recommended by the President of the World Jewish Economic Federation, and now in unquestionably hostile terms our President declared a political war. In his diary, Secretary of Defense James Forrestal recorded that he was told by Joseph P. Kennedy, our Ambassador to Britain, that Prime Minister Chamberlain "stated that America and the world Jews had forced England into the war" (*The Forrestal Diaries*, ed. by Walter Millis, The Viking Press, New York, 1951, pp. 121-122).

Censorship, governmental and other (Chapter V), was tight in America by 1937. It had blocked out the reasons for Mr. Roosevelt's *public* change of policy between summer and autumn, and it blacked out the fact that the President's threatening attitude caused Germany to make, and make a second time, an appeal for peace. *These appeals did not become known to the American public for more than ten years.* Here is the story, summarized from an article by Bertram D. Hulen in the *New York Times* of December 17, 1948:

In 1937, and again in 1938, the German government made "a sincere effort to improve relations with the United States, only to be rebuffed." The U.S. Government's alleged reason was "a fear of domestic political reactions in this country unfavorable to the Administration." Germany was told that *the American public would not tolerate a conference.* Some officials favored exploring the German offer "after the congressional elections in the fall" (1938). *The sequel, of course, is that the Roosevelt administration blocked Germany's further efforts for peace by withdrawing our ambassador from Berlin and thus peremptorily preventing future negotiations.* Germany then had to recall her Ambassador "who was personally friendly toward Americans" and, according to the *New York Times*, "was known in diplomatic circles here at the time to be working for international understanding in a spirit of good will". Here, to repeat for emphasis, is the crux of the matter: *The whole story of Germany's appeal for negotiations and our curt refusal and severance of diplomatic relations was not published in*

1937 or 1938, when Germany made her appeals, but was withheld from the public until ferreted out by the House Committee on Un-American Activities after World War II and by that committee released to the press more than ten years after the facts were so criminally suppressed. Parenthetically, it is because of services such as this on behalf of truth that the Committee on Un-American Activities has been so frequently maligned. In fact, in our country since the 1930's there seems little question that the best criterion for separating true Americans from others is a recorded attitude toward the famous Martin Dies Committee.

Economically strangled by an international boycott headed up in New York, and outlawed politically even to the extent of being denied a conference, the Germans in the late 1930's faced the alternatives of mass unemployment from loss of world trade or working in government-sponsored projects. They accepted the latter. The workers who lost their jobs in export businesses were at once employed in Hitler's armament industries (see the special edition of the *Illustrirte Zeitung* for November 25, 1936), which were already more than ample for the size and resources of the country, and soon became colossal.

Thus by desperate measures, advertised to the world in the phrase "guns instead of butter," Hitler prepared to cope with what he considered to be the British-French-American-Soviet "encirclement." Stung by what he considered President Roosevelt's insulting language and maddened by the contemptuous rejection of his diplomatic approaches to the United States, he made a deal (August 1939) against Poland with the Soviet Union, a power he had taught the German people to fear and hate! With the inevitability of a Sophoclean tragedy, this betrayal of his own conscience brought him to ruin – and Germany with him. Such is the danger which lurks for a people when they confide their destiny to the whims of a dictator!

The war, which resulted from Franklin D. Roosevelt's policy is well remembered, especially by those American families whose sons lie beneath white crosses – at home or afar. Its pre-shooting phase, with all the weavings back and forth, is analyzed in Professor Beard's volume, already referred to. Its causes are the subject of Frederic R. Sanborn's *Design for War* (Devin-Adair New York, 1951). Its progress is surveyed in William Henry Chamberlin's *America's Second Crusade* (Henry Regnery Company, Chicago, 1950). Details cannot be here presented.

This much, however, is evident. With some secret facts now revealed and with the foul picture now nearing completion, we can no longer wonder at a clean trustful young soldier or an honorable general being unable to give a satisfactory reason for our part in promoting and participating in World War II.

As the "unnecessary war" progressed, we adopted an increasingly horrible policy. Our government's fawning embrace of the Communist dictator of Russia, and his brutal philosophy which we called "democratic," was the most "unnecessary" act of our whole national history, and could have been motivated only by the most reprehensible political considerations – such, for instance, as holding the 100 percent Communist support at a price proposed by Mr. Browder. Among those who learned the truth and remained silent, with terrible consequences to himself and his country, was James V. Forrestal. In an article, "The Forrestal Diaries," *Life* reveals (October 15, 1951) that in 1944 Forrestal wrote thus to a friend about the "liberals" around him:

> I find that whenever any American suggests that we act in accordance with the needs of our own security he is apt to be called a [profane adjective deleted] fascist or imperialist, while if Uncle Joe suggests that he needs the Baltic Provinces, half of Poland, all of Bessarabia and access to the Mediterranean, all hands agree that he is a fine, frank, candid and generally delightful fellow who is very easy to deal with because he is so explicit in what he wants.

Among those who saw our madness, and spoke out, were Senator Robert A. Taft of Ohio and Winston Churchill.

Senator Taft's radio address of June 29, 1941, a few days after Hitler invaded Russia, included the following passage:

> How can anyone swallow the idea that Russia is battling for democratic principles? Yet the President on Monday announced that the United States would give all possible aid to Russia, the character and quantity of the aid to await only a disclosure of Russian needs... To spread the four freedoms throughout the world we will ship airplanes and tanks and guns to Communist Russia. But no country was more responsible for the present war and Germany's aggression than Russia itself. Except for the Russian pact with Germany there would have been no invasion of Poland. Then Russia proved to be as much of an aggressor as Germany. In the name of democracy we are to make a Communist alliance with the most ruthless dictator in the world...
>
> But the victory of Communism in the world would be far more dangerous to the United States than the victory of Fascism. There has never been the slightest danger that the people of this country would ever embrace Bundism or Nazism... But Communism masquerades, often successfully, under the guise of democracy (*Human Events*, March 28, 1951).

The Prime Minister of Britain, the Right Honorable Winston Churchill, was alarmed at President Roosevelt's silly infatuation for Stalin and the accompanying mania for serving the interests of world Communism. "It would be a measureless disaster if Russian barbarism overlaid the culture and independence of the ancient states of Europe," he wrote on Oct. 21, 1942, to the British Foreign Secretary, Anthony Eden. Churchill also wanted an invasion of the Balkans, which Roosevelt and Marshall opposed, apparently to please Stalin (Elliott Roosevelt, *As He Saw It*, Duell, Sloan and

Pearce, New York, 1946, *passim*). This is no place and the author assumes no competence for analyzing the strategy of individual campaigns; but according to Helen Lombard's *While They Fought* (Charles Scribner's Sons, 1947, p. 148), General Marshall stated to a Congressional Committee that the "purpose" of the Italian campaign was to draw "German forces away from the Russian front," and according to the same source, General Mark Clark when questioned "about American political aims" found himself "obliged to state that his country was seeking nothing except ground in which to bury her dead." Such being true, one may wonder why – except for the furtherance of Stalin's aims – the forces devoted to strategically unimportant Italy, the winning of which left the Alps between our armies and Germany, were not landed, for instance, in the Salonika area for the historic Vardar Valley invasion route which leads without major obstacles to the heart of Europe and would have helped Stalin defeat Hitler without giving the Red dictator all of Christian Eastern Europe as a recompense.

It is widely realized now that Churchill had to put up with much indignity and had to agree to many strategically unsound policies to prevent the clique around Roosevelt from prompting him to injure even more decisively Britain's world position vis-a-vis with the Soviet Union. Sufficient documentation is afforded by General Elliott Roosevelt's frank and useful *As He Saw It*, referred to above. Determined apparently to present the truth irrespective of its bearing on reputations, the general (p. 116) quotes his father's anti-British attitude as expressed at Casablanca: "I will work with all my might and main to see to it that the United States is not wheedled into the position of accepting any plan … that will aid or abet the British Empire in its imperial ambitions." This was the day before Roosevelt's "Unconditional Surrender" proclamation (Saturday, Jan. 23, 1943). The next day Roosevelt again broached the subject to his son, telling him the British "must never get the idea that we're in it just to help them hang on to the archaic, medieval Empire ideas."

This attitude toward Britain, along with a probably pathological delight in making Churchill squirm, explains the superficial reason for Roosevelt's siding with the Stalinites on the choice of a strategically insignificant area for the Mediterranean front. As implied above, the deeper reason, beyond question, was that in his frail and fading condition he was a parrot for the ideas which the clique about him whispered into his ears, with the same type of flattery that Mr. Untermeyer had used so successfully in initiating the Jewish boycott. No reason more valid can be found for the feeble President's interest in weakening the British Empire while strengthening the Soviet Empire – either in the gross or in such specific instances as the Roosevelt-Eisenhower policy in Germany. This policy, initiated by Roosevelt and implemented by Eisenhower, was well summarized in a speech, "It Is Just Common Sense to Ask Why We Arrived at Our Present Position," by Congressman B. Carroll Reece of Tennessee in the House of Representatives on March 19, 1951 (*Congressional Record*, pp. A1564 to A1568):

... We could have easily gotten to Berlin first. But our troops were first halted at the Elbe. They were then withdrawn from that river in a wide circle – far enough westward to make Stalin a present of the great Zeiss optical and precision instrument works at Jena, the most important V-1 and V-2 rocket laboratory and production plant in Nordhausen, and the vital underground jet plant in Kahla. Everywhere we surrendered to the Soviets intact thousands of German planes, including great masses of jet fighters ready for assembly, as well as research centers, rocket developments, scientific personnel, and other military treasures. When it was all over, a large part of the formidable Russian militarism of today was clearly marked "Made in America" or "donated by America from Germany." But where Roosevelt left off President Truman resumed.

At Potsdam, Truman maintaining intact Roosevelt's iron curtain of secret diplomacy, played fast and loose with American honor and security. He agreed to an enlargement of the boundaries of a Poland already delivered by Roosevelt and Churchill to Russian control through addition of areas that had for centuries been occupied by Germans or people of German origin. Some 14,000,000 persons were brutally expelled from their homes with the confiscation of virtually all their property. Only 10,000,000 finally reached the American, French, and British zones of Germany. Four million mysteriously disappeared, though the finger points toward Russian atrocities. Thus Truman approved one of the greatest mass deportations in history, which for sheer cruelty is a dark page in the annals of history.

At Potsdam, Truman also sanctioned Russian acquisition of Eastern Germany, the food bin of that nation before the war. It then became impossible for the remaining German economy in British, French, and American hands to feed its people. Germany, like Japan, also went on our bounty rolls.

Like Roosevelt, Truman did not neglect to build up Russian military strength when this opportunity came at Potsdam. He provided her with more factories, machines, and military equipment, though at the time he attended Potsdam Truman knew that through lend-lease we had already dangerously expanded Russia's military might and that, in addition, we had given the Soviets some 15,000 planes – many of them our latest type – and 7,000 tanks.

But at Potsdam Truman gave to Russia the entire zone embracing the Elbe and Oder Rivers, excepting Hamburg, which lies within the British zone. Naval experts had known from the early days of World War II that it was along these rivers and their tributaries that the Germans had set up their submarine production line. The menace which the Nazi underwater fleet constituted during World War II is still remembered by residents along the Atlantic coast who saw oil tankers, merchant ships, and even a troop transport sunk within sight of our shores. Convoy losses during the early years of the war were tremendous. And special defensive methods had to be devised by our Navy to get our supplies across the Atlantic.

But in spite of this, the President agreed at Potsdam to deliver to Russia the parts [of Germany containing] plants sufficient for her to fabricate hundreds of submarines. In addition to this, he agreed to give to Russia 10 of the latest snorkel-tube long-range German submarines for experimental purposes.

Why did Churchill consent to the initiation of such a program? Why did he allow Roosevelt to give an ideologically hostile power a foothold as far West as the Elbe River, which flows into the North Sea?

Since Churchill was characteristically no weak-kneed yes-man (witness his "blood and tears" speech which rallied his people in one of their darkest hours), Roosevelt and his clique must have confronted him with terrible alternatives to secure his consent to the unnatural U.S. decisions in the last months of the war. Wrote George Sokolsky in his syndicated column of March 22, 1951, "The pressure on him (Churchill) from Roosevelt, who was appeasing Stalin, must have been enormous… But why was Roosevelt so anxious to appease Stalin?" And also at Potsdam, why was Truman so ready to adopt the same vicious policy which, as a former field grade officer of the army, he must have known to be wrong?

A study of our Presidential "policies" from 1933, and especially from 1937, on down to Potsdam, leads to a horrible answer.

To one who knows something of the facts of the world and knows also the main details of the American surrender of security and principles at Tehran, Yalta, and Potsdam, and other conferences, three ghastly purposes come into clear focus:

(1) *As early as 1937, our government determined upon war against Germany for no formulated purpose beyond pleasing the dominant Eastern European element and allied elements in the National*

Democratic Party, and holding "those votes," as Roosevelt II put it (Chapter III, above).

The President's determination to get into war to gratify his vanity of having a third term of office is touched on by Jesse H. Jones, former Secretary of Commerce and head of the Reconstruction Finance Corporation, in his book, *Fifty Billion Dollars* (The Macmillan Company, New York, 1951). In this comprehensive and carefully documented volume, which is obligatory background reading on U.S. politics in the years 1932-1945, Mr. Jones throws much light on Roosevelt, the "Total Politician." On Roosevelt's desire for getting into World War II, these (p. 260) are Mr. Jones's words: "Regardless of his oft repeated statement 'I hate war,' he was eager to get into the fighting since that would insure a third term." The most notorious instance of the President's Dr. Jekyll and Mr. Hyde character was his unblushing promise, as he prepared for intervention, that there would be no war. The third-term candidate's "again and again and again" speech (Boston, October 30, 1940) is invariably quoted, but even more inclusive was his broadcast statement of October 26 that no person in a responsible position in his government had "ever suggested in any shape, manner, or form the remotest possibility of sending the boys of American mothers to fight on the battlefields of Europe." We are thus confronted by a dilemma. Was Roosevelt the scheming ruiner of his country or was he a helpless puppet pulled by strings from hands which wielded him beyond any power of his to resist?

A continuing lack of any policy beyond the corralling of minority votes blighted the entire world effort of our devoted and self-sacrificing soldiers, and frustrated the hopes of those of our lower echelon policy-makers who were trying to salvage something useful to civilization from our costly world-wide war. Our diplomatic personnel, military attachés, and other representatives abroad were confused by what they took to be rudderless drifting. In one foreign country diametrically opposed statements were issued simultaneously by heads of different U.S. missions. In Washington, the Office of War Information issued under the same date line completely conflicting instructions to two sets of its representatives in another Asiatic country. A United States military attaché with the high rank of brigadier general made an impassioned plea (in the author's hearing) for a statement of our purposes in the war; but, asking the bread of positive strategic policy, he got the stone of continued confusion. Some of the confusion was due to the fact that officials from the three principal kinds of Democrats (Chapter III) were actuated by and gave voice to different purposes; most of it, however, resulted from the actual lack of any genuine policy except to commit our troops and write off casualties with the smoke of the President's rhetoric. Yes, we were fighting a war, not to protect our type of civilization or to repel an actual or threatened invasion, but for Communist and anti-German *votes. Thus when our ailing President went to Yalta, he is said to have carried no American demands, to have presented no positive plans to counter the proposals of Stalin.* In his feebleness, with Alger Hiss nearby, he yielded with scarcely a qualm to the strong and determined Communist leader. For fuller details see the carefully documented article, "America Betrayed at Yalta," by Hon. Lawrence H. Smith, U.S. Representative from Wisconsin (*National Republic,* July, 1951).

(2) *The powerful Eastern European element dominant in the inner circles of the Democratic Party regarded with complete equanimity, perhaps even with enthusiasm, the killing of as many as possible of the world-ruling and Khazar-hated race of "Aryans"* (Chapter II); that is, native stock Americans of English, Irish, Scotch, Welsh, German, Dutch, Scandinavian, Latin, and Slavic descent. This non-Aryan power bloc therefore endorsed "Unconditional Surrender" and produced the Morgenthau Plan (see below), both of which were certain to stiffen and prolong the German resistance at the cost of many more American lives, much more desolation

in Germany, and many more German lives – also "Aryan." The plans of the prolongers of the war were sustained by those high Democratic politicians who saw nothing wrong in the spilling of blood in the interest of votes. Unfortunately, President Roosevelt became obsessed with the idea of killing Germans (*As He Saw It*, pp. 185-186) rather than defeating Hitler, and reportedly set himself against any support of anti-Hitler elements in Germany. Perhaps taking his cue from his Commander-in-Chief – a term Roosevelt loved – General Mark Clark told American soldiers of the Fifth Army that German "assaults" were "welcome," since "it gives you additional opportunity to kill your hated enemy in large numbers." The general drove the point home. "It is open season on the Anzio bridgehead," he continued, "and there is no limit to the number of Germans you can kill" (*New York Times*, February 13, 1944).

Such a sentiment for men about to make the supreme sacrifice of their lives has – in the author's opinion – an unnatural ring to ears attuned to the teachings of Christianity. Such a stress on "killing" or "kill" rather than on a "cause" or on "victory" is definitely at variance with the traditions of Western Christian civilization. It is also costly in the life blood of America, for "killing" is a two-edged sword. An enemy who would surrender in the face of certain defeat will fight on to the end when truculently promised a "killing" – and more Americans will die with him.

The underlying philosophy of "killing" was incidentally hostile to the second largest racial strain in America. Germans have from the beginning been second only to the English and Scotch in the make-up of our population. "In 1775 the Germans constituted about 10 per cent of the white population of the colonies" (*The Immigration and Naturalization Systems of the United States*, p. 233). The total of Dutch, Irish, French "and all others" was slightly less than the Germans, the great bulk of the population being, of course, the English-speaking people from England, Scotland, and Wales. In the first three quarters of the nineteenth century,

"German immigration outdistanced all other immigration," and as of 1950 "the Germans have contributed over 25 per cent of the present white population of the United States. The English element – including Scots, North Irish, and Welsh – alone exceeds them with about 33 per cent of the present white population. The Irish come third with about 15 per cent" (*op. cit.,* p. 233).

Thus in his desire for shedding German blood, apart from military objectives, Roosevelt set himself not against an enemy government but against the race which next to the English gave America most of its life-blood. The general merely copied his "commander-in-chief." Another tragic factor in any announced stress on "killing" was, of course, that the Germans whom we were to "kill" rather than merely "defeat" had exactly as much to do with Hitler's policies as our soldiers in Korea have to do with Acheson's policies.

Why did the thirty-four million Americans of German blood make no loud protest? The answer is this: in physical appearance, in culture, and in religion, Protestant or Catholic, they were so identical with the majority that their amalgamation had been almost immediate. In 1945 there was a great strain of German blood in America, but there was no significant vote-delivering body of political "German-Americans."

Meanwhile, the ships which took American soldiers to kill Germans and meet their own death in Europe brought home "refugees" in numbers running in many estimates well into seven figures. According to Assistant Secretary of State Breckenridge Long (testimony before House Committee on Foreign Affairs, Nov. 26, 1943), the number of *officially* admitted aliens fleeing "Hitler's persecution" had reached 580,000 as early as *November, 1943.* Those refugees above quotas were admitted on "visitors' visas." These facts were released by Congressman Sol Bloom, Democrat of New York, Chairman of the House Committee on Foreign Affairs, on December 10 (article by Frederick Barkley, *New York*

Times, Dec. 11, 1943). On December 11, Congressman Emanuel Celler, Democrat of New York, complained that Mr. Long was, in all the State Department, the man "least sympathetic to refugees," and added indignantly that United States ships had returned from overseas ports "void of passengers" (*New York Times*, December 12, 1943). Incidentally, in 1944 Mr. Long ceased to be Assistant Secretary of State.

The influx of refugees continued. So great was the number of these people that even with the closing of thousands of American homes by our casualties, the housing shortage after the war was phenomenal. For the lack of homes available to veterans, some writers blamed capital, some blamed labor, and some found other causes; but none, to the knowledge of the author, counted the homes which had been pre-empted by "refugees," while our soldiers were fighting beyond the seas. By 1951 the situation showed no amelioration, for on August 20 Senator Pat McCarran, chairman of a Senate sub-committee on internal security, said that "possibly 5,000,000 aliens had poured into the country illegally, creating a situation 'potentially more dangerous' than an armed invasion" (AP dispatch in *New York Times*, August 20, 1951). This statement should be pondered thoughtfully by every true American.

And there are more aliens to come. On September 7, 1951, a "five-year program for shifting 1,750,000 of Europe's 'surplus' population to new homes and opportunities in the Americas and Australia was disclosed" by David A. Morse, head of the International Labor Office of the UN (*New York Times*, Sept. 8, 1951). Needless to say, few of those 1,750,000 persons are likely to be accepted elsewhere than in the United States (for data on Mr. Morse, see *Economic Council Letter*, No. 200, October 1, 1948, or *Who's Who in America*, 1950-1951). Congressman Jacob K. Javits of New York's Twenty-first District, known to some as the Fourth Reich from the number of its "refugees" from Germany, also wishes still more immigrants. In an article, "Let Us Open the

Gates" (*New York Times Magazine,* July 8, 1951), he asked for ten million immigrants in the next twenty years.

(3) *Our alien-dominated government fought the war for the annihilation of Germany, the historic bulwark of Christian Europe* (Chapter I, above). The final phase of this strategically unsound purpose sprouted with the cocky phrase "Unconditional Surrender," already mentioned. It was "thrown out at a press conference by President Roosevelt at Casablanca on January 24, 1943. ... President Roosevelt went into the press conference in which he 'ad-libbed' the historic phrase" (Raymond Gram Swing in "Unconditional Surrender," *The Atlantic Monthly,* September 1947). According to General Elliott Roosevelt, the President repeated the phrase, "thoughtfully sucking a tooth" (*As He Saw It,* p. 117), and added that "Uncle Joe might have made it up himself."

Our foul purpose of liquidating Germany flowered with the implementation of the Morgenthau Plan, an implementation, which allowed "widespread looting and violence" by "displaced persons" and brought Germans to the verge of starvation, according to Prof. Harold Zink, who served as American Editor of the *Handbook for Military Government in Germany* in 1944 and was subsequently Consultant on U.S. Reorganization of German Government, U.S. Troop Control Council for Germany, 1944-1945 (*Who's Who in America,* Vol. 25, 1948-1949, p. 2783). In his book, *American Military Government in Germany* (Macmillan, 1947, pp. 106 and 111), Prof. Zink writes as follows:

> The Germans were forced to furnish food for the displaced persons at the rate of 2,000 calories per day when they themselves could have only 900-1100 calories...
>
> The amount available for German use hardly equalled the food supplied by the Nazis at such notorious concentration camps as Dachau ... most of the urban German population suffered severely from lack of food.

The hunger at Dachau was war-time inhumanity by people who were themselves desperately hungry because their food stocks and transportation systems had been largely destroyed by American air bombardment; but the quotation from Professor Zink refers to peace-time inhumanity, motivated by vengeance partly in its conception and even more so in its implementation (see *Potsdam Agreement*, Part III, paragraph 156 in *Berlin Reparations Assignment*, by Ratchford and Ross, The University of North Carolina Press, Chapel Hill, p. 206).

Why did inhumanity in Germany go on? Because "a little dove," according to President Roosevelt, flew in the President's window and roused him against a "too 'easy' treatment of the Germans," the "little dove" being "actually Secretary Morgenthau's personal representative in the ETO" (Zink, *op. cit.*, pp. 131-132)! Further testimony to the President's desire for an inhuman treatment of "German people" is found in former Secretary of State James F. Byrnes's book, *Speaking Frankly* (Harper and Brothers, New York, 1947). The President stated to his Secretary of State that the Germans "for a long time should have only soup for breakfast, soup for lunch, and soup for dinner" (p. 182).

The fruits of the Morgenthau Plan were not all harvested at once. The persistence of our mania for destroying the historic heart of Germany was shown vividly in 1947. With Prussia already being digested in the maw of the Soviet, the Allied Control Council in Berlin (March 1) added a gratuitous insult to an already fatal injury when it "formally abolished" Prussia, the old homeland of the Knights of the Teutonic Order. This could have had no other motive than offending Germans unnecessarily for the applause of certain elements in New York. It was also a shock to all Christians, Catholic or Protestant, who have in their hearts the elementary instincts of Christ-like mercy (*St. Matthew*, V, 7), or know in spite of censorship the great facts of the history of Europe (Chapter I).

Our policy of terrifying the Germans spiritually, and ruining them economically, is understandable only to one who holds his eye in focus upon the nature of the High Command of the National Democratic Party. Vengeance and votes were the sire and dam of the foul monster of American cruelty to the Germans. In the accomplishment of our base purpose there was also a strange pagan self-immolation, for we would not let the West Germans all the way die and spent approximately a billion dollars a year (high as our debt was – and is) to provide for our captives the subsistence they begged to be allowed to earn for themselves! Our wanton dismantling of German industrial plants in favor of the Soviet as late as 1950 and our hanging of Germans as late as 1951 (Chapter V, c), more than six years after the German surrender, had no other apparent motive than the alienation of the German people. Moreover, as the years pass, there has been no abandonment of our policy of keeping in Germany a number of representatives who, whatever their personal virtues, are *personae non gratae* to the Germans (Chapters III and VI). Our many-facetted policy of deliberately alienating a potentially friendly people violates a cardinal principle of diplomacy and strategy and weakens us immensely to the advantage of Soviet Communism.

The facts and conclusions thus far outlined in this chapter establish fully the validity of Churchill's phrase, "The Unnecessary War." The war was unnecessary in its origin, unnecessarily cruel in its prolongation, indefensible in the double-crossing of our ally Britain, criminal in our surrender of our own strategic security in the world, and all of this the more monstrous because it was accomplished in foul obeisance before the altar of anti-Christian power in America.

The facts and conclusions outlined in this chapter raise the inevitable question: "How were such things possible?" The answer is the subject of the next chapter.

CHAPTER V

THE BLACK HOOD
OF CENSORSHIP

Over his head, face, and neck the medieval executioner sometimes wore a loose-fitting hood of raven black. The grim garment was pierced by two eye-holes through which the wearer, himself unrecognized, caused terror by glancing among the onlookers while he proceeded to fulfill his gruesome function. In similar fashion today, under a black mask of censorship, which hides their identity and their purpose, the enemies of our civilization are at once creating fear and undermining our Constitution and our heritage of Christian civilization. In medieval times, the onlookers at least knew what was going on, but in modern times the people have no such knowledge. Without the ignorance and wrong judging generated by this hooded propaganda, an alert public and an informed Congress would long since have guided the nation to a happier destiny.

The black-out of truth in the United States has been effected (I) by the executive branch of the national government and (II) by non-government power.

I

In the mention of government censorship, it is not implied that our national government suppresses newspapers, imprisons editors, or in other drastic ways prevents the actual publication of news

103

which has already been obtained by periodicals. It is to be hoped that such a lapse into barbarism will never befall us.

Nevertheless, since the mid-thirties, a form of censorship has been applied at will by many agencies of the United States government. Nothing is here said against war-time censorship of information on United States troop movements, military plans, and related matters. Such concealment is necessary for our security and for the surprise of the enemy, and is a vital part of the art of war. Nothing is said here against such censorship as the government's falsification of the facts about our losses on December 7, 1941, at Pearl Harbor (*Pearl Harbor, The Story of the Secret War*, by George Morgenstern, The Devin-Adair Company, New York, 1947), though the falsification was apparently intended to prevent popular hostility against the administration rather than to deceive an enemy who already knew the facts.

Unfortunately, however, government censorship has strayed from the military field to the political. Of the wide-spread flagrant examples of government blackout of truth before, during, and after World War II the next five sections (a to e) are intended as samples rather than as even a slight survey of a field, the vastness of which is indicated by the following:

> Congressman Reed (N.Y., Rep.) last week gave figures on the number of publicity people employed in all the agencies of the Government. "According to the last survey made," he said, "there were 23,000 permanent and 22,000 part-time" (From "Thought Control," *Human Events*, March 19, 1952.)

(a)

Our grossest censorship concealed the Roosevelt administration's maneuvering our people into World War II. The blackout of Germany's appeal to settle our differences has been fully enough presented in Chapter IV. Strong evidence of a similar censorship of an apparent effort of the administration to start a war in the Pacific is voluminously presented in Frederic R. Sanborn's heavily documented *Design for War* (already referred to). Testimony of similar import has been furnished by the war correspondent, author, and broadcaster, Frazier Hunt. Addressing the Dallas Womans Club late in 1950, he said, "American propaganda is whitewashing State Department mistakes ... the free American mind has been sacrificed... We can't resist because we don't have facts to go on."

For a startling instance of the terrible fact of censorship in preparing for our surrender to the Soviet and the part played by Major General Clayton Bissell, A.C. of S., G-2 (the Chief of Army Intelligence), Ambassador to Moscow W. Averell Harriman, and Mr. Elmer Davis, Director of the Office of War Information, see "The Truth About the Katyn Forest Massacre," by Arthur Bliss Lane, former U.S. Ambassador to Poland (*The American Legion Magazine*, February, 1952). There has been no official answer to Mr. Lane's question:

> Who, at the very top levels of the United States Government, ordered the hiding of *all* intelligence reports unfavorable to the Soviets, and the dissemination only of lies and communist propaganda?

Professor Harry Elmer Barnes's pamphlet, "Was Roosevelt Pushed Into War by Popular Demand in 1941?" (Freeman's Journal Press, Cooperstown, New York, 1951, 25¢) furnishes an important observation on the fatal role of government censorship in undermining the soundness of the public mind and lists so well the significant matters on which knowledge was denied the people that an extensive quotation is here used as a summary of this section:

> Fundamental to any assumption about the relation of public opinion to political action is this vital consideration: It is not only

what the people think, but the *soundness* of their opinion which is most relevant. The founders of our democracy assumed that, if public opinion is to be a safe guide for statecraft, the electorate must be honestly and adequately informed. I do not believe that any interventionist, with any conscience whatever, would contend that the American public was candidly or sufficiently informed as to the real nature and intent of President Roosevelt's foreign policy from 1937 to Pearl Harbor. Our public opinion, however accurately or inaccurately measured by the polls, was not founded upon full factual information.

Among the vital matters not known until *after* the War was over were: (1) Roosevelt's statement to President Benes in May, 1939, that the United States would enter any war to defeat Hitler; (2) the secret Roosevelt-Churchill exchanges from 1939 to 1941; (3) Roosevelt's pressure on Britain, France and Poland to resist Hitler in 1939; (4) the fact that the Administration lawyers had decided that we were legally and morally in the War after the Destroyer Deal of September, 1940; (5) Ambassador Grew's warning in January, 1941, that, if the Japanese should ever pull a surprise attack on the United States, it would probably be at Pearl Harbor, and that Roosevelt, Stimson, Knox, Marshall and Stark agreed that Grew was right; (6) the Anglo-American Joint-Staff Conferences of January-March, 1941; (7) the drafting and approval of the Washington Master War Plan and the Army-Navy Joint War Plan by May, 1941; (8) the real facts about the nature and results of the Newfoundland Conference of August, 1941; (9) the devious diplomacy of Secretary Hull with Japan; (10) Konoye's vain appeal for a meeting with Roosevelt to settle the Pacific issues; (11) Roosevelt's various stratagems to procure an overt act from Germany and Japan; (12) Stimson's statement about the plan to maneuver Japan into firing the first shot; (13) the idea that, if Japan crossed a certain line, we would have to shoot; (14) the real nature and implications of Hull's ultimatum of November 26, 1941; and (15) the criminal failure to pass on to Admiral Kimmel and General Short information about the impending Japanese attack.

If the people are to be polled with any semblance of a prospect for any intelligent reaction, they must know what they are voting for. This was conspicuously *not* the case in the years before Pearl Harbor.

(b)

Almost, if not wholly, as indefensible as the secret maneuvering toward war, was the wholesale deception of the American people by suppressing or withholding facts on the eve of the presidential election of 1944. Three examples are here given.

First of all, the general public got no hint of the significance of the pourparlers with the "left," which led to the naming of the same slate of presidential electors by the Democratic, American Labor, and Liberal parties in New York – a deal generally credited with establishing the fateful grip (Executive Order of December 30, 1944) of Communists on vital power-positions in our government. Incidentally, the demands of the extreme left were unassailable under the "We need those votes" political philosophy; for Dewey, Republican, received 2,987,647 votes to 2,478,598 received by Roosevelt, Democrat – and Roosevelt carried the state only with the help of the 496,405 American Labor (Marcantonio) votes and the 329,236 Liberal votes, both of which were cast for the Roosevelt electors!

As another example of catering to leftist votes, the President arrantly deceived the public on October 28, 1944, when he "boasted of the amplitude of the ammunition and equipment which were being sent to American fighting men in battle." The truth, however, was that our fighting men would have sustained fewer casualties if they had received some of the supplies which at the time were being poured into Soviet Russia in quantities far beyond any current Soviet need. It was none other than Mrs. Anna Rosenberg, "an indispensable and ineradicable New Deal ideologist, old friend of Mrs. Roosevelt" who, about a month before the election, "went to Europe and learned that ammunition was being rationed" to our troops. "It apparently did not occur to Mrs. Rosenberg to give this information to the people before election day." After the election and before the end of the same tragic November, the details were made public, apparently to stimulate production (all quotes from Westbrook Pegler's column "Fair Enough," Nov. 27, 1944, Washington *Times-Herald* and other papers).

A third example of apparent falsification and deception had to do with President Roosevelt's health in the summer and autumn of 1944. His obvious physical deterioration was noted in the foreign press and was reported to proper officials by liaison officers to the White House (personal knowledge of the author). Indeed, it was generally believed in 1944, by those in a position to know, that President Roosevelt never recovered from his illness of December, 1943, and January, 1944, despite a long effort at convalescence in the spring weather at the "Hobcaw Barony" estate of his friend Bernard Baruch on the South Carolina coast. The imminence of the President's death was regarded as so certain that, after his nomination to a fourth term, Washington newspaper men passed around the answer "Wallace" to the spoken question "Who in your opinion will be the next president?" Former Postmaster General James A. Farley has testified that Roosevelt "was a dying man" at the time of his departure for Yalta ("America Betrayed at Yalta," by Congressman Lawrence H. Smith, *National Republic,* July, 1951). The widespread belief that Roosevelt was undergoing rapid deterioration was shortly to be given an appearance of certitude by the facts of physical decay revealed at the time of his death, which followed his inauguration by less than three months.

Nevertheless, Vice Admiral Ross T. McIntire, Surgeon-General of the Navy and Roosevelt's personal physician, was quoted thus in a *Life* article by Jeanne Perkins (July 21, 1944, p. 4) during the campaign: "The President's health is excellent. I can say that unqualifiedly."

(c)

In World War II, censorship and falsification of one kind or another were accomplished not only in high government offices but in lower echelons as well. Several instances, of which three are here given, were personally encountered by the author.

(1) Perhaps the most glaring was the omission, in a War Department report (prepared by two officers of Eastern European background), of facts uncomplimentary to Communism in vital testimony on UNRRA given by two patriotic Polish-speaking congressmen (both Northern Democrats) returning from an official mission to Poland for the House Foreign Affairs Committee. An investigation was initiated but before it could be completed both officers had been separated from the service.

(2) News was slanted as much as by a fifty-to-one pro-Leftist ratio in a War Department digest of U.S. newspaper opinion intended, presumably, to influence thought including the thought of U.S. soldiers. For example, the leftist *PM* (circulation 137,100) in one issue (Bureau of Publications Digest, March 14, 1946) was represented by 616 columnar inches of quoted matter in comparison with 35½ columnar inches from the non-leftist N.Y. *World-Telegram* (circulation 389,257). There was also a marked regional slant. Thus in the issue under consideration 98.7 per cent of the total space was given to the Northeastern portion of the United States, plus Missouri, while only 1.3 per cent was given to the rest of the country, including South Atlantic States, Gulf States, Southwestern States, Prairie States, Rocky Mountain States, and Pacific Coast States.

(3) Late in 1945 the former Secretary of War, Major General Patrick D. Hurley, resigned as Ambassador to China to tell the American government and the American people about Soviet Russia's ability to "exert a potent and frequently decisive influence

in American politics and in the American government, including the Department of Justice" (for details, see Chapter VI, a). General Hurley was expected to reveal "sensational disclosures" about certain members of the State Department's Far Eastern staff in particular (quoted passages are from the Washington *Times-Herald,* December 3, 1945); but he was belittled by high government agencies including the Chairman of the Foreign Relations Committee of the Senate, and large sections of the press connived to smother his message. A scheduled Military Intelligence Service interview arranged with General Hurley by the author was cancelled by higher authority. Be it said for the record, however, that the colonels and brigadier generals immediately superior to the author in Military Intelligence were eager seekers for the whole intelligence picture and at no time during the author's conducting over 2,000 interviews made any effort to suppress the collection of information – except to transmit the order just referred to.

Incidentally the brush-off of General Hurley suggests that the leftist palace guard which was inherited from the Roosevelt administration had acquired in eight months a firmer grip on Mr. Truman that it ever had on the deceased president until he entered his last months of mental twilight. Roosevelt's confidence in Hurley is several times attested by General Elliott Roosevelt in *As He Saw It.* In Tehran the morning after the banquet at the Russian Embassy the President said:

> I want you to do something for me, Elliott. Go find Pat Hurley, and tell him to get to work drawing up a draft memorandum guaranteeing Iran's independence... I wish I had more men like Pat, on whom I could depend. The men in the State Department, those career diplomats ... half the time I can't tell whether I should believe them or not (pp. 192-193).

At the second Cairo Conference, the President told his son:

That Pat Hurley... He did a good job. If anybody can straighten out the mess of internal Chinese politics, he's the man... Men like Pat Hurley are invaluable. Why? Because they're loyal. I can give him assignments that I'd *never* give a man in the State Department because I can depend on him... Any number of times the men in the State Department have tried to conceal messages to me, delay them, hold them up somehow, just because some of those career diplomats aren't in accord with what they know I think (pp. 204-205).

The above passages not only throw light on the enormity of the offense against America of preventing the testimony of General Hurley, but give on the Department of State a testimony that cannot be regarded as other than expert.

(d)

With the passing of the years, government censorship has become so much more intensive that it was a principal topic of the American Society of Newspaper Editors at its meeting (April 21, 1951) in Washington. Here is an excerpt (*The Evening Star,* Washington, April 21, 1951) from the report of the Committee on Freedom of Information:

Most Federal offices are showing exceptional zeal in creating rules, regulations, directives, classifications and policies which serve to hide, color or channel news...

We editors have been assuming that no one would dispute this premise: That when the people rule, they have a right to know all their Government does.

This committee finds appalling evidence that the guiding credo in Washington is becoming just the opposite: That it is dangerous and unwise to let information about Government leak out in any unprocessed form.

In spite of this protest, President Truman on September 25, 1951, extended government censorship drastically by vesting in other government agencies the authority and obligation to classify information as "Top Secret," "Secret," and "Confidential" – a right and a responsibility previously enjoyed only, or principally, by the departments of State and Defense. Again the American Society of Newspaper Editors made a protest (AP, September 25, 1951). The President assured the public that no actual censorship would be the outcome of his executive order.

To anyone familiar with the use of "Secret" and "Confidential" not for security but for "playing safe" with a long or not fully understood document, or for suppressing information, the new order cannot, however, appear as other than a possible beginning of drastic government-wide censorship.

The day after the President's executive order, "Some 250 members of the Associated Press Managing Editors Association" voiced their fears and their determination to fight against the "tightening down of news barriers" (AP, September 1, 1951). Kent Cooper, executive director of the Associated Press and a well-known champion of the freedom of the press, said: "I'm really alarmed by what is being done to cover up mistakes in public office."

The reaction, after the censorship order was several weeks old, was thus summarized by *U.S. News and World Report* (October 19, 1951):

> Newspaper men and others deeply fear that this authority may be broadened in application, used to cover up administrative blunders and errors of policy, to conceal scandals now coming to light, or to hide any information unfavorable to the administration, especially as the presidential campaign draws near.

It is to be hoped that the newspapers of the country will keep the issue alive in the minds of the American people. (It is to be hoped also that they will take concerted action to deal with censorship imposed by some of their advertisers. See section II, a, below.)

(e)

During World War II, the Congress of the United States was the victim of censorship to almost as great a degree as the general public. By virtue of his official position, the author was sent by his superiors to brief members of the Congress about to go abroad, and he also interviewed them on their return from strategic areas. He was also sometimes invited to a conference by members with whom he had in his official capacity become acquainted. He found them, including some Northern Democrats, restive at the darkness of censorship and indignant at the pressure upon them to vote funds for such projects as the extension of UNRRA without any full knowledge of its significance. With regard to secret data, the Congress was really in an awkward position. Because several Senators and Representatives, including members of the most sensitive committees, were indiscreet talkers and because of the possibility that some, like the Canadian Member of Parliament, Fred Rose (Rosenberg), might be subversive, the Congress could make no demands for full details on secret matters. The alternative was the twilight in which patriotic Senators and Representatives had to work and vote.

Alarmed by the threat of Communism, however, the Congress has made investigations and published a number of pamphlets and books (Superintendent of Documents, Government Printing Office, Washington 25, D.C.) intended to acquaint the American people with the danger to this country from Communists in general as well as from those embedded in the departments and agencies of the government. It is suggested that you write to your own Congressman or to one of your Senators for an up-to-date list of these publications. One of a series of ten-cent books (see below in this chapter) is actually entitled "100 Things You Should

Know About Communism and Government." How pathetic and how appalling that a patriotic Congress, denied precise facts even as the people are denied them, has to resort to such a means to stir the public into a demand for the cleanup of the executive branch of our government!

II

Censorship, however, has by no means been a monopoly of the administration. Before, during, and since World War II, amid ever-increasing shouts about the freedom of the press, one of the tightest censorships in history has been applied by non-government power to the opinion-controlling media of the United States. A few examples follow under (a) newspapers, (b) motion pictures, and (c) books. These examples are merely samples and in no case are to be considered a coverage of the field. The subject of the chapter is concluded by observations on three other subjects (d, e, f) pertinent to the question of censorship.

(a)

Newspaper censorship of news is applied to some extent in the selection, rejection, and condensation of factual AP, UP, INS, and other dispatches. Such practices cannot be given blanket condemnation, for most newspapers receive from the agencies far more copy than they can publish; a choice is inevitably hurried; and selection on the basis of personal and institutional preferences is legitimate – provided there is no blackout of important news. The occasional use of condensation to obscure the point of a news story is, however, to be vigorously condemned.

Still worse is a deliberate news slanting, which is accomplished by the "editing" – somewhere between fact and print – of such dispatches as are printed. During World War II the author at one time had under his supervision seven War Department teletype machines and was astounded to learn that dispatches of the news agencies were sometimes re-worded to conform to the policy or the presumed policy of a newspaper, or to the presumed attitude of readers or advertisers, or possibly to the prejudices of the individual journalist who did the re-wording! Thus, when Field Marshall von Mackensen died, a teletype dispatch described him as the son of a "tenant farmer." This expression, presumably contrary to the accepted New York doctrine that Germany was undemocratic, became in one great New York morning paper "son of a minor landholder" and in another it became "son of a wealthy estate agent." It is not here implied that the principal owners of these papers knew of this or similar instances. The changed dispatches, however, show the power of the unofficial censor even when his infiltration is into minor positions.

The matter of securing a substantially different meaning by changing a word or a phrase was, so far as the author knows, first brought to the attention of the general public late in 1951 when a zealous propagandist substituted "world" for "nation" in Lincoln's "Gettysburg Address." The revamping of Lincoln's great words "that this nation, under God, shall have a new birth of freedom" would have made him a "one worlder," except for the fact that some Americans knew the Gettysburg Address by heart! Their protests not only revealed the deception in this particular instance, but brought into daylight a new form of falsification that is very hard to detect – except, of course, when the falsifiers tamper with something as well known as the Gettysburg Address!

Occasionally during World War II the abuse of rewriting dispatches was habitual. One foreign correspondent told the author that the correspondent's paper, a "liberal" sheet which was a darling of our government, virtually threw away his dispatches, and wrote what they wished and signed his name to it. Be it said to this man's credit that he resigned in protest.

Sometimes the censorship is effected not by those who handle news items, but by the writer. Thus the known or presumed attitude of his paper or its clientèle may lead a correspondent to send dispatches designed, irrespective of truth, to please the recipients. This practice, with especial emphasis on dispatches from West Germany, was more than once noted by the newsletter, *Human Events* (1710 Rhode Island Avenue, N.W., Washington 6, D.C.) during the year 1950. See the issue of December 20, 1950, which contains an analysis of the dim-out in the United States on the German reaction to the naming of General Eisenhower, the first implementer of the Morgenthau Plan, as Supreme Commander of our new venture in Europe.

In the early summer of 1951, the American public was treated to a nation-wide example of one form of distortion or falsification in certain sections of the press and by certain radio commentators. This was the presentation *as fact* of the individual columnist's or commentator's thesis that General MacArthur wanted war, or wanted World War III, or something of the sort – a thesis based on the General's request for the use of Nationalist Chinese troops as allies and for the removal of the blindfold which prevented his even reconnoitering, much less bombing, the trans-Yalu forces of the enemy armies, vastly more numerous than his own (see Chapter VI, d, below), who were killing his men. The presentation of such a thesis is a writer's privilege, which should not be denied him, but it should be labeled as a viewpoint and not as a fact.

One powerful means of effecting censorship in the United States was mentioned as early as 1938 by William Allen White, nationally known owner and editor of the Emporia (Kansas) *Gazette*, in a speech at the University of Pennsylvania. These are his words:

> The new menace to the freedom of the press, a menace to this country vastly more acute than the menace from government, may come through the pressure not of one group of advertisers, but a wide sector of advertisers. Newspaper advertising is now placed somewhat, if not largely, through nationwide advertising

agencies... As advisers the advertising agencies may exercise unbelievably powerful pressure upon newspapers..." (Quoted from Beaty's *Image of Life*. Thomas Nelson and Sons, New York, 1940).

Details of the pressure of advertisers on newspaper publishers rarely reach the public. An exception came in January, 1946, when the local advertising manager of the Washington *Times-Herald* wrote in his paper as follows: "Under the guise of speaking of his State Department career in combination with a preview of FM and Television Broadcasting, Mr. Ira A. Hirschmann today, at a meeting of the Advertising Club of Washington at the Statler Hotel, asked the Jewish merchants to completely boycott the *Times-Herald* and the New York *Daily News*." It is interesting to note that Mrs. Eleanor M. Patterson, the owner of the *Times-Herald*, published the following statement: "I have only this comment to make: This attack actually has nothing to do with racial or religious matters. It is merely a small part of a planned, deliberate Communist attempt to divide and destroy the United States of America." She refused to yield to pressure, and before long those who had withdrawn their advertisements asked that the contracts be renewed. The outcome prompts the question: May the advertiser not need the periodical more than the periodical needs the advertiser?

(b)

Propaganda attitudes and activities in the United States motion picture output cannot be adequately discussed here. The field is vast and the product, the film, cannot, like the files of newspapers or shelves of books, be consulted readily at an investigator's convenience. Some idea of the power of organized unofficial censorship may be gained, however, from the vicissitudes of one film which has engaged the public interest because it is based on a long-recognized classic by the most popular novelist of the English-speaking world.

As originally produced, the J. Arthur Rank motion picture, *Oliver Twist*, was said to be faithful to the text of the Dickens novel of that name. The picture was shown in Britain without recorded disorder, but when it reached Berlin, "the Jews and police fought with clubs, rocks and firehoses around the Karbel theater in Berlin's British sector." The door of the theater was "smashed by Jewish demonstrators who five times broke through police cordon established around playhouse." These things happened although "not once in the picture ... was Fagin *called* a Jew." Needless to say, the Jews prevailed over the Berlin police and the British authorities, and the exhibitors ceased showing the film (all quotes from the article, "Fagin in Berlin Provokes a Riot." *Life*, March 7, 1949, pp. 38-39).

The barring of Mr. Rank's *Oliver Twist* from its announced appearance (1949) in the United States is explained thus by Arnold Forster in his book, *A Measure of Freedom* (Doubleday and Co., Inc., 1950, p. 10):

> American movie distributors refused to become involved in the distribution and exhibition of the motion picture after the Anti-Defamation League and others expressed the fear that the film was harmful. The Rank Organization withdrew the picture in the United States.

Finally it was announced in the spring of 1951 that the British film "after seventy-two eliminations" and with a prologue by Dr. Everett R. Clinchy of the National Conference of Christians and Jews might be "accepted as a filming of Dickens without anti-semitic intentions" (*Dallas Morning News*). But is there any Charles Dickens left anywhere around?

On the question of Communism in Hollywood, there is available in pamphlet form a remarkably informative broadcast of a dialogue (*Facts Forum Radio Program*, WFAA, Dallas, January 11, 1952) between Mr. Dan Smoot of Dallas and the motion picture star,

Adolphe Menjou. Replying dramatically to a series of questions climatically arranged, Mr. Menjou begins with Lenin's "We must capture the cinema," shows Americans their "incredible ignorance" of Communism, lists Congressional committees which issue helpful documents, and recommends a boycott of "motion pictures which are written by Communists, produced by Communists, or acted in by Communists," – the term *Communists* including those who support the Communist cause. For a free copy of this valuable broadcast, write to Facts Forum, 718 Mercantile Bank building, Dallas, Texas. See also *Red Treason in Hollywood* by Myron C. Fagan (Cinema Educational Guild, P. O. Box 8655, Cole Branch, Hollywood 46, California), and do not miss "Did the Movies Really Clean House?" in the December, 1951, issue of *American Legion Magazine.*

(c)

Censorship in the field of books is even more significant than in periodicals, motion pictures, and radio (not here considered), and a somewhat more extended discussion is imperative.

With reference to new books, a feature article, "Why You Buy Books That Sell Communism," by Irene Corbally Kuhn in the *American Legion Magazine* for January, 1951, shows how writers on the staffs of two widely circulated New York book review supplements are influential in controlling America's book business. To school principals, teachers, librarians, women's clubs – indeed to parents and all other Americans interested in children, who will be the next generation – this article is necessary reading. It should be ordered and studied in full and will accordingly not be analyzed here (*American Legion Magazine*, 580 Fifth Avenue, New York 18, New York; 10¢ per copy; see also "The Professors and the Press" in the July, 1951, number of this magazine). Important also is "A Slanted Guide to Library Selections," by Oliver Carlson, in *The Freeman* for January 14, 1952.

Dealing in more detail with books in one specific field, the China theater, where our wrong policies have cost so many young American lives, is an article entitled "The Gravediggers of America, Part I: The Book Reviewers Sell Out China," by Ralph de Toledano (*The American Mercury*, July, 1951, pp. 72-78. See also Part II in the August number). Mr. de Toledano explains that America's China policy – whether by coincidence or as "part of a sharply conceived and shrewdly carried out plan" – has led to the fact that "China is Russia's." Mr. de Toledano then turns his attention to the State Department:

> Meanwhile the real lobby – the four-plus propagandists of a pro-Communist line in Asia – prospered. Its stooges were able to seize such a stranglehold on the State Department's Far Eastern division that to this day, as we slug it out with the Chinese Reds, they are still unbudgeable. Working devotedly at their side has been a book-writing and book-reviewing cabal.

With regard to books, book reviewers, and book-reviewing periodicals, Mr. de Toledano gives very precise figures. He also explains the great leftist game in which one pro-Communist writer praises the work of another – an old practice exposed by the author of *The Iron Curtain Over America* in the chapter, "Censorship, Gangs, and the Tyranny of Minorities" in his book *Image of Life* (pp. 146-147):

> Praise follows friendship rather than merit. Let a novelist, for instance, bring out a new book. The critic, the playwright, the reviewers, and the rest in his gang hail it as the book of the year. Likewise all will hail the new play by the playwright – and so on, all the way around the circle of membership. Provincial reviewers will be likely to fall in step. The result is that a gang member will sometimes receive national acclaim for a work, which deserves oblivion, whereas a nonmember may fail to receive notice for a

truly excellent work. Such gangs prevent wholly honest criticism and are bad at best, but they are a positive menace when their expressions of mutual admiration are poured forth on obscene and subversive books.

For still more on the part played by certain book-reviewing periodicals in foisting upon the American public a ruinous program in China, see "A Guidebook to 10 Years of Secrecy in Our China Policy," a speech by Senator Owen Brewster of Maine (June 5, 1951). The tables on pp. 12 and 13 of Senator Brewster's reprinted speech are of especial value.

The unofficial arbiters and censors of books have not, however, confined themselves to contemporary texts but have taken drastic steps against classics. Successful campaigns early in the current century against such works as Shakespeare's play *The Merchant of Venice,* are doubtless known to many older readers of *The Iron Curtain Over America.* The case of Shakespeare was summed up effectively by George Lyman Kittredge (*The Merchant of Venice,* by William Shakespeare, edited by George Lyman Kittredge, Ginn and Company, Boston, 1945, pp. ix-x), long a professor of English in Harvard University:

> One thing is clear, however: *The Merchant of Venice* is no anti-Semitic document; Shakespeare was not attacking the Jewish people when he gave Shylock the villain's rôle. If so, he was attacking the Moors in *Titus Andronicus,* the Spaniards in *Much Ado,* the Italians in *Cymbeline,* the Viennese in *Measure for Measure,* the Danes in *Hamlet,* the Britons in *King Lear,* the Scots in *Macbeth,* and the English in *Richard the Third.*

Much more significant than attacks on individual masterpieces, however, was a subtle but determined campaign begun a generation ago to discredit our older literature under charges of Jingoism and didacticism (*Image of Life,* Chapter III). For documentary indication of a nation-wide minority boycott of books as early as 1933, write to the American Renaissance Book Club (P. O. Box 1316, Chicago 90, Illinois).

Still it was not until World War II that the manipulators of the National Democratic Party hit on a really effective way of destroying a large portion of our literary heritage and its high values of morality and patriotism. Since most classics have a steady rather than a rapid sale and are not subject to quick reprints even in normal times, and since many potential readers of these books were not in college, but in the armed forces, few editions of such works were reprinted during the war. At this juncture the government ordered plates to be destroyed on all books not reprinted within four years. The edict was almost a death blow to our culture, for as old books in libraries wear out very few of them can be reprinted at modern costs for printing and binding. Thus, since 1946 the teacher of advanced college English courses has had to choose texts not, as in 1940, from those classics which he prefers but from such classics as are available. The iniquitous practice of destroying plates was reasserted by "Directive M-65, dated May 31, 1951, of the National Production Authority," which provides that "plates which have not been used for more than four years or are otherwise deemed to be obsolete" must be delivered "to a scrap metal dealer" (letter to the author from Appleton-Century-Crofts, Inc., June 15, 1951). In this connection, Upton Close wrote (*Radio Script,* August 12, 1951) that he "was a writer on the Orient who stood in the way of the Lattimore-Hiss gang and Marshall's giving of China to the Communists," and that such an order "wiped out" all his books on China and Japan. Mr. Close continued as follows:

> The order to melt book plates on the pretense that copper is needed for war is the smartest way to suppress books ever invented. It is much more clever than Hitler's burning of books. The public

never sees the melting of plates in private foundries. All the metal from all the book plates in America would not fight one minor engagement. But people do not know that. They do not even know that book plates have been ordered melted down!

Censorship is applied even to those classics which are reprinted. Let us look at only one author who lived long ago, Geoffrey Chaucer (c. 1340-1400). In both of the two fluent and agreeable verse translations at hand as this is written, the fact that the Knight belonged to the Teutonic Order (Chapter I) is eliminated in the wording. Perhaps this is excusable, for the translator into verse faces many difficulties. Of different import, however, are the omissions in two other editions. The Heritage Press edition of the *Canterbury Tales* omits with no explanation the "Tale of the Prioress," the one in which Chaucer, more than 550 years ago, happened to paint – along with the several Gentile poisoners and other murderers of his stories – one unflattering portrait, a version of the popular ballad "Sir Hugh and the Jew's Daughter," of one member of the Jewish race, and that one presumably fictitious! Professor Lumiansky's edition (Simon and Schuster, 1941, preface by Mark Van Doren) of the *Canterbury Tales* likewise omits the Prioress's tale, and tells why: "Though anti-Semitism was a somewhat different thing in the fourteenth century from what it is today, the present-day reader has modern reactions in literature no matter when it was written. From this point of view the Prioress's story of the little choir-boy who is murdered by the Jews possesses an unpleasantness which overshadows its other qualities" (*op. cit.*, p. xxiii).

No criticism of the translators, editors, and publishers is here implied. They may have merely bent to pressure as so many other publishers and so many other publishers and so many periodicals have done – to the author's certain knowledge. One cannot, however, escape the question as to what would happen to American and English literature if persons of English, Scotch,

Irish, German, Italian, or other decent, took the same attitude toward "defamation" of persons of their "races," including those who lived more than 500 years ago! There would be no motion pictures or plays, and except for technical treatises, there would be no more books.

One of the most horrible results of the types of censorship illustrated above is the production, by writers without honor, of works which will "pass" the unofficial censor. The result is a vast output of plays, non-fiction prose, and especially novels, worthless at best and degraded and subversive at the worst, which will not be reviewed here.

Time and space must be given, however, to the blackout of truth in history. Fortunately the way has been illuminated by Professor Harry Elmer Barnes in his pamphlet *The Struggle Against the Historical Blackout* (Freeman's Journal Press, Cooperstown, N.Y. 1951, 50¢). Professor Barnes defines the historical craft's term "revisionism" as the "readjustment of historical writing to historical facts relative to the background and causes of the first World War" and later equates the term "revisionism" with "truth."

After mentioning some of the propaganda lies of World War I and the decade thereafter and citing authorities for the fact that "the actual causes and merits of this conflict were very close to the reverse of the picture presented in the political propaganda and historical writings of the war decade," Professor Barnes states – again with authorities and examples – that by 1928 "everyone except the die-hards and bitter-enders in the historical profession had come to accept revisionism, and even the general public had begun to think straight in the premises."

Unfortunately, however, before the historical profession had got to be as true to history as it was prior to 1914, World War II was ushered in and propaganda again largely superseded truth in the writing of history. Here are several of Professor Barnes's conclusions:

If the world policy of today [1951] cannot be divorced from the mythology of the 1940's, a third World War is inevitable... History has been the chief intellectual casualty of the second World War and the cold war which followed... In this country today, and it is also true of most other nations, many professional historians gladly falsify history quite voluntarily...

Why? To get a publisher, and to get favorable reviews for their books? The alternative is either oblivion or the vicious attack of a "smearbund," as Professor Barnes puts it, of unofficial censors "operating through newspaper editors and columnists, 'hatchet-men' book reviewers, radio commentators, pressure-group intrigue and espionage, and academic pressures and fears." The "powerful vested political interest" is strong enough to smother books by a truthful writer. "Powerful pressure groups have also found the mythology helpful in diverting attention from their own role in national and world calamity." Professor Barnes is not hopeful of the future:

Leading members of two of the largest publishing houses in the country have frankly told me that, whatever their personal wishes in the circumstances, they would not feel it ethical to endanger their business and the property rights of their stockholders by publishing critical books relative to American foreign policy since 1933. And there is good reason for their hesitancy. The book clubs and the main sales outlets for books are controlled by powerful pressure groups, which are opposed to truth on such matters. These outlets not only refuse to market critical books in this field but also threaten to boycott other books by those publishers who defy their blackout ultimatum.

Bruce Barton (San Antonio *Light*, April 1, 1951) expresses the same opinions in condensed form and dramatic style, and adds some of the results of the "historical blackout":

We have turned our backs on history; we have violated the Biblical injunction, "remove not the ancient landmarks"; we have lost our North Star. We have deliberately changed the meaning of words... More and more bureaucracy, tighter and tighter controls over Freedom and Democracy. Lying to the people becomes conditioning the public mind. Killing people is peace. To be for America First is to be an undesirable citizen and a social outcast... Crises abroad that any student of history would normally anticipate, hit the State Department and the Pentagon as a complete surprise.

Thus the study of falsified history takes its toll even among fellow-workers of the falsifiers.

(d)

The propagation of Marxism and other alien ideas is accomplished not only by persons in those businesses which control public opinion but also by the actual infiltration of aliens, or their captives among Americans of old stock, into the periodical-selecting and book-selecting staffs of a wide variety of institutions. The penetration is especially notable in the book-selecting personnel of bookstores, libraries, schools, and colleges.

The National Council for American Education (1 Maiden Lane, New York 38, N.Y.) is effectively showing the grip which persons tolerant of Communism and hostile to the American government have upon U.S. universities, and is also exposing Communist-inclined textbooks used in schools and colleges. Needless to say, such great facts of history as those outlined in Chapters I and II, above, have not been found in school history texts examined by the author. The menace is recognized by our own United States Congress, which offers a pertinent booklet entitled "100 Things You Should Know About Communism and Education" (Superintendent of Documents, Government Printing Office, Washington, D.C., 10¢).

The question of Communist workers in the ranks of American clergy is not to be taken up here. Suffice it to say that many well-meaning but gullible members of the clergy have been lured into various "American" and "National" and other well sounding conferences, councils, and committees, many (but not all) of which are subversive.

In this connection, persons favorable to Western Christian civilization should be warned about carelessly joining an organization, even though it has an innocent-sounding or actually a seemingly praiseworthy name. The following organizations by their names suggest nothing subversive, yet each of them is listed by the Senate of the United States ("Hearings before the Subcommittee on Immigration and Naturalization of the Committee on the Judiciary, United States Senate," 81st Congress, Part 3, pp. A8 and A9) as being not merely subversive, but Communist:

Abraham Lincoln School, Chicago, Ill.
American League Against War and Fascism
American Committee for Protection of Foreign Born
American Peace Mobilization
American Russian Institute (of San Francisco)
American Slav Congress
American Youth Congress
American Youth for Democracy
Civil Rights Congress and its affiliates
Congress of American Women
Council for Pan-American Democracy
Jefferson School of Social Science, New York City
Jewish Peoples Committee
Joint Anti-Fascist Refugee Committee
League of American Writers
Nature Friends of America (since 1935)
Ohio School of Social Sciences

People's Educational Association
Philadelphia School of Social Science and Art
Photo League (New York City)
School of Jewish Studies, New York City
Veterans of the Abraham Lincoln Brigade
Walt Whitman School of Social Science, Newark, N.J.
Washington Bookshop Association
Wisconsin Conference on Social Legislation
Workers Alliance

Each of the above-named organizations is also listed, along with many others, in the valuable book, *Guide to Subversive Organizations and Publications* (May 14, 1951), issued by the House Committee on Un-American Activities (82nd Congress). As one example of the menace that may lurk behind an innocent name, read the Committee's "Report on the Congress of American Women" (October 23, 1949, Superintendent of Documents, Government Printing Office, Washington 25, D.C.).

The patriotic American should not be deceived by the fact that there is no pressure-group censorship on the open expression of pro-Communist views (witness the continued publication of the official Communist Party organ, *The Daily Worker*, New York) or on gross indecency, pseudo-Freudian or other (witness some titles on your drugstore rack of 25-cent books). The obvious lack of censorship in these fields merely helps conceal it elsewhere. "Corrupt and conquer" is an ancient adage. Thus, according to the columnist, Constantine Brown (*The Evening Star,* Washington, D.C., December 27, 1948), "The Kremlin men rely on subversion and immorality. The only reason they have not plunged the world into another blood bath is that they hope moral disintegration will soon spread over the western world."

The Kremlin masters are right. Men cannot live by bread, by science, by education, or by economic might. As Washington knew, when he was found on his knees in prayer at Valley Forge, they can live only by a body of ideals and a faith in which they believe. These things our unofficial censors would deny us.

To all "censorships," governmental and other, there is an obvious corollary. As long as information received by the public – including those who poll public opinion – is, in vital aspects, incomplete and is often distorted for propaganda purposes, the most well-intentioned polls intended to reflect public opinion on foreign affairs or domestic affairs are to be relied on only with extreme caution. The perhaps unavoidable "leading question" tendency in certain types of opinion polls has rarely been illustrated better than in an article "What the GOP Needs to Win in 1952" by George Gallup in the September 25, 1951, issue of *Look*. Legitimately laying aside for the purposes of the article the commonly mentioned Republican presidential possibilities, Eisenhower, Dewey, Taft, Stassen, and Warren, "the American Institute of Public Opinion ... chose nine Americans who might be dark horses in the GOP race." The poll people have, of course, a perfect right to choose such questions as they wish and to select names of individuals about whom to ask questions. The nine chosen in the poll under discussion were Paul G. Hoffman, Henry Cabot Lodge, Jr., Charles E. Wilson (of General Electric), James Bryant Conant, Robert Patterson, James H. Duff, Margaret Chase Smith, Alfred E. Driscoll, and John J. McCloy. Five of these are or have been functionaries under the New Deal and scarcely one of them is a Republican in the historical sense of the term.

Moreover, in dealing with the possibility of appealing to independent voters, why was no mention made of Senators Mundt, Brewster, Bridges, Martin, Bricker, Jenner, Capehart, Dirksen, Ecton, Millikin, Nixon, and Knowland, all of whom have drawn praise *outside* the Republican party? As to "independent" voters of *leftist* leanings, they may storm into precinct conventions or vote in Republican primaries to force the choice of a candidate to their liking, but how many will *vote* for the Republican nominee, and, especially, how many will vote for *non-leftist candidates* for the Senate and the House in the general election?

(e)

Several of the instances of censorship mentioned in this Chapter call attention to the deplorable fact that many persons in the United States who have fought Communism aggressively with facts have been branded as anti-Semitic. Under this form of censorship, it is permissible to rail vaguely against Communism in the abstract, particularly if unnamed Communists are denounced along with "Fascists," "Nazis," and "America Firsters"; but a speaker who calls by name the foreign-born organizers of Communistic atomic espionage in Canada (1946), or mentions the common alien background of the first group of Americans convicted of atomic espionage (1950, 1951) is, in the experience of the author, subject to a vicious heckling from the floor and to other forms of attempted intimidation on the charge of anti-Semitism. For information on Communist tactics, every American should read "Menace of Communism," a statement of J. Edgar Hoover, Director of the Federal Bureau of Investigation, before the Committee on Un-American Activities of the House of Representatives, March 26, 1947. Mr. Hoover said in part:

> Anyone who opposes the American Communist is at once branded as a "disrupter," a "Fascist," a "Red baiter," or a "Hitlerite," and becomes the object of a systematic campaign of character assassination. This is easily understood because the basic tactics of the Communist Party are deceit and trickery.

See also, "Our New Privileged Class," by Eugene Lyons (*The American Legion Magazine,* September, 1951).

The label of anti-Semitic is tossed not only at those who mention

Jewish Communists by name; it is tossed also at the opponents of government ventures which are Jewish-sponsored or Jewish-endorsed. For an official Jewish attitude toward an opponent of American involvement in the program of political Zionism and an opponent of the Morgenthau plan, see Arnold Forster's *A Measure of Freedom* (pp. 62 to 86). In this connection, it is interesting to recall that in the 1940 campaign the third term presidential candidate made much sport of "Martin, Barton, and Fish." At a conference of Democrats at Denver, Colorado, launching the 1952 campaign, Secretary of Agriculture Brannan recalled the success of the phrase and suggested for a similar smear in 1952 the "off-key quartet" of "Taft and Martin, McCarthy and Cain." Would an opposing candidate dare crack back with humorous jibes at "Frankfurter, Morgenthau, and Lehman"? Your answer will reveal to you something you should know as to who wields *power* in the United States.

A zealous approach to securing the *co-operation* of Gentiles is shown in an article, "Glamorous Purim Formula: Exterminate Anti-Semitic Termites...," by Rabbi Leon Spitz (*The American Hebrew*, March 1, 1946): "American Jews ... must come to grips with our contemporary anti-Semites. We must fill our jails with anti-Semitic gangsters. We must fill our insane asylums with anti-Semitic lunatics..."

The Khazar Jew's frequent equating of anti-Communism with so-called "anti-Semitism" is unfortunate in many ways. In the first place, it is most unfair to loyal American Jews. Charges of "anti-Semitism" are absurd, moreover, because the Khazar Jew is himself not a Semite (Chapter II, above). The blood of Abraham, Isaac, and Jacob flows not at all (or to a sporadic degree, as from immigrant merchants, fugitives, etc.) in the veins of the Jews who have come to America from Eastern Europe. On the contrary, the blood of Old Testament people does flow in the veins of Palestine Arabs and others who live along the shores of the eastern Mediterranean. Palestinians, true descendants of Old Testament people, are refugees today from the barbarity of non-Semitic Khazars, who are the rapers – not the inheritors – of the Holy Land!

Charges of "anti-Semitism" are usually made by persons of Khazar stock, but sometimes they are parroted by shallow people, or people who bend to pressure in Protestant churches, in educational institutions, and elsewhere.

Seeking the bubble reputation in the form of publicity, or lured by thirty pieces of silver, many "big-time" preachers have shifted the focus of their "thinking" from the "everlasting life" of St. John III, 16, to the "no man spake openly of him" of St. John VII, 13. In their effort to avoid giving offense to non-Christians, or for other reasons, many preachers have also placed their own brand of "social-mindedness over individual character," their own conception of "human welfare over human excellence," and, in summary, "pale sociology over Almighty God" (quotes from "This morning" by John Temple Graves, Charleston, S.C., *News and Courier,* February 10, 1951).

Similar forces inimical to Western Christian civilization are at work in England. In that unhappy land, worn out by wars and ridden almost to death by Attlee's socialist government (1945-1951), the "Spring 1950 Electoral Register" form dropped the traditional term "Christian name" for the new "Forename" presumably inoffensive to British Jews, Communists, atheists, and other non-Christians. In America, of course, "Christian name" and "Family name" have long since yielded to "first," "middle," and "last." These instances are trivial, if you like, but though mere straws, they show the way the wind is blowing.

Realizing the vast penetration of anti-Christian power – communist, atheist, and what not – into almost every thought-influencing activity in America, a commendable organization known as The Christophers (18 East 48th St., New York 17, N.Y.) has suggested a Christian counter-penetration into vital spots for shaping the future of our children and our land.

Here in their own words, with emphasis supplied by their own italics, is a statement of the purpose of the Christophers:

Less than 1% of humanity have caused most of the world's recent major troubles. This handful, which hates the basic truth on which this nation is founded, usually strives to get into fields that touch the lives of *all* people: (1) education, (2) government, (3) the writing end of newspapers, magazines, books, radio, motion pictures, and television, (4) trade unions, (5) social service, and (6) library work.

If another 1% go (or encourage others to go) as Christophers or *Christ-bearers* into these same 6 fields and work as hard to restore the fundamental truth which the other 1% are working furiously to eliminate, we will soon be on the high road to lasting peace.

Each Christopher works as an individual. He takes out *no* membership, attends *no* meetings, pays *no* dues. Tens of thousands have already gone as Christ-bearers into the marketplace. Our aim is to find a *million*. Positive, constructive action is needed. *"It is better to light one candle than to curse the darkness."*

The Christophers publish "News Notes" (monthly, free of charge). By these notes (circulation 700,000) and by several books, including *Careers That Change Your World* and *Government Is Your Business,* their effort has already made substantial progress. Their movement is worthy of support and imitation. Be it noted that the Christophers are not "anti-" anything. Their program is positive – they are *for* Christian civilization.

(f)

This chapter may well be closed by a reference to the most far-reaching plan for thought-control, or censorship of men's minds, ever attempted in the United States. Mrs. Anna Rosenberg's triumphal entry into the Pentagon in late 1950 was not her first. With the administration's blessing, she appeared there once before to present a plan for giving each World War II soldier an ideological disinfecting before releasing him from service, she to be in charge, presumably, of the ideas to be removed and those to be inculcated. Fortunately (or unfortunately, according to viewpoint) all general officers in the Pentagon were summoned to hear Mrs. Rosenberg, and their unconcealed disgust, along with the humorous and devastating attack of the Washington *Times-Herald*, killed the proposal. A recent account of Mrs. Rosenberg's "scheme to establish reorientation camps for American soldiers at the close of the World War II, on the theory they would be unfit to resume their normal lives at home" appeared in the Washington *Times-Herald* for November 13, 1950.

The public is entitled to know what facts have been blacked out and what ideological doctrines have been inculcated in propaganda fed to our soldiers by the foreign-born Mrs. Rosenberg while in the manpower saddle in the wider field of our unified Department of Defense. In a song by William Blake used in their successful campaign in 1945, British Socialists pledged that they would not abstain from "mental fight" until they had made "Jerusalem" of England (*Time*, November 5, 1951).

According to *Who's Who in America* (Vol. 25), Mrs. Rosenberg's interests include "mental hygiene." Can it be that her strong effort for lowering the draft age to eighteen was due to the known fact that boys of that age are more susceptible than older boys to propaganda?

Who is it that has enjoyed the highest military position held by woman since Joan of Arc led the French armies against the English in the fifteenth century? For a partial answer, see the article on Mrs. Rosenberg in the *Reader's Digest* of February, 1951. For a portrait of another modern woman who has wielded power over armed men, see the similar article on Ana Rabinsohn Pauker in the same magazine, April, 1949.

The issue – so alive in American hearts – of using the draft, or universal military training, for sinister political propaganda was bluntly stated by Major General William B. Ruggles, Editor-in-Chief of the Dallas *Morning News*, on March 3, 1951:

> If the nation is to draft or even to enlist its manpower in national defense, the nation owes some sort of guarantee to the cannon fodder that it will not be sacrificed to forward devious methods of foreign policy or of war policy that somebody in high office is unwilling to lay on the line. They [U.S. soldiers] face the hazards of death with sublime courage. But they have a right to demand that their own leaders must not stack the cards or load the dice against them.

In 1952, however, the "thought-controllers" grew bolder. "The Pentagon received a jolt in the past week when it scanned a proposal from the State Department that the Army should install 'political officers,' one to each unit down to the regimental level" (*Human Events*, April 9, 1952).

Comparing the startling proposal with the Soviet use of "political commissars," *Human Events* states further that "the current daring attempt ... to gain control over the minds of youths in uniform" is "embodied in the bill for Universal Military Training, which was shaped and supported by Assistant Secretary of Defense, Anna Rosenberg."

Surely censorship is at its peak in America today. We must pass quickly into a thought-dictatorship which out-Stalins Stalin – or begin *now* to struggle as best we can for our ancient liberties of political freedom and freedom of thought.

In the temple in ancient Jerusalem, Christ said: "And ye shall know the truth, and the truth shall make you free" (*St. John*, VIII, 32). This is true not only for religion but for national safety. J. Edgar Hoover, Director of the Federal Bureau of Investigation, wrote recently: "Communism can be defeated only by the truth" (*The Educational Forum*, May, 1950).

To become free then we must demand the truth from a government which spends monthly a king's ransom in propaganda to cover its mistakes and sugar-coat its policies. We must achieve, also, a relaxation of that unofficial censorship which perverts our school books, distorts our histories and our classics, and denies us vital facts about world affairs.

CHAPTER VI

THE FOREIGN POLICY
OF THE TRUMAN ADMINISTRATION

For many of President Truman's early mistakes in foreign policy, he cannot rightly be blamed. As a Senator he had specialized in domestic problems and was not at any time a member of the Foreign Relations Committee. Nor had he by travel or scholarship built up a knowledge of world affairs. Elevated to second place on the National Democratic ticket by a compromise and hated by the pro-Wallace leftists around Franklin Roosevelt, he was snubbed after his election to the Vice-Presidency in 1944 and was wholly ignorant of the tangled web of our relations with foreign countries when he succeeded to the Presidency on April 12, 1945 – midway between the Yalta and Potsdam conferences.

Not only was Mr. Truman inexperienced in the field of foreign affairs; it has since been authoritatively stated that much vital information was withheld from him by the hold-over Presidential and State Department cabals.

This is not surprising in view of the deceased President's testimony to his son Elliott on his difficulty (Chapter V) in getting the truth from "the men in the State Department, those career diplomats." Significantly, the new President was not allowed to know of his predecessor's reputed despair at learning that his wisecracks and blandishing smiles had not induced Stalin to renounce the tenets of bloody and self-aggrandizing dialectic materialism, a state-religion of which he was philosopher, pontiff, and commander-in-chief.

President Truman brought the war to a quick close. His early changes in the cabinet were on the whole encouraging. The nation appreciated the inherited difficulties under which the genial Missourian labored and felt for him a nearly unanimous good will.

In the disastrous Potsdam Conference decisions (July 17-August 2, 1945), however, it was evident (Chapter IV) that anti-American brains were busy in our top echelon. Our subsequent course was equally ruinous. Before making a treaty of peace, we demobilized – probably as a part of the successful Democratic-leftist political deal of 1944 – in such a way as to reduce our armed forces quickly to ineffectiveness. Moreover, as one of the greatest financial blunders in our history, we gave away, destroyed, abandoned, or sold for a few cents on the dollar not merely the no longer useful portion of our war matériel but many items such as trucks and precision instruments which we later bought back at market value! These things were done in spite of the fact that the Soviet government, hostile to us by its philosophy from its inception, and openly hostile to us after the Tehran conference, was keeping its armed might virtually intact.

Unfortunately, our throwing away of our military potential was but one manifestation of the ineptitude or disloyalty which shaped our foreign policy. Despite Soviet hostility, which was not only a matter of old record in Stalin's public utterances, but was shown immediately in the newly launched United Nations, we persisted in a policy favorable to world domination by the Moscow hierarchy. Among the more notorious of our pro-Soviet techniques was our suggesting that "liberated" and other nations which wanted our help should be ruled by a coalition government including leftist elements. This State Department scheme tossed one Eastern European country after another into the Soviet maw, including finally Czechoslovakia.

This foul doctrine of the left coalition and its well-known results of infiltrating Communists into key positions in the governments of Eastern Europe will not be discussed here, since the damage is done beyond repair as far as any possible immediate American action is concerned. Discussion here is limited to our fastening of the Soviet clamp upon the Eastern Hemisphere in three areas still the subject of controversy. These are (a) China, (b) Palestine, and (c) Germany. The chapter will be concluded by some observations (d) on the war in Korea.

(a)

The Truman policy on China can be understood only as the end-product of nearly twenty years of American-Chinese relations. President Franklin D. Roosevelt felt a deep attachment to the Chiangs and deep sympathy for Nationalist China – feelings expressed as late as early December, 1943, shortly after the Cairo Declaration (November 26, 1943), by which Manchuria was to be "restored" to China, and just before the President suffered the mental illness from which he never recovered. It was largely this friendship and sympathy which had prompted our violent partisanship for China in the Sino-Japanese difficulties of the 1930's and early 1940's. More significant, however, than our freezing of Japanese assets in the United States, our permitting American aviators to enlist in the Chinese army, our gold and our supplies sent in by air, by sea, and by the Burma road, was our ceaseless diplomatic barrage against Japan in her rôle as China's enemy (see *United States Relations With China, With Special Reference to the Period 1944-1949*, Department of State, 1949, p. 25 and *passim*).

When the violent phase of our already initiated political war against Japan began with the Pearl Harbor attack of December 7, 1941, we relied on China as an ally and as a base for our defeat of the island Empire. On March 6, 1942, Lieutenant General Joseph W. Stilwell "reported to Generalissimo Chiang" (*op. cit.*, p. xxxix).

General Stilwell was not only "Commanding General of United States Forces in the China-Burma-India Theater" but was supposed to command "such Chinese troops as Generalissimo Chiang Kai-Shek might assign him" (*op. cit.,* p. 30) and in other ways consolidate and direct the Allied war effort. Unfortunately, General Stilwell had formed many of his ideas on China amid a coterie of leftists led by Agnes Smedley as far back as 1938 when he, still a colonel, was a U.S. military attaché in Hankow, China (see *The China Story,* by Freda Utley, Henry Regnery Company, Chicago, 1951, $3.50). It is thus not surprising that General Stilwell quickly conceived a violent personal animosity for the anti-Communist Chiang (*Saturday Evening Post,* January 7, 14, 21, 1950). This personal feeling, so strong that it results in amazing vituperative poetry (some of it reprinted in the *Post*), not only hampered the Allied war effort but was an entering wedge for vicious anti-Chiang and pro-Communist activity which was destined to change completely our attitude toward Nationalist China.

The pro-Communist machinations of certain high placed members of the Far Eastern Bureau of our State Department and of their confederates on our diplomatic staff in Chungking (for full details, see *The China Story*) soon became obvious to those in a position to observe. Matters were not helped when "in the spring of 1944, President Roosevelt appointed Vice-President Henry A. Wallace to make a trip to China" (*United States Relations With China,* p. 55). Rebutting what he considered Mr. Wallace's pro-Communist attitude, Chiang "launched into a lengthy complaint against the Communists, whose actions, he said, had an unfavorable effect on Chinese morale... The Generalissimo deplored propaganda to the effect that they were nothing but agrarian democrats and remarked that they were more communistic than the Russians" (*op. cit.,* p. 56).

Our Ambassador to China, Clarence E. Gauss, obviously disturbed by the Wallace mission and by the pro-Communist attitude of his diplomatic staff, wrote as follows (*op. cit.,* p. 561) to Secretary Hull on August 31, 1944:

> ... China should receive the entire support and sympathy of the United States Government on the domestic problem of Chinese Communists. Very serious consequences for China may result from our attitude. In urging that China resolve differences with the Communists, our Government's attitude is serving only to intensify the recalcitrance of the Communists. The request that China meet Communist demands is equivalent to asking China's unconditional surrender to a party known to be under a foreign power's influence (the Soviet Union).

With conditions in China in the triple impasse of Stilwell-Chiang hostility, American pro-Communist versus Chinese anti-Communist sentiment, and an ambassador at odds with his subordinates, President Roosevelt sent General Patrick J. Hurley to Chungking as his Special Representative "with the mission of promoting harmonious relations between Generalissimo Chiang and General Stilwell and of performing certain other duties" (*op. cit.,* p. 57). Ambassador Gauss was soon recalled and General Hurley was made Ambassador.

General Hurley saw that the Stilwell-Chiang feud could not be resolved, and eventually the recall of General Stilwell from China was announced. With regard, however, to our pro-Communist State Department representatives in China, Ambassador Hurley met defeat. On November 26, 1945, he wrote President Truman, who had succeeded to the Presidency in April, a letter of resignation and gave his reasons:

> ... The astonishing feature of our foreign policy is the wide discrepancy between our announced policies and our conduct of international relations. For instance, we began the war with the

principles of the Atlantic Charter and democracy as our goal. Our associates in the war at that time gave eloquent lip service to the principles of democracy. We finished the war in the Far East furnishing lend-lease supplies and using all our reputation to undermine democracy and bolster imperialism and Communism ...

... it is no secret that the American policy in China did not have the support of all the career men in the State Department... Our professional diplomats continuously advised the Communists that my efforts in preventing the collapse of the National Government did not represent the policy of the United States. These same professionals openly advised the Communist armed party to decline unification of the Chinese Communist Army with the National Army unless the Chinese Communists were given control...

Throughout this period the chief opposition to the accomplishment of our mission came from the American career diplomats in the Embassy at Chungking and in the Chinese and Far Eastern Divisions of the State Department.

I requested the relief of the career men who were opposing the American policy in the Chinese Theater of war. These professional diplomats were returned to Washington and placed in the Chinese and Far Eastern Divisions of the State Department as my supervisors. Some of these same career men whom I relieved have been assigned as advisors to the Supreme Commander in Asia (*op. cit.,* pp. 581-582).

President Truman accepted General Hurley's resignation with alacrity. Without a shadow of justification, the able and patriotic Hurley was smeared with the implication that he was a tired and doddering man, and he was not even allowed to visit the War Department, of which he was former Secretary, for an interview. This affront to a great American ended our diplomatic double talk in China. With forthrightness, Mr. Truman made his decision. Our China policy henceforth was to be definitely pro-Communist.

The President expressed his changed policy in a "statement" made on December 15, 1945. Although the Soviet was pouring supplies and military instructors into Communist-held areas, Mr. Truman said that the United States would not offer "military intervention to influence the course of any Chinese internal strife." He urged Chiang's government to give the Communist "elements a fair and effective representation in the Chinese National Government." To such a "broadly representative government" he temptingly hinted that "credits and loans" would be forthcoming (*op. cit.*, pp. 608-609). President Truman's amazing desertion of Nationalist China, so friendly to us throughout the years following the Boxer Rebellion (1900), has been thus summarized (NBC Network, April 13, 1951) by Congressman Joe Martin:

> President Truman, on the advice of Dean Acheson, announced to the world on December 15, 1945, that unless communists were admitted to the established government of China, aid from America would no longer be forthcoming. At the same time, Mr. Truman dispatched General Marshall to China with orders to stop the mopping up of communist forces which was being carried to a successful conclusion by the established government of China.

Our new Ambassador to China, General of the Army George C. Marshall, conformed under White House directive (see his testimony before the Combined Armed Services and Foreign Relations Committees of the Senate, May, 1951) to the dicta of the State Department's Communist-inclined camarilla, and made further efforts to force Chiang to admit Communists to his government in the "effective" numbers, no doubt, which Mr. Truman had demanded in his "statement" of December 15. The great Chinese general, however, would not be bribed by promised "loans" and thus avoided the trap with which our State Department snared for Communism the states of Eastern Europe. He was accordingly paid off by the mishandling of supplies already en route, so that guns and ammunition for those guns did not make proper connection, as well as by the eventual complete withdrawal of American support as threatened by Mr. Truman.

For a full account of our scandalous pro-Communist moves in denying small arms ammunition to China; our charging China $162.00 for a bazooka (whose list price was $36.50 and "surplus" price to other nations was $3.65) when some arms were sent; and numerous similar details, see *The China Story*, already referred to.

Thus President Truman, Ambassador Marshall, and the State Department prepared the way for the fall of China to Soviet control. They sacrificed Chiang, who represented the Westernized and Christian element in China, and they destroyed a friendly government, which was potentially our strongest ally in the world – stronger even than the home island of maritime Britain in this age of air and guided missiles. The smoke-screen excuse for our policy – namely that there was corruption in Chiang's government – is beyond question history's most glaring example of the pot calling the kettle black. For essential background material, see *Shanghai Conspiracy* by Major General Charles A. Willoughby, with a preface by General of the Army Douglas MacArthur (Dutton, 1952).

General Ambassador Marshall became Secretary of State in January, 1947, On July 9, 1947, President Harry S. Truman directed Lieutenant General Albert C. Wedemeyer, who had served for a time as "Commander-in-Chief of American Forces in the Asian Theater" after the removal of Stilwell, to "proceed to China without delay for the purpose of making an appraisal of the political, economic, psychological and military situations – current and projected." Under the title, "Special Representative of the President of United States," General Wedemeyer worked with the eight other members of his mission from July 16 to September 18 and on September 19 transmitted his report (*United States Relations with China*, pp. 764-814) to the appointing authority, the President.

In a section of his Report called "Implications of 'No Assistance' to China or Continuation of 'Wait and See' Policy," General Wedemeyer wrote as follows:

> To advise at this time a policy of "no assistance" to China would suggest the withdrawal of the United States Military and Naval Advisory Groups from China and it would be equivalent to cutting the ground from under the feet of the Chinese Government. Removal of American assistance, without removal of Soviet assistance, would certainly lay the country open to eventual Communist domination. It would have repercussions in other parts of Asia, would lower American prestige in the Far East and would make easier the spread of Soviet influence and Soviet political expansion not only in Asia but in other parts of the world.

Here is General Wedemeyer's conclusion as to the strategic importance of Nationalist China to the United States:

> Any further spread of Soviet influence and power would be inimical to United States strategic interests.
>
> In time of war the existence of an unfriendly China would result in denying us important air bases for use as staging areas for bombing attacks as well as important naval bases along the Asiatic coast. Its control by the Soviet Union or a regime friendly to the Soviet Union would make available for hostile use a number of warm water ports and air bases.
>
> Our own air and naval bases in Japan, Ryukyus, and the Philippines would be subject to relatively short range neutralizing air attacks. Furthermore, industrial and military development of Siberia east of Lake Baikal would probably make the Manchurian area more or less self-sufficient.

Here are the more significant of the Wedemeyer recommendations:

It is recommended:

That the United States provide as early as practicable moral, advisory and material support to China in order to prevent Manchuria from becoming a Soviet satellite, to bolster opposition to Communist expansion and to contribute to the gradual development of stability in China...

That arrangements be made whereby China can purchase military equipment and supplies (particularly motor maintenance parts), from the United States.

That China be assisted in her efforts to obtain ammunition immediately...

The [sic] military advice and supervision be extended in scope to include field forces, training centers and particularly logistical agencies.

Despite our pro-Communist policy in the previous twenty months, *the situation in China was not beyond repair at the time of the Wedemeyer survey.* In September, 1947, the "Chiang government had large forces still under arms and was in control of all China south of the Yangtze River, of much of North China, with some footholds in Manchuria" (W. H. Chamberlin, *Human Events,* July 5, 1950). General Wedemeyer picked 39 Chinese divisions to be American-sponsored and these were waiting for our supplies and our instructors – in case the Wedemeyer program was accepted.

But *General Wedemeyer had reported that which his superiors did not wish to hear.* His fate was a discharge from diplomacy and an exile from the Pentagon. Moreover, *the Wedemeyer Report was not released until August, 1949.*

Meanwhile, *in the intervening two years our pro-Communist policy of withdrawing assistance from Chiang, while the Soviet rushed supplies to his enemies, had tipped the scales in favor of those enemies,* the Chinese Communists.

Needless to say, under Mr. Dean Acheson, who succeeded Marshall as Secretary of State (January, 1949), our pro-Soviet policy in China was not reversed! Chiang had been holding on somehow, but Acheson slapped down his last hope. In fact, our Secretary of State – possibly by some strange coincidence – pinned on the Nationalist Government of China the term "reactionary" (August 6, 1949), a term characteristically applied by Soviet stooges to any unapproved person or policy, and said explicitly that the United States would give the Nationalist Government no further support.

Meanwhile, the Soviet had continued to supply the Chinese Communists with war matériel at a rate competently estimated at eight to ten times the amount per month we had furnished – at the peak of our aid – to Chiang's Nationalists. Chiang's troops, many of them without ammunition, were thus defeated, as virtually planned by our State Department, whose Far Eastern Bureau was animated by admirers of the North Chinese Communists. But the defeat of Chiang was not the disgrace his enemies would have us believe. His evacuation to Formosa and his reorganization of his forces on that strategic island were far from contemptible achievements. Parenthetically, as our State Department's wrong-doing comes to light, there appears a corollary re-evaluation of Chiang. In its issue of April 9, 1951, *Life* said editorially that "Now we have only to respect the unique tenacity of Chiang Kai Shek in his long battle against Communism and take full advantage of whatever the Nationalists can do now to help us in this struggle for Asia." It should be added here that any idea of recognizing Communist China as the representative government of China is absurd. According to a Soviet Politburo report (*This Week,* September 30, 1951), the membership of the Chinese Communist Party is 5,800,000. The remainder of China's 450,000,000 or 475,000,000 people, in so far as they are actually under Communist control, are slaves.

But – back to the chronology of our "policy" in the Far East.

On December 23, 1949, the State Department sent to five hundred American agents abroad (New York *Journal-American,*

June 19, 1951, p. 18) a document entitled "Policy Advisory Staff, Special Guidance No. 38, Policy Information Paper – Formosa." As has been stated in many newspapers, the purpose of this policy memorandum was to prepare the world for the United States plan for yielding Formosa (Taiwan, in Japanese terminology) to the Chinese Communists. Here are pertinent excerpts from the surrender document which, upon its release in June, 1951, was published in full in a number of newspapers:

> Loss of the island is widely anticipated, and the manner in which civil and military conditions there have deteriorated under the Nationalists adds weight to the expectation...
>
> Formosa, politically, geographically, and strategically is part of China in no way especially distinguished or important...

Even the small United States military advisory group sent there at British government request was completely withdrawn a year ago...

> Treatment: ... All material should be used best to counter the impression that ... its [Formosa's] loss would seriously damage the interests of the United States or of other countries opposing Communism [and that] the United States is responsible for or committed in any way to act to save Formosa...
>
> Formosa has no special military significance...
>
> China has never been a sea power and the island is of no special strategic advantage to Chinese armed forces.

This State Department policy paper contains unbelievably crass lies such as the statement that the island of Formosa is, in comparison with other parts of China, "in no way especially distinguished or important" and the claim that the island would be "of no special strategic advantage" to its Communist conquerors. It contains an unwarranted slam at our allies, the Chinese Nationalists, and strives to put upon our ally Britain the onus for our slight interest in the island – an interest the "policy memorandum" was repudiating! It is hard to see how the anonymous writer of such a paper could be regarded as other than a scoundrel. No wonder the public was kept in ignorance of the paper's existence until the MacArthur investigation by the Senate raised momentarily the curtain of censorship!

In a "Statement on Formosa" (*New York Times,* January 6, 1950), President Truman proceeded cautiously on the less explosive portions of the "Policy Memorandum," but declared Formosa a part of China – obviously, from the context, the China of Mao Tse-Tung – and continued: "The United States has no desire to obtain special rights or privileges or to establish military bases on Formosa at this time. Nor does it have any intention of utilizing its armed forces to interfere in the present situation." The President's statement showed a dangerous arrogation of authority, for the wartime promises of the dying Roosevelt had not been ratified by the United States Senate, and in any case a part of the Japanese Empire was not at the personal disposal of an American president. More significantly, the statement showed an indifference to the safety of America or an amazing ignorance of strategy, for any corporal in the U.S. army with a map before him could see that Formosa is the virtual keystone of the U.S. position in the Pacific. It was also stated by our government officially and definitely that our aid to South Korea would be "a limited number of arms for internal security."

Six days later (January 12, 1950) in an address at a National Press Club luncheon, Secretary Acheson announced a "new motivation of United States foreign policy," which confirmed the President's statement a week before, including specifically the "hands off" policy in Formosa. Acheson also expressed the belief that we need not worry about the Communists in China since they would naturally grow away from the Soviet on account of the Soviet's "attaching"

North China territory to the great Moscow-ruled imperium (article by Walter H. Waggoner, *New York Times,* January 13, 1950).

Also, according to the *New York Times* (whose issues from January 3 to January 10, 1950, are important reading for students of our Far Eastern "policy"), Mr. Acheson said "he had been in the business of foreign relations too long to believe anyone could be sure of results, and he had been dealing with the subject matter of the Far East too briefly to believe in the infallibility of his own judgment."

These sentiments must have appealed to Governor Thomas E. Dewey, of New York, for at Princeton University on April 12 he called for Republican support of the Truman-Acheson foreign policy and specifically commended the appointment of John Foster Dulles (for the relations of Dulles with Hiss, see Chapter VIII) as a State Department "consultant."

Mr. Acheson's partly concealed and partly visible maneuverings were thus summed up by Walter Winchell (Dallas *Times-Herald,* April 16, 1951):

> These are the facts. Secretary Acheson ... is on record as stating we would not veto Red China if she succeeded in getting a majority vote in the UN... As another step, Secretary Acheson initiated a deliberate program to play down the importance of Formosa.

Mr. Winchell also mentioned Senator Knowland's "documentary evidence" that those who made State Department policy had been instructed by Secretary Acheson to "minimize the strategic importance of Formosa."

All of this was thrown into sharp focus by President Truman when he revealed in a press conference (May 17, 1951) that his first decision to fire General MacArthur a year previously had been strengthened when the Commander in Japan protested in the summer of 1950 that the proposed abandonment of Formosa would weaken the U.S. position in Japan and the Philippines!

"No matter how hard one tries," *The Freeman* summarized on June 4, 1951, "there is no way of evading the awful truth: *The American State Department* wanted Marxist Communists to win for Marxism and Communism in China." Also, *The Freeman* continued, "On his own testimony, General Marshall supported our pro-Marxist China policy with his eyes unblinkered with innocence."

Thus, in the first half of 1950, our Far Eastern policy, made by Acheson and approved by Truman and Dewey, was based on (1) the abandonment of Formosa to the expected conquest by Chinese Communists, (2) giving no battle weapons to the Nationalist Chinese or to the South Koreans, in spite of the fact that the Soviet was known to be equipping the North Koreans with battle weapons and with military skills, (3) the mere belief – at least, so stated – of our Secretary of State, self-confessedly ignorant of the matter, that the Communists of China would become angry with the Soviet. The sequel is outlined in section (d) below.

(b)

Our second great mistake in foreign policy – unless votes in New York and other Northern cities are its motivation – was our attitude toward the problem of Palestine. In the Eastern Mediterranean, on the deck of the heavy cruiser, U.S.S. Quincy, which was to bring him home from Yalta, President Roosevelt in February, 1945, received King Ibn Saud of Saudi Arabia. According to General Elliott Roosevelt (*As He Saw It*, p. 245): "It had been father's hope that he would be able to convince Ibn Saud of the equity of the settlement in Palestine of the tens of thousands of Jews driven from their European homes." But, as the ailing President later told Bernard Baruch, "of all the men he had talked to in his life, he had got least satisfaction from this iron-willed Arab monarch." General Roosevelt concludes thus: "Father ended by promising Ibn Saud that he would sanction no American move hostile to the Arab people." This may be considered the four-term President's legacy on the subject, for in less than two months death had completed its slow assault upon his frame and his faculties.

But the Palestine problem, like the ghost in an Elizabethan drama, would not stay "down." In the post-war years (1945 and after), Jewish immigrants mostly from the Soviet Union or satellite states poured into the land once known as "Holy." These immigrants were largely Marxist in outlook and principally of Khazar antecedents. As the immigration progressed, the situation between Moslems and this new type of Jew became tense.

The vote-conscious American politicians became interested. After many vacillations between "non-partition" which was recommended by our strategists and "partition" which was clamored for by many American Jewish organizations and highly placed individual Jews, the United States – which has many Zionist voters and few Arab voters – decided to sponsor the splitting of Palestine, which was predominantly Arab in population, into Arab and Jewish zones. In spite of our lavish post-war tossing out of hundreds of millions and sometimes billions to almost any nation – except a few pet "enemies" such as Spain – for almost any purpose, the United Nations was inclined to disregard our sponsorship and reject the proposed new member. On Wednesday, November 26, 1947, our proposition received 25 votes out of 57 (13 against, 17 abstentions, 2 absent) and was defeated. Thus the votes had been taken and the issue seemed settled. But, no!

Any reader who wishes fuller details should by all means consult the microfilmed *New York Times* for November 26-30, and other pertinent periodicals, but here are the highlights:

> The United Nations General Assembly postponed a vote on the partition of Palestine yesterday after Zionist supporters found that they still lacked an assured two-thirds majority (article by Thomas J. Hamilton, *New York Times,* November 27, 1947).

> Yesterday morning Dr. Aranha was notified by Siamese officials in Washington that the credentials of the Siamese delegation, which had voted against partition in the Committee, had been canceled (November 27, 1947).
>
> Since Saturday [November 22] the United States Delegation has been making personal contact with other delegates to obtain votes for partition... The news from Haiti ... would seem to indicate that some persuasion has now been brought to bear on home governments ... the result of today's vote appeared to depend on what United States representatives were doing in faraway capitals (from an article by Thomas J. Hamilton, *New York Times*, November 28, 1947).

The result of our pro-"Israeli" pressures, denounced in some instances by representatives of the governments who yielded, was a change of vote by nine nations: Belgium, France, Haiti, Liberia, Luxemburg, The Netherlands, New Zealand, Paraguay, and the Philippines. Chile dropped – to "not voting" – from the pro-"Israeli" twenty-five votes of November 26, and the net gain for U.S.-"Israeli" was 8. Greece changed from "not voting" to "against," replacing the dismissed Siamese delegation, and the "against" vote remained the same, 13. Thus the *New York Times* on Sunday, November 30, carried the headline,

ASSEMBLY VOTES PALESTINE PARTITION;
MARGIN IS 33-13; ARABS WALK OUT...

The Zionist Jews of Palestine now had their seacoast and could deal with the Sovietized Black Sea countries without further bother from the expiring British mandate. The selection of immigrants of which over-populated "Israel" felt such great need was to some extent, if not entirely, supervised by the countries of origin. For instance, a high "Israeli" official visited Bucharest to coordinate

153

with the Communist dictator of Rumania, Ana Rabinsohn Pauker, the selection of immigrants for "Israel." "Soviet Bloc Lets Jews Leave Freely and Take Most Possessions to Israel," the *New York Times* headlined (November 26, 1948) a UP dispatch from Prague. The close ties between Communism and "Israel" were soon obvious to any penetrating reader of the *New York Times*. A notable example is afforded in an article (March 12, 1948) by Alexander Feinberg, entitled "10,000 in Protest on Palestine Here: Throng Undaunted by Weather Mustered by Communist and Left-Wing Labor Leaders." Here is a brief quotation from this significant article:

> Youthful and disciplined Communists raised their battle cry of "solidarity forever" as they marched... The parade and rally were held under the auspices of the United Committee to Save the Jewish State and the United Nations, formed recently after the internationally minded Communists decided to "take over" an intensely nationalistic cause, the partition of Palestine. The grand marshal of the parade was Ben Gold, president of the Communist-led International Fur and Leather Workers Union, CIO.

With the Jewish immigrants to Palestine came Russian and Czecho-slovak (Skoda) arms. "Israel Leaning Toward Russia, Its Armorer," the New York *Herald-Tribune* headlined on August 5, 1948. Here are quotations on the popularity of the Soviet in "Israel" from Correspondent Kenneth Bilby's wireless dispatch from Tel Aviv:

> Russian prestige has soared enormously among all political factions... Certain Czech arms shipments which reached Israel at critical junctures of the war, played a vital role in blunting the invasion's five Arab armies... The Jews, who are certainly realists, know that without Russia's nod, these weapons would never have been available.

Mr. Bilby found that "the balance sheet" read "much in Russia's favor" and found his conclusion "evidenced in numerous ways – in editorials in the Hebrew press praising the Soviet Union," and also "in public pronouncements of political and governmental leaders." Mr. Bilby concluded also that the "political fact" of "Israeli" devotion to the Soviet might "color the future of the Middle East" long after the issues of the day were settled. Parenthetically, the words of the *Herald-Tribune* correspondent were prophetic. In its feature editorial of October 10, 1951, the *Dallas Morning News* commented as follows on the announced determination of Egypt to seize the Sudan and the Suez Canal:

> Beyond question, the Egyptian move is concerned with the understandable unrest stirred in the Arab world by the establishment of the new State of Israel. The United Nations as a whole and Britain and the United States in particular did that. The Moslem world could no more accept equably an effort to turn back the clock 2,000 years than would this country agree to revert to the status quo of 1776.

Showing contempt, and her true colors, "Israel" voted with the Soviet Union and against the United States on the question of admitting Communist China to the UN (broadcast of Lowell Thomas, CBS Network, November 13, 1951). Thus were we paid for the immoral coercion by which we got "Israel" into the United Nations – a coercion which had given the whole world, in the first instance, a horrible but objective and above-board example of the Truman administration's conception of elections!

But back to our chronology. In 1948, strong with Soviet armor and basking in the sunshine of Soviet sympathy, "Israeli" troops mostly born in Soviet-held lands killed many Arabs and drove out some 880,000 others, Christian and Moslem. These wretched refugees apparently will long be a chief problem of the Arab League nations of the Middle East. Though most Americans are unaware, these brutally treated people are an American problem also, for the Arabs blame their tragedy in large part on "the Americans – for pouring money and political support to the Israelis; Harry Truman is the popular villain" ("The Forgotten Arab Refugees," by James Bell, *Life*, September 17, 1951). With such great sympathy for the Soviet Union, as shown above, it is not surprising "Israel" at once began to show features which are extremely leftist – to say the least. For instance, on his return from "Israel," Dr. Frederick E. Reissig, executive director of the Washington (D.C.) Federation of Churches, "told of going to many co-operative communities... Land for each 'kibbutz' – as such communities are called – is supplied by the government. Everything – more or less – is shared by the residents" (Mary Jane Dempsey in Washington *Times-Herald*, April 24, 1951). For fuller details, see "The Kibbutz" by John Hersey in *The New Yorker* of April 19, 1952.

After the "Israeli" seizure of the Arab lands in Palestine, there followed a long series of outrages including the bombings of the British Officers' Club in Jerusalem, the Acre Prison, the Arab Higher Command Headquarters in Jaffa, the Semiramis Hotel, etc. These bombings were by "Jewish terrorists" (*World Almanac*, 1951). The climax of the brutality in "Israel" was the murder of Count Bernadotte of Sweden, the United Nations mediator in Palestine! Here is the *New York Times* story (Tel Aviv, September 18, 1948) by Julian Louis Meltzer:

> Count Folke Bernadotte, United Nations Mediator for Palestine, and another United Nations official, detached from the French Air Force, were assassinated this afternoon [September 17], within the Israeli-held area of Jerusalem.

Also, according to the *New York Times*, "Reuters quoted a Stern Group spokesman in Tel Aviv as having said, 'I am satisfied that it has happened." A United Nations truce staff announcement confirmed the fact that Count Bernadotte had been "killed by two Jewish irregulars," who also killed the United Nations senior observer, Col. André Pierre Serot, of the French Air Force. Despite the fact that the murderers were Jews, and that the murdered UN officers were from countries with no appreciable political influence in the United States, American reaction to the murder of the United Nations mediator was by no means favorable. It was an election year and Dewey droned on about "unity" while Truman trounced the "do-nothing Republican 80th Congress." For a month after the murders neither of them fished in the putrid pond of "Israeli"-dominated Palestine.

Strangely enough, it was Dewey who first threw in his little worm on a pinhook. In a reply to a letter from the Constantinople-born Dean Alfange, Chairman of the Committee which founded the Liberal Party of the State of New York, May 19, 1944 (*Who's Who in America*, Vol. 25, p. 44), Dewey wrote (October 22, 1948):

"As you know, I have always felt that the Jewish people are entitled to a homeland in Palestine which would be politically and economically stable... My position today is the same." On October 24, in a formal statement, Truman rebuked Dewey for "injecting foreign affairs" into the campaign and – to change the figure of speech – raised the Republican candidate's "six-spades" bid for Jewish votes by a resounding "ten-no-trumps":

> So that everyone may be familiar with my position, I set out here the Democratic platform on Israel:
>
> "President Truman, by granting immediate recognition to Israel, led the world in extending friendship and welcome to a people who have long sought and justly deserve freedom and independence.
>
> "We pledge full recognition to the State of Israel. We affirm our pride that the United States, under the leadership of President Truman, played a leading role in the adoption of the resolution

of Nov. 29, 1947, by the United Nations General Assembly for the creation of a Jewish state.

"We approve the claim of the State of Israel to the boundaries set forth in the United Nations' resolution of Nov. 29 and consider that modifications thereof should be made only if fully acceptable to the State of Israel.

"We look forward to the admission of the State of Israel to the United Nations and its full participation in the international community of nations. We pledge appropriate aid to the State of Israel in developing its economy and resources.

"We favor the revision of the arms embargo to accord to the State of Israel the right of self-defense" (*New York Times*, October 25, 1948).

But the President had not said enough. Warmed up, perhaps by audience contact, and flushed with the prospect of victory, which was enhanced by a decision of the organized leftists to swing – after the opinion polls closed – from Wallace to Truman, he swallowed the "Israel" cause, line, sinker and hook – the hook being never thereafter removed. Here from the *New York Times* of Oct. 29, 1948, is Warren Moscow's story:

President Truman made his strongest pro-Israel declaration last night. Speaking at Madison Square Garden to more than 16,000 persons brought there under the auspices of the Liberal Party, the President ignored the Bernadotte Report and pledged himself to see that the new State of Israel be "large enough, free enough, and strong enough to make its people self-supporting and secure."

The President continued:

What we need now is to help the people of Israel and they've proved themselves in the best traditions of hardy pioneers. They have created a modern and efficient state with the highest standards of Western civilization.

In view of the Zionist record of eliminating the Arab natives of Palestine, continuous bombings, and the murder of the United Nations mediator, hardly cold in his grave, Mr. Truman owes the American people a documented exposition of his conception of "best traditions" and "highest standards of Western civilization."

Indeed, our bi-partisan endorsement of Zionist aggression in Palestine – in bidding for the electoral vote of New York – is one of the most reprehensible actions in world history.

The Soviet-supplied "Jewish" troops which seized Palestine had no rights ever before recognized in law or custom except the right of triumphant tooth and claw (see "The Zionist Illusion," by Prof. W. T. Stace of Princeton University, *Atlantic Monthly*, February, 1947).

In the first place the Khazar Zionists from Soviet Russia were not descended from the people of Hebrew religion in Palestine, ancient or modern, and thus not being descended from Old Testament people (*The Lost Tribes*, by Allen H. Godbey, Duke University Press, Durham, N.C., 1930,. pp. 257, 301, and *passim*), they have no Biblical claim to Palestine. Their claim to the country rests solely on their ancestors' having adopted a form of the religion of a people who ruled there eighteen hundred and more years before (Chapter II, above). This claim is thus exactly as valid as if the same or some other horde should claim the United States in 3350 A.D. on the basis of having adopted the religion of the American Indian! For another comparison, the 3,500,000 Catholics of China (*Time*, July 2, 1951) have as much right to the former Papal states in Italy as these Judaized Khazars have to Palestine! (Bible students are referred to the Apocalypse, *The Revelation of St. John the Divine*, Chapter II, Verse 9.)

Moreover, the statistics of both land-ownership and population

stand heavily against Zionist pretensions. At the close of the first
World War, "there were about 55,000 Jews in Palestine, forming
eight percent of the population... Between 1922 and 1941, the
Jewish population of Palestine increased by approximately 380,000,
four-fifths of this being due to immigration. This made the Jews
31 percent of the total population" (*East and West of Suez*, by
John S. Badeau, Foreign Policy Association, 1943, p. 46). Even
after hordes from Soviet and satellite lands had poured in, and
when the United Nations was working on the Palestine problem,
the best available statistics showed non-Jews owning more land
than Jews in all sixteen of the county-size subdivisions of Palestine
and outnumbering the Jews in population in fifteen of the sixteen
subdivisions (*UN Presentations* 574, and 573, November, 1947).

The anti-Communist Arab population of the world was un-
derstandably terrified by the arrival of Soviet-equipped troops
in its very center, Palestine, and was bitter at the presence among
them – despite President Roosevelt's promise to Ibn Saud – of
Americans with military training. How many U.S. army personnel,
reserve, retired, or on leave, secretly participated is not known.
Robert Conway, writing from Jerusalem on January 19, 1948, said:

> More than 2,000 Americans are already serving in Haganah, the
> Jewish Defense Army, highly placed diplomatic sources revealed
> today.

Conway stated further that a "survey convinced the Jewish agency
that 5,000 Americans are determined to come to fight for the Jewish
state even if the U.S. government imposes loss of citizenship upon
such volunteers." The expected number was 50,000 if no law on
forfeiting citizenship was passed by the U.S. Congress (N.Y. *News*
cable in Washington *Times-Herald,* January 20, 1948).

Among Americans who cast their lot with "Israel" was David
Marcus, a West Point graduate and World War II colonel. Col.

Marcus's service with the "Israeli" army was not revealed to the public until he was "killed fighting with Israeli forces near Jerusalem" in June, 1948. At the dedication of a Brooklyn memorial to Colonel Marcus a "letter from President Truman ... extolled the heroic roles played by Colonel Marcus in two wars" (*New York Times,* Oct. 11, 1948). At the time of his death, Colonel Marcus was "supreme commander of Israeli military forces on the Jerusalem front" (AP dispatch, Washington *Evening Star,* June 12, 1948).

The Arab vote in the United States is negligible – as the Zionist vote is *not* – and after the acceptance of "Israel" by the UN the American government recognized as a sovereign state the new nation whose soil was fertilized by the blood of many people of many nationalities from the lowly Arab peasant to the royal Swedish United Nations mediator. "You can't shoot your way into the United Nations," said Warren Austin, U.S. Delegate to the UN, speaking of Communist China on January 24, 1951 (Broadcasts of CBS and NBC). Mr. Austin must have been suffering from a lapse of memory, for that is exactly what "Israel" did!

Though the vote of Arabs and other Moslem peoples is negligible in the United States, the significance of these Moslem peoples is not negligible in the world (see the map entitled "The Moslem Block" on p. 78 of Badeau's *East of Suez*). Nor is their influence negligible in the United Nations. The friendly attitude of the United States toward Israel's bloody extension of her boundaries and other acts already referred to was effectively analyzed on the radio (NBC Network, January 8, 1951) by the distinguished philosopher and Christian (so stated by the introducer, John McVane), Dr. Charles Malik, Lebanese Delegate to the United Nations and Minister of Lebanon to the United States. Dr. *Charles* Malik of Lebanon is not to be confused with Mr. *Jacob* (Jakov, Yakop) Malik, Soviet Delegate with Andrei Y. Vishinsky to the 1950 General Assembly of the United Nations (*The United Nations – Action for Peace,* by Marie and Louis Zocca, Rutgers University Press, New Brunswick,

N.J., 1951). To his radio audience Dr. Malik of Lebanon spoke, in part, as follows:

> MR. MALIK: The United States has had a great history of very friendly relations with the Arab peoples for about one hundred years now. That history has been built up by faithful missionaries, educators, explorers, and archaeologists and businessmen for all these decades. Up to the moment when the Palestine problem began to be an acute issue, the Arab peoples had a genuine and deep sense of love and admiration for the United States. Then, when the problem of Palestine arose, with all that problem involved, by way of what we would regard as one-sided partiality on the part of the United States with respect to Israel, the Arabs began to feel that the United States was not as wonderful or as admirable as they had thought it was. The result has been that at the present moment there is a real slump in the affection and admiration that the Arabs have had towards the United States. This slump has affected all the relations between the United States and the Arab world, both diplomatic and non-diplomatic. And at the present moment I can say, much to my regret, but it is a fact that throughout the Arab world, perhaps at no time in history has the reputation of the United States suffered as much as it has at the present time. The Arabs, on the whole, do not have sufficient confidence that the United States, in moments of crises, will not make decisions that will be prejudicial to their interests. Not until the United States can prove in actual historical decision that it can withstand certain inordinate pressures that are exercised on it from time to time and can really stand up for what one might call elementary justice in certain matters, would the Arab people really feel that they can go back to their former attitude of genuine respect and admiration for the United States.

Thus the mess of pottage of vote-garnering in New York and other doubtful states with large numbers of Khazar Zionists has cost us the loyalty of *twelve nations*, our *former friends*, the so-called "Arab and Asiatic" block in the UN!

It appears also that the world's troubles from little blood-born "Israel" are not over. An official "Israeli" view of Germany was expressed in Dallas, Texas, on March 18, 1951, when Abba S. Eban, ambassador of the state of "Israel" to the United States and "Israel's" representative at the United Nations, stated that "Israel resents the rehabilitation of Germany." Ambassador Eban visited the Texas city in the interest of raising funds for taking "200,000 immigrants this year, 600,000 within the next three years" (*Dallas Morning News,* March 13, 1951) to the small state of Palestine, or "Israel." The same day that Ambassador Eban was talking in Dallas about "Israel's" resentment at the rehabilitation of Germany, a Reuters dispatch of March 13, 1951, from Tel Aviv (Washington *Times-Herald*) stated that "notes delivered yesterday [March 12] in Washington, London, and Paris and to the Soviet Minister at Tel Aviv urge the occupying powers of Germany not to "hand over full powers to any German government" without express reservations for the payment of reparations to "Israel" in the sum of $1,500,000,000.

This compensation was said to be for 6,000,000 Jews killed by Hitler. This figure has been used repeatedly (as late as January, 1952 – "Israeli" broadcast heard by the author), but one who consults statistics and ponders the known facts of recent history cannot do other than wonder how it is arrived at. According to Appendix VII, "Statistics on Religious Affiliation," of *The Immigration and Naturalization Systems of the United States* (A Report of the Committee on the Judiciary of the United States Senate, 1950), the number of Jews in the world is 15,713,638. The *World Almanac*, 1949, p. 289, is cited as the source of the statistical table reproduced on p. 842 of the government document. The article in the *World Almanac* is headed "Religious Population of the World." A corresponding item, with the title, "Population, Worldwide, by

Religious Beliefs" is found in the *World Almanac* for 1940 (p. 129), and in it the world Jewish population is given as 15,319,359. If the *World Almanac* figures are correct, the world's Jewish population did not decrease in the war decade, but showed a small increase.

Assuming, however, that the figures of the U.S. document and the *World Almanac* are in error, let us make an examination of the known facts. In the first place, the number of Jews in Germany in 1939 was about 600,000 – by some estimates considerably fewer – and of these, as shown elsewhere in this book, many came to the United States, some went to Palestine, and some are still in Germany. As to the Jews in Eastern European lands temporarily overrun by Hitler's troops, the great majority retreated ahead of the German armies into Soviet Russia. Of these, many came later to the U.S., some moved to Palestine, some unquestionably remained in Soviet Russia and may be a part of the Jewish force on the Iranian frontier, *and enough remained in Eastern Europe or have returned from Soviet Russia to form the hard core of the new ruling bureaucracy in satellite countries* (Chapter II).

It is hard to see how all these migrations and all these power accomplishments can have come about with a Jewish population much less than that which existed in Eastern Europe before World War II. Thus the known facts on Jewish migration and Jewish power in Eastern Europe tend, like the *World Almanac* figures accepted by the Senate Judiciary Committee, to raise a question as to where Hitler got the 6,000,000 Jews he is said to have killed. This question should be settled once and for all before the United States backs any "Israeli" claims against Germany. In this connection, it is well to recall also that the average German had no more to do with Hitler's policies than the average American had to do with Franklin Roosevelt's policies; that *5,000,000 Germans are unaccounted for* – 4,000,000 civilians (see the quote from Congressman B. Carroll Reece in Chapter IV, above, pp. 92-94) and 1,000,000 soldiers who never returned from Soviet labor camps (see section c, below, p. 167); and that *a permanent hostile attitude toward Germany on our part is the highest hope of the Communist masters of Russia*.

In spite of its absurdity, however, the "Israeli" claim for reparations from a not yet created country, whose territory has been nothing but an occupied land through the entire life of the state of "Israel," may well delay reconciliation in Western Europe; and the claim, even though assumed under duress by a West German government, would almost certainly be paid – directly or indirectly – by the United States. The likelihood of our paying will be increased if a powerful propaganda group puts on pressure in our advertiser-dominated press.

As to Ambassador Eban's 600,000 more immigrants to "Israel": Where will these people go – unless more Arab lands are taken and more Christians and Moslems are driven from their homes?

And of equal significance: Whence will Ambassador Eban's Jewish immigrants to "Israel" come? As stated above, a large portion of pre-war Germany's 600,000 Jews came, with other European Jews, to the United States on the return trips of vessels which took American soldiers to Europe. Few of them will leave the United States, for statistics show that of all immigrants to this country, the Jew is least likely to leave. The Jews now in West Germany will probably contribute few immigrants to "Israel," for these Jews enjoy a preferred status under U.S. protection. It thus appears that Ambassador Eban's 600,000 reinforcements to "Israel" – apart from stragglers from the Arab world and a possible mere handful from elsewhere – can come only from Soviet and satellite lands. If so, they will come on permission of and by arrangement with some Communist dictator (Chapter II, above). Can it be that many of the 600,000 will be young men with Soviet military training? Can it be that such permission will be related to the Soviet's great concentration of Jews in 1951 inside the Soviet borders adjacent to the Soviet-Iranian frontier?

Can it be true further that an army in Palestine, Soviet-supplied and Soviet-trained, will be one horn of a giant pincers movement ("Keil und Kessel" was Hitler's term) and that a thrust southward into oil-rich Iran will be the other? The astute Soviet politicians know that the use of a substantial body of Jewish troops in such an operation might be relied on to prevent any United States moves, diplomatic or otherwise, to save the Middle East and its oil from the Soviet. In fact, if spurred on by a full-scale Zionist propaganda campaign in this country our State Department (Chapter IX, below, pp. 272-273), following its precedent in regard to "Israel," might be expected to support the Soviet move.

To sum it up, it can only be said that there are intelligence indications that such a Soviet trap is being prepared. The Soviet foreign office, however, has several plans for a given strategic area, and will activate the one that seems, in the light of changing events, to promise most in realizing the general objective. Only time, then, can tell whether or not the Kremlin will thrust with Jewish troops for the oil of Iran and Arabia.

Thus the Middle East flames – in Iran, on the "Israeli" frontier, and along the Suez Canal.

Could we put out the fires of revolt which are so likely to lead to a full scale third World War? A sound answer was given by *The Freeman* (August 13, 1950), which stated that "all we need to do to insure the friendship of the Arab and Moslem peoples is to revert to our traditional American attitudes toward peoples who, like ourselves, love freedom." This is true because the "Moslem faith is founded partly upon the teachings of Christ." Also, "Anti-Arab Policies Are Un-American Policies," says William Ernest Hocking in *The Christian Century* ("Is Israel A 'Natural Ally'?" September 19, 1951).

Will we work for peace and justice in the Middle East and thus try to avoid World War III? Under our leftist-infested State Department, the chance seems about the same as the chance of the

Moslem voting population and financial power surpassing those of the Zionists during the next few years in the State of New York!

(c)

The Truman administration's third great mistake in foreign policy is found in its treatment of defeated Germany. In China and Palestine, Mr. Truman's State Department and Executive Staff henchmen can be directly charged with sabotaging the future of the United States; for despite the surrender at Yalta the American position in those areas was still far from hopeless when Roosevelt died in April, 1945. With regard to Germany, however, things were already about as bad as possible, and the Truman administration is to be blamed not for creating but for tolerating and continuing a situation dangerous to the future security of the United States.

At Yalta the dying Roosevelt, with Hiss at his elbow and General Marshall in attendance, had consented to the brutality of letting the Soviet use millions of prisoners of war as slave laborers – one million of them still slaves or dead before their time. We not only thus agreed to the revival of human slavery in a form far crueler than ever seen in the Western world; we also practiced the inhumanity of returning to the Soviet for Soviet punishment those Western-minded Russian soldiers who sought sanctuary in areas held by the troops of the once Christian West! The Morgenthau plan for reviving human slavery by its provision for "forced labor outside Germany" after the war (William Henry Chamberlin, *America's Second Crusade*, Henry Regnery Company, Chicago, 1950, p. 210) was the basic document for these monstrous decisions. It seems that Roosevelt initiated this plan at Quebec without fully knowing what he was doing (*Memoirs of Cordell Hull*, Vol. II) and might have modified some of the more cruel provisions if he had lived and regained his strength. Instead, he drifted into the twilight, and at Yalta Hiss and Marshall were in attendance upon him, while Assistant Secretary of State Acheson was busy in Washington.

After Roosevelt's death the same officials of sub-cabinet rank or high non-cabinet rank carried on their old policies and worked sedulously to foment more than the normal amount of post-war unrest in Western Germany. Still neglected was the sound strategic maxim that a war is fought to bring a defeated nation into the victor's orbit as a friend and ally. Indeed, with a much narrower world horizon than his predecessor, Mr. Truman was more easily put upon by the alien-minded officials around him. To all intents and purposes, he was soon their captive.

From the point of view of the future relations of both Germans and Jews and of our own national interest, we made a grave mistake in using so many Jews in the administration of Germany. Since Jews were assumed not to have any "Nazi contamination," the "Jews who remained in Germany after the Nazi régime were available for use by military government" (Zink, *American Military Government in Germany*, p. 136). Also, many Jews who had come from Germany to this country during the war were sent back to Germany as American officials of rank and power. Some of these individuals were actually given on-the-spot commissions as officers in the Army of the United States. Unfortunately, not all refugee Jews were of admirable character. Some had been in trouble in Germany for grave non-political offenses and their repatriation in the dress of United States officials was a shock to the German people. There are testimonies of falsifications by Jewish interpreters and of acts of vengeance. The extent of such practices is not here estimated, but in any case the employment of such large numbers of Jews – whether of good report, or bad – was taken by Germans as proof of Hitler's contention (heard by many Americans as a shortwave song) that America is a "Jewish land," and made rougher our road toward reconciliation and peace.

A major indelible blot was thrown on the American shield by the Nuremberg war trials in which, in clear violation of the spirit of our own Constitution, we tried people under *ex post facto* laws for actions performed in carrying out the orders of their superiors. Such a travesty of justice could have no other result than teaching the Germans – as the Palestine matter taught the Arabs – that our government had no sense of justice. The persisting bitterness from this foul fiasco is seen in the popular quip in Germany to the effect that in the third World War England will furnish the navy, France the foot soldiers, America the airplanes, and Germany the war-criminals.

In addition to lacking the solid foundation of legal precedent our "war trials" afforded a classic example of the "law's delay." Seven German soldiers, ranging in rank from sergeant to general, were executed as late as June 7, 1951. Whatever these men and those executed before them may or may not have done, the long delay had two obvious results – five years of jobs for the U.S. bureaucrats involved and a continuing irritation of the German people – an irritation desired by Zionists and Communists.

The Germans had been thoroughly alarmed and aroused against Communism and used the phrase "Gegen Welt Bolshewismus" ("Against World Communism") on placards and parade banners while Franklin Roosevelt was courting it ("We need those votes"). Consequently the appointment of John J. McCloy as High Commissioner (July 2, 1949) appeared as an affront, for this man was Assistant Secretary of War at the time of the implementation of the executive order which abolishes rules designed to prevent the admission of Communists to the War Department; and also, before a Congressional Committee appointed to investigate Communism in the War Department, he testified that Communism was not a decisive factor in granting or withholding an army commission. Not only McCloy's record (Chapter VIII, c) but his manner in dealing with the Germans tended to encourage a permanent hostility toward America. Thus, as late as 1950, he was still issuing orders to them not merely plainly but "bluntly" and "sharply" (Drew Middleton in the *New York Times,* Feb. 7, 1950).

Volumes could not record all our follies in such matters as dismantling German plants for the Soviet Union while spending nearly a billion a year to supply food and other essentials to the German people, who could have supported themselves by work in the destroyed plants. For details on results from dismantling a few chemical plants in the Ruhr, see "On the Record" by Dorothy Thompson, Washington *Evening Star*, June 14, 1949. The crowning failure of our policy, however, came in 1950. This is no place for a full discussion of our attitude toward the effort of 510,000 Jews – supported, of course, from the outside as shown in Chapter IV, above – to ride herd on 62,000,000 Germans (1933, the figures were respectively about 600,000 and 69,000,000 by 1939) or the ghastly sequels. It appeared as sheer deception, however, to give the impression, as Mr. Acheson did, that we were doing what we could to secure the cooperation of Western Germany, when Mr. Milton Katz was at the time (his resignation was effective August 19, 1951) our overall Ambassador in Europe and, under the far from vigorous Marshall, the two top assistant secretaries of Defense were the Eastern European Jewess, Mrs. Anna Rosenberg, and Mr. Marx Leva! Nothing is said or implied by the author against Mr. Katz, Mrs. Rosenberg, or Mr. Marx Leva, or others such as Mr. Max Lowenthal and Mr. Benjamin J. Buttenwieser, who have been prominent figures in our recent dealings with Germany, the former as Assistant to Commissioner McCloy and the latter as Assistant High Commissioner of the United States. As far as the author knows, all five of these officials are true to their convictions. The sole point here stressed is the unsound policy of sending unwelcome people to a land whose good will we are seeking – or perhaps only *pretending* to seek.

According to Forster's *A Measure of Freedom* (p. 86), there is a "steady growth of pro-German sentiment in the super-Patriotic press" in the United States. The context suggests that Mr. Forster is referring in derision to certain pro-American sheets of small circulation, most of which do not carry advertising. These English-language papers with their strategically sound viewpoints can, however, have no appreciable circulation in Germany, if any at all, and Germans are forced to judge America by its actions and its personnel. In both, we have moved for the most part rather to repel them than to draw them into our orbit as friends.

If we really wish friendship and peace with the German people, and really want them on our side in case of another world-wide war, our choice of General Eisenhower as Commander-in-Chief in Europe was most unfortunate. He is a tactful, genial man, but to the Germans he remains – now and in history – as the Commander who directed the destruction of their cities with civilian casualties running as high as a claimed 40,000 in a single night, and directed the U.S. *retreat* from the outskirts of Berlin. This retreat was both an affront to our victorious soldiers and a tragedy for Germany, because of the millions of additional people it placed under the Soviet yoke, and because of the submarine construction plants, guided missile works, and other factories it presented to the Soviet. Moreover, General Eisenhower was Supreme Commander in Germany during the hideous atrocities perpetrated upon the German people by displaced persons after the surrender (Chapter IV, above). There is testimony to General Eisenhower's lack of satisfaction with conditions in Germany in 1945, but he made – as far as the author knows – no strong gesture such as securing his assignment to another post. Finally, according to Mr. Henry Morgenthau (*New York Post*, November 24, 1947), as quoted in *Human Events* and in W. H. Chamberlin's *America's Second Crusade*, General Eisenhower said: "The whole German population is a synthetic paranoid," and added that the best cure would be to let them stew in their own juice.

All in all, sending General Eisenhower to persuade the West Germans to "let bygones be bygones" (CBS, January 20, 1951), even before the signing of a treaty of peace, was very much as if

President Grant had sent General Sherman to Georgia to placate the Georgians five years after the burning of Atlanta and the march to the sea – except that the personable Eisenhower had the additional initial handicap of Mr. Katz breathing on his neck, and Mrs. Anna Rosenberg in high place in the Department of Defense in Washington! The handicap may well be insurmountable, for many Germans, whether rightly or not, believe Jews are responsible for all their woes. Thus, after the Eisenhower appointment, parading Germans took to writing on their placards not their old motto "Gegen Welt Bolshewismus" but "Ohne mich" (AP dispatch from Frankfurt-am-Main, Germany, February 4, 1951), which may be translated "Leave me out."

In this Germany, whose deep war wounds were kept constantly festering by our policy, our government has stationed some six divisions of American troops. Why? In answering the question remember that Soviet Russia is next door, while our troops, supplies, and reinforcements have to cross the Atlantic! Moreover, if the Germans, fighting from and for their own homeland, "failed with a magnificent army of 240 combat divisions" (ex-President Herbert Hoover, broadcast on "Our National Policies in This Crisis," Dec. 20, 1950) to defeat Soviet Russia, what do we expect to accomplish with *six divisions?* Of course, in World War II many of Germany's divisions were used on her west front and America gave the Soviet eleven billion dollars worth of war matériel; still by any comparison with the number of German divisions used against Stalin, six is a very small number *for any military purpose envisioning victory.* Can it be that the six divisions have been offered by some State Department schemer as World War III's European parallel to the "sitting ducks" at Pearl Harbor and the cockle shells in Philippine waters? (See Chapter VII, d, below and *Design for War,* by Frederic R. Sanborn, The Devin-Adair Company, New York, 1951.) According to the military historian and critic, Major Hoffman Nickerson, our leaders have some "undisclosed purpose of their own, or if they foresee war they intend that war to begin either with a disaster or a helter-skelter retreat" (*The Freeman*, July 2, 1951). In any case the Soviet Union – whether from adverse internal conditions, restive satellites, fear of our atomic bomb stockpile, confidence in the achievement of its objectives through diplomacy and infiltration, or other reasons – has not struck violently at our first bait of six divisions. But, under our provocation the Soviet has *quietly* got busy.

For five years after the close of World War II, we maintained in Germany two divisions and the Soviet leaders made little or no attempt to prepare the East German transportation network for possible war traffic (*U.S. News and World Report*, January 24, 1951). Rising, however, to the challenge of our four additional divisions (1951), the Soviet took positive action. Here is the story (AP dispatch from Berlin in Washington *Times-Herald*, April 30, 1951):

> Russian engineers have started rebuilding the strategic rail and road system from Germany's Elbe River, East German sources disclosed today.
>
> The main rail lines linking East Germany and Poland with Russia are being double-tracked, the sources said.
>
> The engineers are rebuilding Germany's highway and bridge network to support tanks and other heavy artillery vehicles.

The Soviet got busy not only in transportation but in personnel and equipment. According to Drew Middleton (*New York Times*, August 17, 1951), "All twenty-six divisions of the Soviet group of armies in Eastern Germany are being brought to full strength for the first time since 1946." Also, a "stream of newly produced tanks, guns, trucks, and light weapons is flowing to divisional and army bases." There were reports also of the strengthening of satellite armies.

These strategic moves *followed* our blatantly announced plans to increase our forces in Germany. Moreover, according to Woodrow Wyatt, British Undersecretary for War, the Soviet Union had "under arms" in the summer of 1951 "215 divisions and more than 4,000,000 men" (AP dispatch in *New York Times,* July 16, 1951). Can it be possible that our State Department is seeking ground conflict with this vast force not only on their frontier but on the particular frontier which is closest to their factories and to their most productive farm lands?

In summary, the situation of our troops in Germany is part of a complex world picture which is being changed daily by new world situations such as our long delayed accord with Spain and a relaxing of the terms of our treaty with Italy. There are several unsolved factors. One of them is our dependence – at least in large part – on the French transportation network which is in daily jeopardy of paralysis by the Communists, who are numerically the strongest political party in France. Another is the nature of the peace treaty which will some day be ratified by the government of West Germany and the Senate of the United States – and thereafter the manner of implementing that treaty.

As we leave the subject, it can only be said that the situation of our troops in Germany is precarious and that the question of our relations with Germany demands the thought of the ablest and most patriotic people in America – a type not overly prominent in the higher echelons of our Department of State in recent years.

(d)

Having by three colossal "mistakes" set the stage for possible disaster in the Far East, in the Middle East, and in Germany, we awaited the enemy's blow which could be expected to topple us to defeat. It came in the Far East.

As at Pearl Harbor, the attack came on a Sunday morning – June 25, 1950. On that day, North Korean Communist troops crossed the

38th parallel from the Soviet Zone to the recently abandoned U.S. Zone in Korea and moved rapidly to the South. Our government knew *from several sources* about these Communist troops before we moved our troops out on January 1, 1949, leaving the South Koreans to their fate. For instance, in March, 1947, Lieutenant General John R. Hodge, U.S. Commander in Korea, stated "that Chinese Communist troops were participating in the training of a Korean army of 500,000 in Russian-held North Korea" (*The China Story*, p. 51).

Despite our knowledge of the armed might of the forces in North Korea; despite our vaunted failure to arm our former wards, the South Koreans; despite our "hands off" statements placing Formosa and Korea outside our defense perimeter and generally giving Communists the green light in the Far East; and despite President Truman's statement as late as May 4, 1950, that there would be "no shooting war," we threw United States troops from Japan into that unhappy peninsula – without the authority of Congress – to meet the Communist invasion.

Our troops from Japan had been trained for police duty rather than as combat units and were "without the proper weapons" (P. L. Franklin in *National Republic*, January, 1951). This deplorable fact was confirmed officially by former Defense Secretary, Louis Johnson, who testified that our troops in Korea "were not equipped with the things that you would need if you were to fight a hostile enemy. They were staffed and equipped for occupation, not for war or an offensive" (testimony before combined Armed Services and Foreign Relations Committees of the Senate, June, 1951, as quoted by *U.S. News and World Report*, June 22, 1951, pp. 21-22). Our administration had seen to it also that those troops which became our South Korean allies were also virtually unarmed, for the Defense Department "had no establishment for Korea. It was under the State Department at that time" (Secretary Johnson's testimony).

Under such circumstances, *can any objective thinker avoid the conclusion that the manipulators of United States policy confidently anticipated the defeat and destruction of our forces, which Secretary Acheson advised President Truman to commit to Korea* in June, 1950?

But the leftist manipulators of the State Department – whether in that department or on the outside – were soon confronted by a miracle they had not foreseen. The halting of the North Korean Communists by a handful of men under such handicaps was one of the remarkable and heroic pages in history – credit for which must be shared by our brave front-line fighting men; their field commanders including Major General William F. Dean, who was captured by the enemy, and Lieutenant General Walton H. Walker, who died in Korea; and their Commander-in-Chief, General of the Army Douglas MacArthur.

The free world applauded what seemed to be a sudden reversal of our long policy of surrender to Soviet force in the Far East, and the United Nations gave its endorsement to our administration's venture in Korea. But the same free world was stunned when it realized the significance of our President's order to the U.S. Seventh Fleet to take battle station between Formosa and the Chinese mainland and stop Chiang from harassing the mainland Communists. Prior to the Communist aggression in Korea, Chiang was dropping ammunition from airplanes to unsubdued Nationalist troops (so-called "guerrillas"), whose number by average estimates of competent authorities was placed at approximately 1,250,000; was bombing Communist concentrations; was making hit-and-run raids on Communist-held ports, and was intercepting supplies which were being sent from *Britain and the United States* to the Chinese Communists. Repeated statements by Britain and America that such shipments were of no use to the Communist armies were demolished completely by Mr. Winston Churchill, who revealed on the floor of the House of Commons (May 7, 1951,

UP dispatch) that the material sent to the Chinese Communists included 2,500 tons of Malayan rubber per month!

Chiang's forces – despite frequent belittlings in certain newspapers and by certain radio commentators – were and are by no means negligible. His failure on the mainland had resulted directly from our withholding of ammunition and other supplies but, as shown above, he successfully covered his retreat to Formosa. According to Major General Claire Chennault of the famed "Flying Tigers" and Senator Knowland of California – a World War II Major and member of the Senate Armed Services Committee – who investigated independently, Chiang late in 1950 had about 500,000 trained troops on Formosa and considerable matériel. The number was placed at 600,000 by General MacArthur in his historic address to the two houses of the Congress on April 19, 1951.

Our action against Chiang had one effect, so obvious as to seem planned. By our order to the Seventh Fleet, the Communist armies which Chiang was pinning down were free to support the Chinese Communist forces assembled on the Korean border to watch our operations. Despite our State Department's "assumption" that the Chinese Communists would not fight, those armies seized the moment of their reinforcement from the South, which coincided with the extreme lengthening of our supply lines, and entered the war in November, 1950, thirteen days after the election of a pro-Acheson Democratic congress. In his appearance before the combined Armed Services and Foreign Relations Committees of the Senate in May, 1951, General MacArthur testified that *two Chinese Communist armies which had been watching Chiang had been identified among our enemies in Korea.* Thus our policy in the Strait of Formosa was instrumental in precipitating the Chinese Communist attack upon us when victory in Korea was in our grasp.

Here then, in summary, was the situation when the Chinese Communists crossed the Yalu River in November, 1950: – *We had virtually supplied them with the sinews of war by preventing*

Chiang's interference with their import of strategic materials. We had released at least two of their armies for an attack on us by stopping Chiang's attacks on them. We not only, for "political" reasons, had refused Chiang's offer of 33,000 of his best troops when the war broke out ("How Asia's Policy Was Shaped: Civilians in the State Department Are Dictating Military Strategy of Nation, Johnson confirms," by Constantine Brown, *The Evening Star,* Washington, June 16, 1951), but even in the grave crisis in November, 1950, we turned down General MacArthur's plea that he be allowed to "accept 60,000 of Chiang's troops."

These truths, which cannot be questioned by anyone, constitute a second barrage of evidence that the shapers of our policy sought defeat rather than victory. Had General MacArthur been permitted to use them, Chiang's loyal Chinese troops would not only have fought Communists, but, being of the same race and speaking the same or a related language, "would no doubt have been able to induce many surrenders among the Red Chinese forces" (see "Uncle Sam, Executioner," *The Freeman,* June 18, 1951). If we had accepted the services of Chiang's troops, we would have also secured the great diplomatic advantage of rendering absurd, and probably preventing, the outcry in India, and possibly other Asiatic countries, that our operation in Korea was a new phase of Western imperialism.

But this was not all that our State Department and Presidential coterie did to prevent the victory of our troops in Korea. Despite the fact that the United Nations on October 7, 1950, voted by a big majority for crossing the 38th parallel to free North Korea, up to the Yalu River, we denied MacArthur's army the right to use air reconnaissance for acquiring intelligence indications of the Chinese Communist troops and facilities across that river. This amazing denial of a commander's elementary right to take a reasonable precaution in saving soldiers' lives at last made clear to many Americans that we were fighting for some other objective besides victory. Coming, as it did, as one of a series of pro-Communist moves, this blindfolding of General MacArthur prompted Representative Joe Martin of Massachusetts, former Speaker of the House, to ask pointedly in his Lincoln Day Speech in New York (February 12, 1951): "What are we in Korea for – to win or to lose?"

The denial of the right to reconnoiter and to bomb troop concentrations and facilities, after whole Chinese armies were committed against us, was very close to treason under the Constitutional prohibition (Article III, Section 3, paragraph 1) of giving "aid and comfort" to an enemy. In fact, if a refusal to let our troops take in defense of their lives measures always recognized in warfare as not only permissible but obligatory does not constitute "aid and comfort" to the enemy, it is hard to conceive any action which might be so construed. The pretense that by abstaining from reconnaissance and from the bombing of enemy supply lines we kept the Soviet out of the war makes sense only to the very ignorant or to those in whose eyes our State Department can do no wrong. A country such as the Soviet Union will make war when the available matériel is adequate, when its troops have been trained and concentrated for the proposed campaign, and when the government decides that conditions at home and abroad are favorable – not when some of its many catspaws are bombed on one side or the other of an Asiatic river.

The only logical conclusion, therefore – and a conclusion arrived at by a whole succession of proofs – is that *for some reason* certain people with influence in high places wanted heavier American casualties in Korea, the final defeat of our forces there, and the elimination of MacArthur from the American scene.

But once again, MacArthur did not fail. Once again, under terrible odds, MacArthur first evaded and then stopped the enemy – an enemy sent against him by the Far Eastern policy of Truman and Acheson.

179

According to General Bonner Fellers (UP, Baltimore, Md., May 11, 1952, *New York Times*), the Chinese field commanders in Korea in the Spring of 1951 were desperate and "could not hold out much longer." Apparently not wanting victory, the Truman-Acheson-Marshall clique acted accordingly. On April 10, 1951, General Douglas MacArthur was dismissed from his Far Eastern command. With MacArthur's successor, our top echelon executives took no chances. Before a Florida audience, the veteran radio commentator, H. V. Kaltenborn, spoke as follows: "General Ridgway told me in answer to my query as to why we can't win that he was under orders not to win" (article by Emilie Keyes, *Palm Beach Post*, Jan. 30, 1952).

The frantic dismissal of a great general who was also a popular and successful ruler of an occupied country caused a furor all over America. The general was invited to address the two houses of the Congress in joint session and did so on April 19, 1951. During the same hour, the President conferred, as he said later, with Dean Acheson, without turning on radio or television – and Mrs. Truman was at a horse race.

General MacArthur's speech will forever be a classic in military annals and among American State papers. It was followed shortly by an investigation of the circumstances leading to his dismissal – an investigation by the combined Armed Services and Foreign Relations committees of the Senate.

The millions of words of testimony before the combined Senate committees resulted in no action. The volume of questions and answers was so vast that few people or none could follow all of it, but certain good resulted – even over and above the awakening of the more alert Americans to the dangers of entrusting vital decisions to men with the mental processes of the secretaries of State and Defense. After the MacArthur investigation the American people (i) knew more about our casualties in Korea; (ii) learned of the Defense Department's acceptance of the idea of a bloody stalemate, and (iii) got a shocking documentary proof of the ineptitude or virtual treason of our foreign policy. These three topics will be developed in the order here listed.

(i) By May 24, 1951 – eleven months after the Korean Communist troops crossed the 38th parallel – our own publicly admitted battle casualties had reached the recorded total of 69,276, a figure much larger than that for our casualties during the whole first full year (1942) of World War II (*U.S. News and World Report,* April 17, 1951, p. 14). On the subject of our casualties, Senator Bridges of New Hampshire, senior Republican member of the Armed Services Committee of the Senate, revealed the further significant fact that as of April, 1951, Americans had suffered "94.6 per cent of all casualties among United Nations forces aiding South Korea" (UP dispatch from Chicago, April 11, 1951). Parenthetically, the second United Nations member in the number of casualties in Korea was our Moslem co-belligerent, the Republic of Turkey. The casualties of South Korea were not considered in this connection since that unhappy land was not a UN member.

Moreover, on May 24, 1951, General Bradley revealed in his testimony before the combined Armed Services and Foreign Relations Committees of the Senate that non-battle casualties, *including the loss of frozen legs and arms,* which had not been included in lists issued to the public, totaled an *additional* 72,679 casualties, among them 612 dead.

With such terrible casualties admitted and published, President Truman's glib talk of "avoiding war" by a "police action" in Korea appeared to more and more people to be nothing but quibbling with a heartless disregard of our dead and wounded men and their sorrowing relatives. Our battle casualties passed 100,000 by mid-November, 1951.

(ii) Before his dismissal, General MacArthur stressed his conviction that the only purpose of war is victory. In direct contrast, Secretary of Defense Marshall admitted to the Congress, in seeking more drastic draft legislation, that there was no foreseen end to our losses in Korea – a statement undoubtedly coordinated with the State Department. This acceptance of a bloody stalemate with no foreseeable end horrified MacArthur, who is a Christian as well as a strategist, and prompted a protest which was a probable factor in his dismissal. The Marshall "strategy in Korea" was summed up succinctly by *U.S. News and World Report* (April 20, 1951) as a plan "to bleed the Chinese into a mood to talk peace." This interpretation was confirmed by General Marshall, who was still Secretary of Defense, in testimony before the Senate Armed Services and Foreign Relations Committees on May 7, 1951.

What an appalling prospect for America – this fighting a war our leaders do not want us to win, for when every possible drop of our blood has been shed on Korean soil the dent in China's 475,000,000 people (population figures given by Chinese Communist mission to the UN) will not be noticeable. This is true because on a blood-letting basis we cannot kill them as fast as their birth rate will replace them. Moreover, the death of Chinese Communist soldiers will cause no significant ill-effects on Chinese morale, for the Chinese Communist authorities publish neither the names of the dead nor any statistics on their losses.

(iii) Terrible for its full and final exposure of our government's wanton waste of young American lives and of our State Department's destruction of our world position, but fortunate for its complete revelation of treason or the equivalent in high places in our government, a second instalment of the Wedemeyer Report (a, above) was given to the public on May 1, 1951, possibly because of the knowledge that the MacArthur furor would turn the daylight on it anyhow. The full text of the Wedemeyer Report on Korea, as issued, was published in the *New York Times* for May 2, 1951. The report was condensed in an editorial (Washington *Daily News*, April 10, 1951) which Congressman Walter H. Judd of Minnesota included in the *Congressional Record* (May 2, 1951, pp.

A2558-2559). Here is a portion of the *Daily News* editorial with a significant passage from the Wedemeyer Report:

The [Wedemeyer] reports, which presented plans to save China and Manchuria from Communism, were suppressed until July, 1949. The report on Korea was denied to the public until yesterday. It contained this warning:

"The Soviet-equipped and trained North Korean people's (Communist) army of approximately 125,000 is vastly superior to the United States-organized constabulary of 16,000 Koreans equipped with Japanese small arms... The withdrawal of American military forces from Korea would ... result in the occupation of South Korea either by Soviet troops, or, as seems more likely, by the Korean military units trained under Soviet auspices." Those units, General Wedemeyer said, maintained active liaison "with the Chinese Communists in Manchuria."

This was written nearly 4 years ago.

To meet this threat, General Wedemeyer recommended a native force on South Korea, "sufficient in strength to cope with the threat from the North," to prevent the "forcible establishment of a Communist government."

Since 70 per cent of the Korean population was in the American occupation zone south of the thirty-eighth parallel, the manpower advantage was in our favor, if we had used it. But the sound Wedemeyer proposal was ignored, and, when the predicted invasion began, American troops had to be rushed to the scene because sufficient South Korean troops were not available.

The State Department was responsible for this decision.

Thus a long-suppressed document, full of warning and of fulfilled prophecy, joined the spilled blood of our soldiers in casting the shadow of treason upon our State Department. "UN forces, under present restraints, will not be able to win," said *U.S. News and World*

Report, on June 8, 1951. In fact, by their government's plan they were not allowed to win! Here's how *The Freeman* (June 4, 1951) summed up our Korean war:

> So whenever the Chinese Communists feel that they are getting the worse of it, they may simply withdraw, rest, regroup, rearm – and make another attack at any time most advantageous to themselves. They have the guarantee of Messrs. Truman, Acheson, and Marshall that they will be allowed to do all this peacefully and at their leisure; that we will never pursue them into their own territory, never bomb their concentrations or military installations, and never peep too curiously with our air reconnaissance to see what they are up to.

The truce conference between the Communists and the representatives of the American Far East commander, General Matthew B. Ridgway, was protracted throughout the summer and autumn of 1951 and into April, 1952, when General Mark Clark of Rapido River notoriety succeeded (April 28) to the military command once held by Douglas MacArthur! Whatever its outcome may be under General Clark, this conference has so far had one obvious advantage for the Communists; it has given them time in which to build up their resources in matériel, particularly in tanks and jet planes, and time to bring up more troops – *an opportunity capable of turning the scales against us in Korea, since a corresponding heavy reinforcement of our troops was forbidden under our new policy of sending four divisions to Germany!* The potential disaster inherent in our long executive dawdling, while our troops under the pliant Ridgway saw their air superiority fade away, should be investigated by Congress. In letters to public officials and to the press and in resolutions passed in public meetings, the American people should demand such an investigation. Congress should investigate the amount of pre-combat training given our fliers; the question of defective planes; and crashes in the Strategic Air Command under

General LeMay and others, as well as the decline under President Truman of our relative air strength in Korea and the world. For amazing pertinent facts, see "Emergency in the Air," by General Bonner Fellers, in *Human Events*, January 23, 1952.

A peace treaty with Japan (for text, see *New York Times*, July 13, 1951) was proclaimed at San Francisco on September 8, 1951, after the dismissal of General MacArthur. This treaty ratified the crimes of Yalta under which, in defiance of the Atlantic Charter and of every principle of self-interest and humanity, we handed to the Soviet the Kurile Islands and placed Japan perilously in the perimeter of Soviet power. Moreover, the preamble to the treaty provides that Japan shall "strive to realize the objectives of the universal declaration of human rights." Since this declaration is intended to supersede the U.S. Constitution, the Senate's ratification of the treaty (Spring of 1952) is thought by many astute political observers to foreshadow UN meddling within our boundaries (see *Human Events*, December 26, 1951) and other violations of our sovereignty.

On April 28, 1952, Japan, amid a clamor of Soviet denunciation, became a nation again. At best, the new Japan, sorely overpopulated and underprovided with food and other resources cannot for many years be other than a source of grave concern to our country. This is our legacy from Hiss, Acheson, and Dulles!

And what of the South Koreans, a people we are ostensibly helping? Their land is a bloody shambles and three million of them are dead. It was thus that we joined Britain in "helping" Poland in World War II. The best comment is a haunting phrase of the Roman historian, Publius Cornelius Tacitus, "Ubi solitudinem faciunt, pacem appellant" ("Where they create a wasteland, they call it peace"). Thus with no visible outcome but a continuing bloody stalemate, and continuing tragedy for the South Koreans, more and more clean young Americans are buried under white crosses in Korea.

Perhaps the best summary of our position in Korea was given by Erle Cocke, Jr., National Commander of the American Legion, after a tour of the battle lines in Korea ("Who Is Letting Our GI's Down?" *American Legion Magazine,* May, 1951):

Our present-day Benedict Arnolds may glibly argue that it is necessary to keep Chiang and his armies blockaded on Formosa, but these arguments make no sense to our soldiers, sailors, airmen and marines who have to do the fighting and dying. They see in Chiang's vast armies a way of saving some of the 250 lives that are being needlessly sacrificed each week because certain furtive people expound that Chiang isn't the right sort of person, and therefore we cannot accept his aid. Our fighting men are not impressed by these false prophets because they haven't forgotten that these same people not long ago were lauding Mao's murdering hordes as "agrarian reformers."

For the life of them – and "life" is meant in a very literal sense – they can't understand why our State Department and the United Nations make it necessary for them to be slaughtered by red armies which swarm down on them from territory which our own heads of Government make sacrosanct...

Agents of the Kremlin, sitting in the councils of the United Nations, in Washington and elsewhere, must laugh up their sleeves at our utter idiocy. But you may be sure that our GI's are not amused. They see the picture as clearly as the Soviet agents do, but, unlike our stateside leaders, they see the results of this criminal skulduggery in the blood they shed and in the mangled corpses of their buddies.

What they cannot understand, though, is the strange apathy of the people back home. As they listen to radio reports of what is happening thousands of miles to the east of them, they are puzzled. Isn't the American public aware of what is going on? Don't they realize that their sons and husbands and sweethearts are fighting a ruthless enemy who has them at a terrible disadvantage, thanks to stupid or traitorous advisors and inept diplomacy?

This brings us to Delegate Warren Austin's statement (NBC, January 20, 1951) that the UN votes with us "usually 53 to 5" but runs out on us when the question rises of substantial help in Korea. The reader is now ready for and has probably arrived at the truth. The free nations vote with us because we are obviously preferable to the Soviet Union as a friend or ally, for the Soviet Union absorbs and destroys its allies.

But according to the Lebanon delegate to the United Nations, quoted above, the nations of Asia are withholding their full support of U.S. policy because they are pained and bewildered by it. They do not understand a foreign policy which (a) *applauds* the landing of Russian-trained troops on a *Palestine* beachhead and amiably tolerates the bloody "liquidation" of natives *and UN officials* and (b) goes to war because one faction of *Koreans* is fighting another faction of *Koreans* in *Korea*.

The failure to see any sense in United States policy is not confined to the nations of Asia. In France, our oldest friend among the great powers, there is confusion also. Thus a full-page cartoon in the conservative and dignified *L'Illustration* (issue of January 20, 1951) showed Stalin and Truman sitting over a chess board. Stalin is gathering in chessmen (U.S. Soldiers' lives) while Truman looks away from the main game to fumble with a deck of cards. Stalin asks him: "Finally, my friend, won't you tell me exactly what game we are playing?" ("Enfin, mon cher, me direz-vous à quoi nous jouons exactement?"). This quip should touch Americans to the quick.

Exactly what game *are* we playing?

How can Lebanon or France, or any nation, or anybody, understand a policy which fights Communism on the 38th Parallel and helps it in the Strait of Formosa; which worships aggression in

Palestine and condemns it in Korea? In the *Philadelphia Inquirer* (April 6, 1951) the matter was brilliantly summed up in the headline of a dispatch from Ivan H. Peterman: "U.S. Zig-Zag Diplomacy Baffles Friend and Foe."

Meanwhile, amid smirking complacency in the State Department, more and more of those young men who should be the Americans of the Future are buried beneath white crosses on an endless panorama of heartbreak ridges.

CHAPTER VII

DOES THE NATIONAL DEMOCRATIC PARTY WANT WAR?

Since the suspension of the Age of Honor in 1933, those few patriotic Americans who as linguists, astute historians, or intelligence officers have been privileged to look behind our iron curtain of censorship have had the shock of many times seeing the selfish wishes of a gang or a minority placed ahead of the welfare of the United States. The attempts of those writers and speakers who have tried to share the truth with their fellow citizens have, however, been largely in vain. Publishers and periodicals characteristically refuse to print books and articles that present vital whole truths. Patriotic truth-tellers who somehow achieve print are subject to calumny. "I have been warned by many," said General MacArthur in his speech to the Massachusetts Legislature in Boston (July 25, 1951), "that an outspoken course, even if it be solely of truth, will bring down upon my head ruthless retaliation – that efforts will be made to destroy public faith in the integrity of my views – not by force of just argument but by the application of the false methods of propaganda." Those who have occasion to read leftist magazines and newspapers know the accuracy of the warnings received by General MacArthur.

Why is the average American deceived by such propaganda? He has been taught, in the various and devious ways of censorship, to see no evil except in his own kind, for on radio and in the motion picture the villain is by regular routine a man of native stock. Ashamed and bewildered, then, the poor American citizen takes his position more or less unconsciously against his own people and against the truth – and thereby, against the traditions of Western Christian civilization, which are, or were, the traditions of the United States. It must not be forgotten for a moment, however, that it was the Saviour himself who said, "Ye shall know the truth, and the truth shall make you free." The average citizen of native stock needs nothing so much as to experience the purifying joy of realizing, of knowing, that he is not the villain in America. When the slackening of censorship allows him to enjoy the restored freedom of seeing himself as a worthy man – which he is – he will learn, also, something about the forces which have deceived him in the last forty or fifty years.

The obvious conclusion to be drawn from the facts stated in Chapter VI is that our foreign policy has had no steadfast principal aims apart from pleasing – as in its Palestine and German deals – the Leftists, largely of Eastern European origin, who control the National Democratic Party. Can this be true? If a war should seem necessary to please certain Democrats, to establish controls, and to give the party an indefinite tenure in office, would our leaders go that far? Despite the pervasive influence of censorship, many Americans think so. A member of the House Foreign Affairs Committee, Congressman Lawrence H. Smith of Wisconsin, charged in 1951 that President Truman, Secretary Acheson, and General Marshall – at that time Secretary of Defense – were "conjuring up another war." In an article in *National Republic* (May, 1951) Congressman B. Carroll Reece of Tennessee gave the history of the Democratic Party as the "war party." This haunting terrible question is expressed as follows by E. B. Gallaher in the *Clover Business Letter* (Clover Mfg. Co., Norwalk, Conn.) for August 1951:

As we all should know by this time, when the New Deal was about to crack up in 1941, Roosevelt, to save his hide, deliberately got us into World War II in order to give us something else to think about. The propaganda at that time, due to the global nature of the war, was "don't swap horses when crossing a stream." On this fake propaganda he succeeded in getting himself elected once again.

Now I wonder if history is not repeating itself, this time in a slightly different form.

Could it be possible that Truman, seeing the handwriting on the wall for his "Fair Deal" ... deliberately started the Korean war in order to insure himself of the necessary power to become a dictator? If he could do this, the 1952 elections could become a farce, and his election would become assured.

Let us then objectively examine the question "Does the National Democratic Party Want War?" Let it be noted explicitly at the outset that the question refers to the *controllers* of the *National* Democratic Party and not to the millions of individual Democrats, Northern and Southern – including many Senators, Congressmen, and other officials – whose basic patriotism cannot and should not be challenged. Their wrong judging is based on an ignorance which is the product of censorship (Chapter V) and is not allied to willful treason.

We shall examine in order (a) the testimony of mathematics; (b) the temptation of the bureaucracy-builder; and (c) the politician's fear of dwindling electoral majorities. The chapter is concluded by special attention to two additional topics (d) and (e) closely related to the question of safeguarding the Democratic party's tenure by war.

(a)

In the first half of this century, the United States had five Republican presidents with no wars and three Democratic presidents with three wars. Such a succession of eight coincidences under the laws of mathematics would happen once in 256 times. Even if against such odds this fact could be considered a coincidence, the Democrats are still condemned by chronology. They have no alibi of inheriting these wars, which broke out respectively in the fifth year of Woodrow Wilson, in the ninth year of Franklin Roosevelt, and in the fifth year of Mr. Truman. In each case there was plenty of time to head off a war by policy or preparedness, or both. Mathematics thus clearly suggests that the behind-the-scenes leaders of the Democratic Party have a strong predilection for solving their problems and fulfilling their "obligations" by war.

(b)

A war inevitably leads to a rapid increase in the number of controls. The first result of controls is the enlargement of the bureaucracy. "Defense emergency gives the Democrats a chance to build up for 1952. There are plenty of jobs for good party regulars" (*U.S. News and World Report,* February 9, 1951). But just as an innocent-looking egg may hatch a serpent, controls may produce a dictator, and once a dictator is in power no one (as shown in the case of Hitler) can chart his mad course. Nevertheless, these controls and this centralization of bureaucratic power urged by Mr. Truman as a "Fair Deal" program are so dear to many socialistically inclined "Democrats," Eastern Europeans and others, that they may be willing to pay for them in young men's blood. This sacrifice of blood for what you want is nothing startling. In the Revolutionary War, for instance, our forefathers sacrificed blood for national independence, and we need not be surprised that others are willing to make the same sacrifice for what they want – namely a socialist bureaucracy. The blood sacrifice, moreover, will not be made by those young male immigrants who are arriving from Eastern Europe (see c below) as students or visitors or as undetected illegal entrants. Many students and visitors have in the past found a way to remain. Young immigrants in these categories who manage to remain and the illegal entrants are likely to have passed the age of twenty-five and probable *exemption from the military draft* before cognizance is taken of their situation. Newcomer aliens all too frequently slip into jobs that might have been held by those who died in Korea! Controls are usually introduced somewhat gradually and with an accompaniment of propaganda designed to deceive or lull the people. A return from absence gives an objective outlook, and it is thus not surprising that on touring America, after his years in the Far East, General Douglas MacArthur saw more clearly than most people who remained in America the long strides we had made toward collectivism. In his speech at Cleveland (AP dispatch in Richmond *Times-Dispatch,* September 7, 1951) he testified that he had noted in this country "our steady drift toward totalitarian rule with its suppression of those personal liberties which have . formed the foundation stones to our political, economic and social advance to national greatness."

It is significant that another American who stands at the utmost top of his profession arrived by a different road at a conclusion identical with that of General MacArthur. In a speech entitled "The Camel's Nose Is Under the Tent," before the Dallas Chapter of the Society for the Advancement of Management on October 10, 1951, Mr. Charles Erwin Wilson, President of General Motors – the largest single maker of armament in World War II – gave Americans a much-needed warning: "The emergency of the Korean war and the defense program, however, is being used to justify more and more government restrictions and controls. It is being used to justify more and more state planning. It is being used to justify more and more policies that are inconsistent with the fundamentals of a free society" (Information Rack Service, General Motors, General Motors Bldg., Detroit, Michigan).

The subject of bureaucratic controls cannot be dropped without the testimony of an able and patriotic American, Alfred E. Smith

193

of New York. At the first annual banquet of the American Liberty League (*New York Times*, January 26, 1936) Governor Smith said:

> Just get the platform of the Democratic party and get the platform of the Socialist party and lay them down on your dining-room table, side by side, and get a heavy lead pencil and scratch out the word 'Democratic' and scratch out the word 'Socialist', and let the two platforms lay there, and then study the record of the present administration up to date.
>
> After you have done that, make your mind up to pick up the platform that more nearly squares with the record, and you will have your hand on the Socialist platform… It is not the first time in recorded history that a group of men have stolen the livery of the church to do the work of the devil.

After protesting the New Deal's "arraignment of class against class," and its draining the "resources of our people in a common pool and redistributing them, not by any process of law, but by the whims of a bureaucratic autocracy," Governor Smith condemned the changing of the Democratic Party into a Socialist Party. Since this was said during Franklin Roosevelt's *first* term, Governor Smith is seen to have been not only a wise interpreter of the political scene, but a prophet whose vigorous friendly warning was unheeded by the American people.

In summary, let it be emphasized again that wars bring controls and that some people in high places are so fond of controls that a war may appear a desirable means for establishing them.

(c)

Finally, there is the Democratic controller-politician's worry about the whittling down of his party from a majority to a minority status in the national elections of 1948 and 1950. In each of these elections the Democratic failure to win a clear majority was slight –

but significant. In 1948, Truman received less than a majority of the popular vote cast (24,045,052 out of a total of 48,489,217), being elected by a suitable distribution of the electoral vote, of which Henry Wallace, the fourth man (Strom Thurmond was third), received none, though his electors polled more than a million popular votes (*World Almanac,* 1949, p. 91). In 1950, the Democrats elected a majority of members of the House of Representatives, but the total vote of all Democratic candidates lacked .08 per cent of being as large as the total vote of all the Republicans. Again the Democratic Party remained in power by the mere distribution of votes.

Here is where the grisly facts of Eastern European immigration enter the electoral vote picture. As shown in Chapter III, the great majority of these immigrants join the Democratic Party. They also have a marked tendency to settle in populous doubtful states – states in which a handful of individual votes may swing a large block of electoral votes.

Moreover, the number of immigrants, Eastern European and other, is colossal (Chapter II). For a short account of the problem read "Displaced Persons: Facts vs. Fiction," a statement by Senator Pat McCarran of Nevada, Chairman of the Senate Judiciary Committee, in the Senate, January 6, 1950. Those interested in fuller details should read *The Immigration and Naturalization Systems of the United States,* referred to several times in Chapter II and elsewhere in this book.

Let us now examine the significance of the fact that almost all recent Eastern European immigrants have joined the Democratic Party.

Let us suppose that our present annual crop of immigrants adds each year a mere third of a million votes to the Democratic Party – in gratitude for connivance at their admittance, if for no other reason – and let us suppose also that in a "limited" war, or because of "occupation" duties far from home, a half million

Americans of native stock each year are either killed or prevented from becoming fathers because of absence from their wives or from the homes they would have established if they were not at war.

The suggested figures of 300,000 and 500,000 are merely estimates, but they are extremely conservative. They are based not on a possible global war but on our present world ventures only – including those in Korea, Japan, Okinawa, and Germany. It thus appears that the combination of our loosely administered immigration laws and our foreign policy is changing the basic nature of our population at the rate of more than three-fourths of a million a year. In case of a world-wide war, there would be a rapid rise of the figure beyond 750,000.

To help in an understanding of the significance of the decrease of the native population occasioned by war here are for comparison some population results suffered by our principal opponent in World War II.

In Germany boys expected to leave school in 1952, 1953, 1954, 1955, and 1956 number respectively 836,000, 837,000, 897,000, 820,000 and 150,000. The final startling figure – which is for boys only – reflects the birth drop because of full-scale participation in World War II (Marion Doenhoff in European Supplement to *Human Events*, September, 1950).

Even so, German soldiers were nearer home and had more furloughs than will be possible for our men in Korea or elsewhere overseas *whether or not* a full-scale World War III develops. It is thus seen that a combination of war deaths and fewer births among the native stock along with the immigration of leftist aliens might appear to some manipulators of the National Democratic Party as a highly desired way to a surer grip on power. To such people, the boon of being a wheel in an ever-rolling Socialist machine might be worth more than the lives of soldiers snuffed out in the undertakings of Secretary of State Acheson, or successor of similar ideology.

(d)

It is well to emphasize in this connection that the American sympathy for "Jewish refugees," so carefully whipped up in large segments of the press and the radio, is mostly unjustified, as far as any hardship is concerned. Those "refugees" who arrived in Palestine were well-armed or soon became well-armed with weapons of Soviet or satellite origin, and were able to take care of themselves by killing native Arabs or expelling them from their homes. Those Judaized Khazars arriving in the United States lost no time in forming an "Association of Jewish Refugees and Immigrants from Poland" (*New York Times,* March 29, 1944), which at once began to exert active political pressure. Many refugees were well-heeled with funds, portable commodities, or spoils from the lands of their origin. For instance, an article by the Scripps-Howard Special Writer, Henry J. Taylor, and an editorial in the Washington *Daily News* (July 18, 1945) told of a clean-up by aliens, "most of whom live in New York," of $800,000,000 in profit on the N.Y. Stock Exchange in the Spring of 1945, "to say nothing of real estate investments, commodity speculations, and private side deals," with no capital gains tax because of their favored status as aliens. The Congress soon passed legislation designed to plug such loopholes in our tax laws, but the politically favored alien remains a problem in the field of tax collections. In 1951, for instance, patriotic U.S. Customs Service officials detected several hundred thousands of dollars worth of diamonds in the hollow shoe heels and in the hollow luggage frames of a group of "refugees" (the *Newsletter* of the U.S. Customs Service as quoted in *Washington Newsletter* by Congressman Ed Gossett, April 12, 1951). In one way or another the average arriving refugee is, in a matter of months or in a few years at most, far better off economically than millions of native Americans whose relative status is lowered by the new aliens above them – aliens for whom in many instances native Americans perform menial work. This aspect of immigration has long bothered American-minded members of Congress. A report of the House Committee on Immigration and Naturalization of the Sixty-eighth Congress (1924) expressed the following principle: "Late comers are in all fairness not entitled to special privilege over those who have arrived at an earlier date and thereby contributed more to the advancement of the Nation" (*The Immigration and Naturalization Systems of the United States*, p. 61).

The non-Christian alien of Eastern European origin not only in many cases deserves no sympathy except of course from those who cherish his ideological attachments and endorse his political purposes; he is also often a problem. His resistance to assimilation and his preferred nation-within-a-nation status have already been discussed. Another objectionable feature of "displaced persons" – suggested in the reference to smuggled diamonds – is their all-too-frequent lack of respect for United States law. A large number of future immigrants actually flout our laws before arriving in this country! Investigating in Europe, Senator McCarran found that such laws as we had on "displaced persons" were brazenly violated. He reported to the Senate in a speech, "Wanted: A Sound Immigration Policy for the United States" (February 28, 1950):

> I have stated, and I repeat, that under the administration of the present act persons seeking the status of displaced persons have resorted to fraud, misrepresentation, fictitious documents, and perjury in order to qualify for immigration into the United States. A responsible employee of the Displaced Persons Commission stated to me that he believed one-third of the displaced persons qualifying for immigration to the United States had qualified on the basis of false and fraudulent documents... A former official of Army Intelligence in Germany testified before the full committee that certain voluntary agencies advise displaced persons on how they might best evade our immigration laws... What is more, I was advised by a high official of the inspector general's office of

the European command that they had "positive evidence that two of the religious voluntary agencies had been guilty of the forgery of documents in their own offices."

Senator McCarran quoted a letter (September 9, 1949) from Sam E. Woods, American Consul General at Munich, to the Secretary of State which tells that the alleged payment of "50 marks through the wife of the president of the Jewish committee of the town" (Schwandorf, Bavaria), led to an investigation which showed "that a number of displaced persons, who had already departed for the United States, had previously caused their police records in Schwandorf to be changed." The Senator also gave evidence that the head of the Displaced Persons Commission at Frankfurt in "direct violation of the law" caused to be removed from files those documents which would prevent the acceptance of a displaced person as an immigrant. Senator McCarran's findings were supported by overwhelming testimony. To cite one instance, Mr. Edward M. Slazek, a former "assistant selector" for the Displaced Persons Commission in Germany, testified before a Senate Judiciary sub-committee on immigration that he was fired because he protested the admission of "fake DP's" through "wholesale fraud and bribery" (Washington *Times-Herald*).

In view of findings and testimony, Senator McCarran urged caution on the bill HR 4567 by Mr. Emanuel Celler of New York, which provided for more Jewish immigrants, at Mr. Truman's especial request. The president said his recommendations were in favor of more "Catholics and Jews," but the *Catholic World* stated editorially that Catholics were satisfied with the law as it was.

Senator McCarran's efforts did not prevail. The Celler bill became Public Law 555, 81st Congress, when signed by the President on June 16, 1950. It raised from 205,000 to 415,744 the number of "refugees" *over and above quotas* eligible legally to enter the United States. (The McCarran-Walter bill, designed to regulate immigration in the national interest, was vetoed by President Truman, but became law when the Senate on June 27, 1952, followed the House in overriding the veto.)

An additional serious aspect of "displaced persons" is their disposition to cause trouble. Without exception informed officials interviewed by the author as an intelligence officer in 1945 advised caution on the indiscriminate admission of "refugees," plenty of whom were in difficulty in their own lands for actual crimes and not for their political views. Further light on refugees, Jewish and other, in the period following VE Day is furnished by Major Harold Zink, a former Consultant on U.S. policy in Germany, in his book *American Military Government in Germany* (Macmillan, 1947). After stating that "displaced persons gave military government more trouble than any other problem" and mentioning the agitation to the end that "the best German houses be cleared of their occupants and placed at the disposal of the displaced persons, especially the Jews," Professor Zink continues as follows (p. 122):

Moreover, the displaced persons continued their underground war with the German population… With German property looted, German lives lost, and German women raped almost every day by the displaced persons, widespread resentment developed among the populace, especially when they could not defend themselves against the fire-arms which the displaced persons managed to obtain.

Eastern European "displaced persons," their associates, and their offspring do not always lose, on arriving in hospitable America, their tendency to cause trouble. In a review of *The Atom Spies* by Arthur Pilat (Putnam), *The New Yorker* (May 10, 1952) states that "the most important people involved – Klaus Fuchs, David Greenglass, the Julius Rosenbergs, Harry Gold, and Morton Sobell – were not professional spies and they weren't much interested in money." The review concludes by emphasizing "the clear and continuing danger of having among us an amorphous group of people who can be persuaded at any time to betray their country for what they are told are super-patriotic reasons."

An understanding of Zionism as a "super-patriotic" force – with a focus of interest outside of and alien to America – can be had from an editorial signed by Father Ralph Gorman, C.P., in *The Sign* (November, 1951):

> Zionism is not, at present at least, a humanitarian movement designed to help unfortunate Jewish refugees. It is a political and military organization, based squarely on race, religion, and nation, using brute force against an innocent people as the instrument for the execution of its policies...
>
> The Israelis have already carved a state out of Arab land and have driven 750,000 Arabs out of their homes into exile. Now they look with covetous eyes on the rest of Palestine and even the territory across the Jordan...
>
> The Arabs are not fools. They realize what is being prepared for them – with American approval and money. They know that the sword is aimed at them and that, unless Zionist plans are frustrated, they will be driven back step by step into the desert – their lands, homes, vineyards, and farms taken over by an alien people brought from the ends of the earth for this purpose.

Even worse in some aspects is a political philosophy – put into practice by "drives" to sell "Israeli" bonds, nation-wide propaganda, etc. – to the effect that "Israel is supposed to have a unique jurisdiction over the 10,000,000 to 12,000,000 Jews who live in every country of the world outside it" (Mr. William Zuckerman, reporting, in the *Jewish Newsletter*, on "the recent World Zionist Congress held in Jerusalem," as quoted by Father Gorman).

In view of the passages just quoted, why are America's leftists so anxious for many more "refugees"? Can there be any conceivable reason except for the eager anticipation of their future votes? Can there be any motives other than anti-American in the opposition to the McCarran-Walter law (see above in this section)? Moreover, can anyone believe that continued subservience to "Israeli" aims is other than an invitation to war in the Middle East–a war which we would probably lose?

(e)

Let us once more consider the foreign policy which is responsible for our present peril.

Could it be that *those* who pull the strings from hidden seats behind the scenes, *want* Americans to be killed in Korea indefinitely and for no purpose; *want* the Arab world to turn against us; *want* a few hundred thousand young Americans killed in Germany; and *want* the reviving German state destroyed lest it somehow become again (see Chapter I) a bulwark against the present pagan rulers of Eastern Europe and Northern Asia? Such an eventuality, of course, would be used to bring in from here and there as in World War II a great new horde of politically dependable refugees – a boon to all leftists – a boon so great that no further challenge to their power could be conceivable.

In answering the question "Do those who pull the hidden strings really want war?" remember that the Soviet manpower reserves are many times greater than ours; their birthrate is nearly twice as high; they have millions of Chinese and other puppets willing to fight for rice and clothing. Without reserves from Asia, however, the Soviet strength in the European theater in 1951 was estimated by General Bonner Fellers as "175 divisions, some 25 of which were armored" (*Human Events,* January 21, 1951). In the Soviet's favor also is the nature and extent of Soviet territory, which is character-ized by miles and miles of marshes in summer and impenetrable snow in winter. The vast inhospitable areas of Russia caused even the tremendous Europe-based armies of Napoleon and Hitler to bog down to ultimate defeat. The long-range Soviet strategic aim, according to Stalin, is to induce the United States to follow a policy of self-destruction, and that goal can be best accomplished by our engaging in extended land warfare far from home. Here is testimony from a speech recently delivered at Brown University by Admiral Harry E. Yarnell, former Commander-in-Chief of the United States Asiatic fleet:

> To a Russian war planner, the ideal situation would be a campaign against the Allies in Western Europe, where their army can be used to the greatest advantage, while their submarines can operate not far from home bases against the supply lines from the United States to Europe.

Moreover in answering the question, "Do those who pull the hidden strings want war?" Americans, and particularly women, must remember, alas! that America is no longer "a preeminent-ly Christian and conservative nation," as General MacArthur described it in a speech to the Rainbow Division (1937) as his career as Chief of Staff of the Army was ending (*MacArthur On War,* by Frank C. Waldrop, Duell, Sloan and Pearce, New York, 1942). Americans who adhere doggedly to the idea that traditional Christianity shall not disappear from our land must beware of the fallacy of thinking that, because they are merciful, other people are merciful. Mercy toward all mankind is a product of Christianity and is absent from the dialectic materialism of the new Rulers of Russia, whose tentacles reach to so many countries. Apart from Christ's Sermon on the Mount, the most famous passage on mercy in the English language is Shakespeare's "the quality of mercy." It has been widely suppressed, along with the teaching of the play, *The Merchant of Venice,* which contains it (Chapter V, above).

It is thus well to reflect constantly that Soviet leaders are moved by no consideration of humanity as the term is understood in the

Christian West. Instead of relieving a famine, the rulers of Russia are reported to have let millions of Russians die in order to restore in a given province, or oblast, a safe balance between productivity and population. Similarly, according to Chinese Nationalist sources – and others – the Chinese Communists "backed by Russia" have decided that they must accomplish the "eventual extermination of 150,000,000 Chinese" to reduce Chinese population, now between 450,000,000 and 475,000,000, "to more manageable proportions" (AP dispatch, *Dallas Morning News*, and other papers, March 12, 1951). This is necessary, under the Communist theory, if China is to be a strong country without the permanent internal problem of hordes of people near starvation, or likely to be so by the ravages of drouth and flood.

This brings us again to the testimony before Congress by Secretary of Defense Marshall (May 8 and following, 1951) that our purpose in Korea was to bleed the Chinese until they got tired and cried halt. For Chinese Communist leaders, who "need" a population reduction of 150,000,000 people, there is only delighted amusement in such U.S. official statements, intended to justify our war policy and reassure the American public! Equally amusing for them is the official U.S. statement that we are inflicting casualties much greater than those we are sustaining. Even apart from any Chinese Communist population reduction policy, their present population is three times ours, and they have no plans, as we have, to use elements of their population to save Europe and "police" foreign areas!

The Kremlin laughter at our acceptance of continuing American casualties under such an insane motivation as bleeding the Chinese and at our waste of matériel must have been even more hearty than that of the Chinese Communists. Yet these appalling facts constituted the foreign policy of our top State Department and Defense Department leaders under the Acheson and Marshall régimes!

It appears then that U.S. leftists, including those who control the National Democratic Party, want war, Socialistic controls, and plenty of casualties, and not one fact known to the author points to the contrary. Full-scale war, of course, would be edged into in devious ways with carefully prepared propaganda, calculated to fool average Americans, including ignorant and deluded basically patriotic people in the Democratic Party. There would, of course, be an iron curtain of complete censorship, governmental and other.

Dazed by propaganda verbiage, American boys will not understand – any more than when talking to General Eisenhower during World War II – but they will give their fair young lives:

> Theirs not to reason why,
> Theirs but to do and die.

"Greater love hath no man than this," said the Saviour (*St. John*, XV, 13), "that a man lay down his life for his friends." But nowhere in scripture or in history is there a justification for wasting precious young life in the furtherance of sinister political purposes.

205

CLEANING THE AUGEAN STABLES

In ancient fable one of the giant labors of Hercules was cleaning the labyrinthine stables of King Augeas who possessed "an immense wealth of herds" (*Encyc. Brit.*, II, 677) and twelve sacred bulls. The removal of accumulated filth was accomplished in the specified time and the story of difficulty successfully overcome has been told through the ages for entertainment and for inspiration.

The modern significance of the parable of Hercules may be thus interpreted. King Augeas is Mr. Truman.

The sacred bulls are those high and mighty individuals who control and deliver the votes of minority blocs.

The filth is the nineteen-year accumulation of Communists and fellow-travelers in the various departments, executive agencies, bureaus, and what not, of our government.

To clean out the filth, there can be but one Hercules – an aroused American people.

Exactly how can the American people proceed under our laws to clean out subversives and other scoundrels from our government? There are three principal ways: (a) by a national election; (b) by the constitutional right of expressing their opinion; and (c) by influencing the Congress to exercise certain powers vested in the Congress by the Constitution, including the power of impeachment.

(a)

A national election is the normal means employed by the people to express their will for a change of policy. There are reasons, however, why such a means should not be exclusively relied on. For one thing, a man elected by the people may lose completely the confidence of the people and do irreparable damage by bad appointive personnel and bad policies after one election and before another. In the second place, our two leading parties consist of so many antagonistic groups wearing a common label that candidates for president and vice-president represent compromises and it is hard to get a clear-cut choice as between Democrats and Republicans. For instance, in the campaigns of 1940, 1944, and 1948 the Republicans offered the American voters Wendell Willkie, and Thomas Dewey – twice! Willkie was a sincere but poorly informed and obviously inexperienced "one-worlder," apparently with a soft spot toward Communism, or at least a blind spot, as evidenced in his hiring or lending himself as a lawyer to prevent government action against alleged Communists. Thus, among "the twelve Communist Party leaders" arrested July 26, 1951, was William Schneiderman, "State Chairman of the Communist Party of California and a member of the Alternate National Committee of the Communist Party of the United States." The preceding quotations are from the *New York Times* (July 27, 1951), and the article continues: "With the late Wendell L. Willkie as his counsel, Schneiderman defeated in the Supreme Court in 1943 a government attempt to revoke his citizenship for his political associations. Schneiderman was born in Russia." Likewise, Governor Dewey of New York, campaigning on a "don't bother the Communists" program, won the Oregon Republican presidential primary election in 1948 in a close contest from Harold Stassen, who endorsed anti-Communist legislation. Governor Dewey, largely avoiding issues, except in this instance, moved on to nomination and to defeat. The moral seems to be that the American people see no reason to change from the Democratic Party to the Republican Party with a candidate favorable to or indifferent to Communism. With such a Republican candidate, a Democratic candidate may be favored by some conservatives who rely on the more or less conservative Democrats – who extend from Maryland in an arc through the South around to Nevada – to block the extreme radicalism of a Democratic administration. Governor Dewey followed the Roosevelt path not only in a disinclination to combat Communism; in such matters as the "purge" of Senator Revercomb of West Virginia, he showed evidence of a dictatorial intention to which not even Roosevelt would have presumed.

Thus, however much one may hope for a pair of *strong, patriotic, and able* Democratic candidates or a pair of *strong, patriotic, and able* Republican candidates at the next election, there is no certainty of a realized hope. There is likewise no certainty of success in the move of a number of patriotic people in both parties to effect a merger of American-minded Republicans and non-leftist Democrats in time for a slate of coalition candidates in the next presidential election. This statement is not meant to disparage the movement, whose principal sponsor Senator Karl Mundt represents a state (South Dakota) not in the Union during the Civil War and is therefore an ideal leader of a united party of patriotic Americans both Northern and Southern.

Senator Mundt's proposal deserves active and determined support, because it is logical for people who feel the same way to vote together. Moreover, the effective implementation of the Mundt proposal would certainly be acclaimed by the great body of the people – those who acclaimed General MacArthur on his return from Tokyo.

The stumbling-block, of course, is that it is very hard for the great body of the people to make itself politically effective either in policy or in the selection of delegates to the national nominating conventions, since leaders already in office will, with few exceptions, be reluctant to change the setup (whatever its evil) under which they became leaders.

To sum up, a coalition team – as Senator Mundt proposes – would be admirable. Nevertheless, other methods of effecting a change of our national policy must be explored.

(b)

A possible way for the American public to gain its patriotic ends is by the constitution-protected right of petition (First Amendment). The petition, whether in the form of a document with many signatures or a mere individual letter, is far more effective than the average individual is likely to believe. In all cases the letters received are beyond question tabulated as straws in the wind of public opinion; and to a busy Congressman or Senator a carefully prepared and well documented letter from a person he can trust may well be a guide to policy. The author thus summed up the influence of letters in his book *Image of Life* (Thomas Nelson and Sons, New York, 1940, pp. 207-208):

> It is perhaps unfortunate, but undeniably true that letter-writers wield a powerful influence in America. Along with the constant newspaper and magazine "polls" of citizens and voters, letters are the modern politician's method of keeping his ear to the ground. This fact was startlingly illustrated in 1939 by a high executive's issuing a statement justifying a certain governmental stand by an analysis of the correspondence received on the subject. Since the letter wields this influence, and since it is one of the chief weapons of the organized minority, public-spirited citizens should use it, too. They should write to members of state legislatures, United States Congressmen and Senators, and other government officials endorsing or urging measures which the writers believe necessary for the good of the country. Similar letters of support should of course be written to any others in or out of government service,

who are under the fire of minorities for courageous work in behalf of decency, morality, and patriotism.

The use of the letter for political purposes by organized groups is illustrated by the fact that a certain congressman (his words to the author in Washington) received in one day more than 5,000 letters and other forms of communication urging him to vote for a pending measure favorable to "Israel," and not one post card on the other side!

Letters in great volume cannot be other than effective. To any Congressman, even though he disapproves of the policy or measure endorsed by the letters, they raise the question of his being possibly in error in view of such overwhelming opposition to his viewpoint. To a Congressman who believes sincerely – as some do – that he is an agent whose duty is not to act on his own judgment, but to carry out the people's will, a barrage of letters is a mandate on how to vote. Apparently for the first time, those favoring Western Christian civilization adopted the technique of the opposition and expressed themselves in letters to Washington on the dismissal of General MacArthur.

In addition to writing letters to the President and his staff and to one's own senators and congressmen, the patriotic American should write letters to other senators and congressmen who are members of committees concerned with a specific issue (see c, below). In this way, he will meet and possibly frustrate the new tactics of the anti-American element which, from its newspaper advertisements, seems to be shifting its controlled letters from a writer's "own congressman and senators" to "committee chairmen and committee members." For the greater effectiveness which comes from a knowledge of the structure of the government, the functions of its subdivisions, and the names of its officials, it is exceedingly important that each patriotic citizen possess or have access to a copy of the latest *Congressional Directory* (Superintendent of Documents, Government Printing Office, Washington, D.C., $1.50).

The patriotic citizen should not let his or her letter writing stop with letters to officials in Washington. Letters along constructive lines should be sent to other influential persons such as teachers, columnists, broadcasters, and judges letting them know the writer's views. Persons such as Judge Medina, who presided in a fair and impartial manner over a trial involving charges of communism, are inundated by letters and telegrams of calumny and vilification (his words to the author and others at a meeting of the Columbia Alumni in Dallas). To such officials, a few letters on the other side are heartening.

Letters to newspapers are especially valuable. Whether published or not, they serve as opinion-indicators to a publisher. Those that are published are sometimes clipped and mailed to the White House and to members of the Congress by persons who feel unable to compose letters of their own. The brevity of these letters and their voice-of-the-people flavor cause them also to be read by and thus to influence many who will not cope with the more elaborate expressions of opinion by columnist and editorial writers.

(c)

As the ninth printing of The Iron Curtain Over America was being prepared (summer of 1952) for the press, it became a fact of history that President Truman would not succeed himself for the presidential term, 1953-1957. The following pages of this chapter should therefore be read not as a specific recommendation directed against Mr. Truman but as a general consideration of the question of influencing executive action through pressure upon Congressional committees and – in extreme cases – by impeachment, with the acts and policies of Mr. Truman and his chief officials used as illustrative material.

If the pressure of public opinion by a letter barrage or otherwise is of no avail, because of already existing deep commitments as a pay-off for blocs of votes or for other reasons, there are other procedures.

The best of these, as indicated under (b) above, is to work through the appropriate committees of the Congress.

Unfortunately, the Foreign Affairs Committee of the Senate has a majority of members willing to play along with almost any vote-getting scheme. It was only by the skillful maneuvering of the Chairman, Senator Tom Connally of Texas, that the Committee was prevented from passing during World War II a pro-Zionist resolution on the Middle East which might have prejudiced the American victory in the war. Despite Mr. Acheson's record, every Republican on the Committee approved the nomination of that "career man" to be Secretary of State (telegram of Senator Tom Connally to the author; see also the article by C. P. Trussell, *New York Times,* January 19, 1949). Thus with no Republican opposition to attract possible votes from the Democratic majority, the committee vote on Acheson's confirmation was unanimous! Parenthetically, a lesson is obvious – namely, that both political parties should in the future be much more careful than in the past in according committee membership to a Senator, or to a Representative, of doubtful suitability for sharing the committee's responsibilities.

Despite one very unfortunate selection, the Republican membership of the House Committee on Foreign Affairs averages up better than the Republican membership of the Senate Committee on Foreign Relations. The House Committee is not so influential, however, because of the Constitution's express vesting of foreign policy in the Senate.

In contrast, however, the House Appropriations Committee is under the Constitution more influential than the Appropriations Committee in the Senate, and might under public pressure withhold funds (U.S. Constitution, Article I, Section 9, Paragraph 6) from a government venture, office, or individual believed inimical to the welfare of the United States (see George Sokolsky's syndicated column, *Dallas Morning News* and other papers, Jan. 23, 1951). In the matter of appropriations, the Senate Committee on Appropriations has, however, made a great record in safeguarding what it believes to be the public interest. For example, in 1946 the senior Republican member of this vital Senate Committee was instrumental in achieving the Congressional elimination from the State Department budget of $4,000,000 earmarked for the Alfred McCormack unit – an accomplishment which forced the exit of that undesired "Special Assistant to the Secretary of State." There is no reason why this thoroughly Constitutional procedure should not be imitated in the 1950's. The issue was raised for discussion by Congressman John Phillips of California, a member of the House Appropriations Committee, in May 1951 (AP dispatch in the *Times-Herald,* Dallas, May 14, 1951).

In mid-1950 the House Committee on Un-American Activities seemed to need prodding by letters from persons in favor of the survival of America. The situation was described thus in a Washington *Times-Herald* (November 26, 1950) editorial entitled "Wake the Watchman":

> The reason the committee has gone to sleep is that it is now, also for the first time in its history, subservient to the executive departments which have so long hid the Communists and fought the committee.
>
> For evidence, compare the volume entitled *Hearings Regarding Communism in the United States Government – Part 2,* that record committee proceedings of Aug. 28 and 31, and Sept. 1 and 15, 1950, with the records of comparable inquiries any year from the committee's origin in 1938 down to 1940 when the present membership took over.
>
> The witnesses who appeared before the committee in these latest hearings need no explaining. They were: Lee Pressman, Abraham

George Silverman, Nathan Witt, Charles Kramer, John J. Abt and Max Lowenthal. This handsome galaxy represents the very distilled essence of inside knowledge on matters that can help the people of this Republic understand why we are now wondering where Stalin is going to hit us next.

At least one, Max Lowenthal, is an intimate friend of President Truman, regularly in and out of side entrances at the White House.

Perhaps that accounts – of course it does – for the arrogant assurance with which Lowenthal spit in the committee's eye when he was finally brought before it for a few feeble questions.

Incidentally, "Truman was chosen as candidate for Vice President by Sidney Hillman, at the suggestion (according to Jonathan Daniels in his recent book *A Man of Independence*) of Max Lowenthal" ("The Last Phase," by Edna Lonigan, *Human Events,* May 2, 1951).

In fairness to the present membership, however, it is well to add that, from a variety of circumstances, the Committee has suffered from a remarkable and continuing turn-over of membership since the convening of the 81st Congress in January, 1949. New regulations – passed for the purpose by the Democratic 81st Congress, which was elected along with President Truman in 1948 – drove from the Committee two of its most experienced and aggressive members: Mr. Rankin of Mississippi, because he was Chairman of the Committee on Veterans' Affairs, and Mr. Hébert of Louisiana, because he was not a lawyer. In January, 1949, the experienced Congressman Karl Mundt of South Dakota left the House and his membership on the Committee to take his seat in the Senate. Promotion to the Senate (Dec. 1, 1950) likewise cost the Committee the services of Congressman Richard Nixon of California, the member most active in the preliminaries to the trial of Alger Hiss. In the election of 1950, Representative Francis Case of South Dakota was advanced to the Senate. After a single term on the

Committee, Congressman Burr P. Harrison of Virginia became a member of the Ways and Means Committee, an appointment which excluded him from the Committee on Un-American Activities. Thus when the Committee was reconstituted at the opening of the 82nd Congress in January, 1951, only one man, Chairman John S. Wood of Georgia, had had more than one full two-year term of service, and a majority of the nine members were new.

The Committee, like all others, needs letters of encouragement to offset pressure from pro-Communist elements, but there were evidences in 1951 of its revitalization. On April 1, 1951, it issued a report entitled "The Communist Peace Offensive," which it described as "the most dangerous hoax ever devised by the international Communist conspiracy" (see *Red-ucators in the Communist Peace Offensive,* National Council for American Education, 1 Maiden Lane, New York 38, N.Y.). Moreover, in 1951 the committee was again probing the important question of Communism in the motion picture industries at Hollywood, California. Finally, late in 1951, the Un-American Activities Committee issued a "brand new" publication, a *Guide Book to Subversive Organizations,* highly recommended by the Americanism Legion (copies may be had from the National Americanism Division, The American Legion, 700 N. Pennsylvania St., Indianapolis, Ind.; 25¢; in lots of 25 or more, 15¢; see also Chapter V, d, above).

Fortunately, the Senate Judiciary Committee is also accomplishing valuable work in the exposure of the nature and methods of the Communist infiltration. Its work is referred to, its chairman Senator McCarran of Nevada is quoted, and its documents are represented by excerpts here and there in this book.

The Rules Committee of the House was restored to its traditional power by the 82nd Congress in 1951 and may also prove an effective brake on bills for implementing the dangerous policies of an incompetent, poorly advised, or treasonable leadership in the executive departments.

As a last resort, however, a President of the United States or any other member of the Executive or Judicial Branches of the government can be removed by impeachment. Article I, Section 2, paragraph 5; Article I, Section 3, paragraph 6; Article II, Section 1, Paragraph 6; and Article II, Section 4, paragraph 1 of the U.S. Constitution name the circumstances, under which, and provide explicitly the means by which, a majority of the representatives and two-thirds of the senators can remove a president who is guilty of "misdemeanors" or shows "inability" to perform the high functions of his office. Surely some such construction might have been placed upon Mr. Truman's gross verbal attack (1950) upon the United States Marine Corps, whose members were at the time dying in Korea, or upon his repeated refusal to cooperate with Canada, with Congress, or with the Courts in facing up to the menace of the 43,217 known Communists said by J. Edgar Hoover (AP dispatch, Washington *Times-Herald,* March 26, 1951) to be operating in this country, with ten times that many following the Communist line in anti-American propaganda and all of them ready for sabotage in vital areas if the Soviet Union should give the word (AP dispatch, Dallas *Times-Herald,* February 8, 1950).

The matter of President Truman's unwillingness to move against Communism came to a head with the passage of the Internal Security Act of 1950. Under the title, "Necessity for Legislation," the two Houses of Congress found as follows:

(1) There exists a world Communist movement which, in its origins, its development, and its present practice, is a world-wide revolutionary movement whose purpose it is, by treachery, deceit, infiltration into other groups (governmental and otherwise), espionage, sabotage, terrorism, and any other means deemed necessary, to establish a Communist totalitarian dictatorship in the countries throughout the world through the medium of a world-wide Communist organization...

(12) The Communist network in the United States is inspir\
and controlled in large part by foreign agents who are sent into the
United States ostensibly as attachés of foreign legations, affiliates
of international organizations, members of trading commissions,
and in similar capacities, but who use their diplomatic or semi-dip-
lomatic status as a shield behind which to engage in activities
prejudicial to the public security.

(13) There are, under our present immigration laws, numerous
aliens who have been found to be deportable, many of whom are in
the subversive, criminal, or immoral classes who are free to roam
the country at will without supervision or control...

(15) ... The Communist organization in the United States,
pursuing its stated objectives, the recent successes of Communist
methods in other countries, and the nature and control of the
world Communist movement itself, present a clear and present
danger to the security of the United States and to the existence of
free American institutions, and make it necessary that Congress,
in order to provide for the common defense, to preserve the
sovereignty of the United States as an independent nation, and to
guarantee to each State a republican form of government, enact
appropriate legislation recognizing the existence of such world-
wide conspiracy and designed to prevent it from accomplishing
its purpose in the United States.

A measure for curbing Communism in the United States – prepared
in the light of the above preamble – was approved by both Senate
and House. It was then sent to the President. What did he do?

He vetoed it.

Thereupon, both Senate and House (September 22, 1950)
overrode the President's veto by far more than the necessary two-
thirds majorities, and the Internal Security Act became "Public
Law 831 – 81st Congress – Second Session." The enforcement of
the law, of course, became the responsibility of its implacable

enemy, the head of the Executive Branch of our government! But the President's efforts to block the anti-Communists did not end with that historic veto.

> "President Truman Thursday [March 27, 1952] rejected a Senate committee's request for complete files on the State Department's loyalty-security cases on the ground that it would be 'clearly contrary' to the public interest" (AP dispatch, Washington, April 3, 1952).

To what "public" did Mr. Truman refer? The situation was summed up well by General MacArthur in a speech before a joint session of the Mississippi legislature (March 22, 1952). The general stated that our policy is "leading us toward a communist state with as dreadful certainty as though the leaders of the Kremlin themselves were charting our course."

In view of his veto of the Internal Security Act and his concealment of security data on government employees from Congressional committees, it is hard to exonerate Mr. Truman from the suspicion of having more concern for leftist votes than for the safety or survival of the United States. Such facts naturally suggest an inquiry into the feasibility of initiating the process of impeachment.

Another possible ground for impeachment might be the President's apparent violation of the Constitution, Article I, Section 8, Paragraph 11, which vests in Congress the power "To declare war, grant letters of marque and reprisal, and make rules concerning captures on land and water." This authority of the Congress has never been effectively questioned. Thus in his "Political Observations" (1795) James Madison wrote: "The Constitution expressly and exclusively vests in the Legislature the power of declaring a state of war" (quoted from "Clipping of Note," No. 38, The Foundation for Economic Education, Inc., Irvington-on-Hudson, New York). Subsequent interpreters of our basic State Paper, except perhaps some of those following in the footsteps of Supreme Court Justice Brandeis (Chapter III, above), have concurred.

It was seemingly in an effort to avoid the charge of violating this provision of the Constitution that President Truman, except for a reported occasional slip of the tongue, chose to refer to his commitment of our troops in Korea as a "police action" and not a war. Referring to the possibility of President Truman's sending four additional divisions to Europe, *where there was no war*, Senator Byrd of Virginia said: "But if by chance he does ignore Congress, Congress has ample room to exercise its authority by the appropriations method and it would be almost grounds for impeachment" (UP dispatch in Washington *Times-Herald*, March 15, 1951). The distinguished editor and commentator David Lawrence (*U.S. News and World Report*, April 20, 1951) also brought up the question of impeachment:

> If we are to grow technical, Congress, too, has some constitutional rights. It can impeach President Truman not only for carrying on a war in Korea without a declaration of war by Congress, but primarily for failing to let our troops fight the enemy with all the weapons at their command.

The question of President Truman's violation of the Constitution in the matter of committing our troops in Korea has been raised with overwhelming logic by Senator Karl Mundt of South Dakota. Article 43 of the United Nations charter, as the Senator points out, provides that member nations of the UN shall supply armed forces "in accordance with their respective constitutional processes." Thus the starting of the Truman-Acheson war in Korea not only violated the United States Constitution, but completely lacked United Nations authority – until such authority was voted retroactively! (Washington *Times-Herald*, May 17, 1951; also see Chapter VI, d, above.)

The House in the 81st Congress several times overrode a Truman veto by more than the Constitutional two-thirds vote. Even in that 81st Congress, more than five-sixths of the Senators voted to override the President's veto of the McCarran-Mundt-Nixon anti-Communist bill, which became Public Law 831. With the retirement of Mrs. Helen Douglas and other noted administration supporters, and Mr. Vito Marcantonio, the 82nd Congress is probably even less inclined than the predecessor Congress to tolerate the Truman attitude toward the control of subversives and might not hesitate in a moment of grave national peril to certify to the Senate for possible impeachment for a violation of the Constitution the name of a man so dependent on leftist votes or so sympathetic with alien thought that he sees no menace – merely a "red herring" – in Communism.

With the defeat of such "left of center" men – to use a term which President Franklin Roosevelt applied to himself – as Claude Pepper, Frank Graham, and Glen Taylor, and such administration henchmen as Millard Tydings, Scott Lucas, and Francis Myers; with election from the House of new members such as Everett Dirksen, Richard Nixon, and Francis Case; and with other new members such as Wallace F. Bennett, John M. Butler, and Herman Welker, the Senate also might not hesitate in a moment of grave national peril to take appropriate steps toward impeachment under the Constitution.

Incidentally, a rereading of the Constitution of the United States is particularly valuable to anyone who is in doubt as to the relative importance of the Congress, the President, and the Supreme court under the basic law of the land. Whereas the Congress is granted specific authority to remove for cause the President and any other executive or a Justice of the Supreme Court, neither the President nor the Supreme Court has any authority whatsoever over the qualifications or tenure of office of a Senator or a Representative. Good books on the Constitution, both by Thomas James

Norton, are *The Constitution of the United States, Its Sources and Its Application* (World Publishing Company, Cleveland, 1940) and *Undermining The Constitution: A History of Lawless Government* (The Devin-Adair Company, New York, 1951).

In another valuable book, *The Key to Peace* (The Heritage Foundation, Inc., 75 East Wacker Drive, Chicago 1, Illinois), the author, Dean Clarence Manion of Notre Dame Law School, develops the idea that the key to peace is the protection of the individual under our Constitution.

With reference again to impeachment, an examination of the career of other high executives including the Secretary of State might possibly find one or more of them who might require investigation on the suspicion of unconstitutional misdemeanors.

Despite the bitter fruit of Yalta, Mr. Acheson never issued a recantation. He never repudiated his affirmation of lasting fidelity to his beloved friend, Alger Hiss, who was at Yalta as the newly appointed State Department "Director of Special Political Affairs." Despite the Chinese attack on our troops in Korea, Mr. Acheson never, to the author's knowing, admitted the error, if not the treason, of the policy of his department's Bureau of Far Eastern Affairs down to and including the very year of 1950, when these Chinese Communists, the darlings of the dominant Leftists of our State Department, attacked us in the moment of our victory over the Communists of North Korea. "What then will you do with the fact that as concerning Soviet Russia, from Yalta to this day, every blunder in American foreign policy has turned out to be what the Kremlin might have wished this country to do? All you can say is that if there had been a sinister design it would look like this" (*The Freeman,* June 18, 1951).

General Marshall was at Yalta as Chief of Staff of the U.S. Army. According to press reports, he never remembered what he was doing the night before Pearl Harbor. At Yalta, it was not memory but judgment that failed him for he was the Superior Officer who tacitly, if not heartily, approved the military deals along the Elbe and the Yalu – deals which are still threatening to ruin our country. General Ambassador Marshall not only failed miserably in China; Secretary of State Marshall took no effective steps when a Senate Appropriations subcommittee, according to Senator Ferguson of Michigan, handed him a memorandum stating in part: "It becomes necessary due to the gravity of the situation to call your attention to a condition that developed and still flourishes in the State Department under the administration of Dean Acheson. It is evident that there is a deliberate, calculated program being carried out not only to protect communist personnel in high places but to reduce security and intelligence protection to a nullity" (INS, Washington *Times-Herald*, July 24, 1950). The reference to Acheson was to Undersecretary Acheson, as he then was. Unfortunately in late 1951, when General Marshall ceased to be Secretary of Defense, he was replaced by another man, Robert A. Lovett, who, whatever his personal views, carried nevertheless the stigma of having been Undersecretary of State from July, 1947, to January, 1949 (*Congressional Directory*, 82nd Congress, 1st Session, p. 365), when our position in China was being ruined under the then Secretary of State, George C. Marshall.

The pro-Soviet accomplishments of the high-placed leftists and their dupes in our government are brilliantly summed up by Edna Lonigan in *Human Events* (Sept. 8, 1948):

> Our victorious armies halted where Stalin wished. His follow- ers managed Dumbarton Oaks, UN, UNRRA, our Polish and Spanish policies. They gave Manchuria and Northern Korea to Communism. They demoted General Patton and wrote infamous instructions under which General Marshall was sent to China. They dismantled German industry, ran the Nuremberg trials and even sought to dictate our economic policy in Japan. Their greatest victory was the "Morgenthau Plan."

And the astounding thing is that except for the dead (Roosevelt, Hillman, Hopkins, Winant) and Mr. Morgenthau, and Mr. Hiss, and General Marshall, *most of those chiefly responsible* for our policy as described above were *still in power* in June, 1952!

In solemn truth, do not seven persons share most of the responsibility for establishing the Communist grip on the world? Are not the seven: (1) Marx, the founder of violent Communism; (2) Engels, the promoter of Marx; (3, 4, 5) Trotsky, Lenin, and Stalin; (6) Franklin D. Roosevelt, who rescued the tottering Communist empire by recognition (1933), by the resultant financial support, by his refusal to proceed against Communists in the United States, and by the provisions of the Yalta Conference; and (7) Harry S. Truman, who agreed at Potsdam to the destruction of Germany and thereafter followed the Franklin Roosevelt policy of refusing to act against Communists in the United States – the one strong nation which remains as a possible obstacle to Communist world power?

In spite of the consolidation of Stalin's position in Russia by Franklin Roosevelt and by Stalin's "liquidation" of millions of anti-Communists in Russia after Roosevelt's recognition, the Soviet Union in 1937 was stymied in its announced program of world conquest by two roadblocks: Japan in the East and Germany in the West. These countries, the former the size of California and the latter the size of Texas, were small for great powers, and since their main fears were of the enormous, hostile, and nearby Soviet Union, they did not constitute an actual danger to the United States. The men around Roosevelt, many of them later around Truman, not merely defeated but *destroyed the two road-blocks against the spread of Stalinist Communism!* Again we come to the question: Should the United States continue to use the men whose stupidity or treason built the Soviet Union into the one great land power of the world?

In continuing to employ people who were in office during the tragic decisions of Tehran, Yalta, and Potsdam, are we not exactly as sensible as a hypothetical couple who employ the same baby-sitter who has already killed three of their children?

"By What Faith, Then, Can We Find Hope in Those Whose Past Judgments So Grievously Erred?" asked Senator Ecton of Montana on September 7, 1951. "Can We Trust the Future to Those Who Betrayed the Past?" asked Senator Jenner of Indiana in a speech in the Senate of the United States on September 19, 1950. Whatever the cause of our State Department's performances, so tragic for America in 1945 and thereafter (see also Chapter VI, above), the answer to Senator Jenner's point blank question is an incontrovertible "No."

Congressmen, the patriotic elements in the press, and the let-ter-writing public should continually warn the President, however, that a mere shuffling around of the same old cast of Yalta actors and others "whose past judgments so grievously erred" will not be sufficient. We must not again have tolerators of extreme leftism, such as Mr. John J. McCloy, who was Assistant Secretary of War from April, 1941, to November, 1945, and Major General Clayton Bissell, who was A.C. of S., G.-2, i.e., the Army's Chief of Intelligence, from February 5, 1944, "to the end of the war" (*Who's Who in America*, 1950-1951, pp. 1798 and 232). In February, 1945, these high officials were questioned by a five-man committee created by the new 79th Congress to investigate charges of communism in the War Department.

In the *New York Times* of February 28 (article by Lewis Wood), Mr. McCloy is quoted as follows:

> The facts point to the difficulties of legal theory which are involved in taking the position that mere membership in the Communist party, present or past, should exclude a person from the army or a commission. But beyond any questions of legal theory, a study of the question and our experience convinced me that we were not

on sound ground in our investigation when we placed emphasis solely on Communist affiliation.

According to some newspapers, Mr. McCloy's testimony gave the impression that he did not care if 49% of a man's loyalty was elsewhere provided he was 51% American. The validity of Christ's "No man can serve two masters" was widely recalled to mind. Edward N. Scheiberling, National Commander of the American Legion, referring to Assistant Secretary of War McCloy's testimony, stated (*New York Times*, March 2, 1945):

> That the Assistant Secretary had testified that the new policy of the armed forces would admit to officer rank persons 49 per cent loyal to an alien power, and only 51 per cent loyal to the United States.

The Legion head asserted further:

> Fifty-one per cent loyalty is not enough when the security of our country is at stake... The lives of our sons, the vital military secrets of our armed forces must not be entrusted to men of divided loyalty.

The Washington *Times-Herald* took up the cudgels against Mr. McCloy and he was shifted to the World Bank and thence to the post of High Commissioner of Germany (Chapter VI, above).

With sufficient documentation to appear convincing, *The Freeman* as late as August 27, 1951, stated that "Mr. McCloy seems to be getting and accepting a kind of advice that borders on mental disorder."

General Bissell was moved from A.C. of S., G-2, to U.S. Military Attaché at London. He received, a little later, a *bon voyage* present of a laudatory feature article in the Communist *Daily Worker*. Below the accompanying portrait (*Daily Worker*, June 20, 1947) was the legend: "Maj. Gen. Clayton Bissell, wartime head of the

U.S. Army Intelligence Corps, who defended Communist soldiers from the attacks of Washington seat-warmers during the war."

What of the Congressional Committee? Though it had been created and ordered to work by a coalition of patriotic Republicans and Southern Democrats, each party chose its own committee members. The Democratic majority in the House chose members to its "left-of-center" liking, and the committee (Chairman: Mr. Thomason of Texas!) by a strict party vote of 3-2 expressed itself as satisfied with the testimony of McCloy and Bissell.

Surely the American public wants no high officials tolerant of Communists or thanked by Communists for favors rendered.

Surely Americans will not longer be fooled by another shuffling of the soiled New Deal deck with its red aces, deuces, knaves, and jokers. This time we will not be blinded by a spurious "bipartisan" appointment of Achesonites whose nominal membership in the Republican Party does not conceal an ardent "me-too-ism." Americans surely will not, for instance, tolerate actors like twee-dle-dum John Foster Dulles who goes along with tweedle-dee Acheson right down the line even to such an act as inviting Hiss to New York to become President of the Carnegie Endowment for International Peace, of which Dulles was the new Chairman of the Board. It might have been expected that with Hiss away, his trouble in Washington would blow over – but it did not.

The reference to high-placed War Department officials whose loyalty or judgment has been questioned by some of their fellow Americans brings us to an evaluation of the reception given in all parts of this nation to General MacArthur after his dismissal by President Truman in April, 1951. It seems that General MacArthur's ovation was due not to his five stars, for half a dozen generals and admirals have similar rank, but to his being a man of unquestioned integrity, unquestioned patriotism, and – above all – to his being avowedly a Christian.

Long before the spring crisis of 1951 General MacArthur was

again and again featured in the obscure religious papers of many Christian denominations as a man who asked for more Christian missionaries for Japan and for New Testaments to give his soldiers. MacArthur's devout Christianity was jeered in some quarters but it made a lasting impression on that silent majority of Americans who have been deeply wounded by the venality and treason of men in high places.

"I was privileged in Tokyo," wrote John Gunther in *The Riddle of MacArthur*, "to read through the whole file of MacArthur's communications and pronouncements since the occupation began, and many of these touch, at least indirectly, on religious themes. He constantly associates Christianity with both democracy and patriotism."

MacArthur is a Protestant, but to the editor of the Brooklyn *Tablet*, a Catholic periodical, he wrote as follows:

> Through daily contact with our American men and women who are here engaged in the reshaping of Japan's future, there are penetrating into the Japanese mind the noble influences which find their origin and their inspiration in the American home. These influences are rapidly bearing fruit, and apart from the great numbers who are coming formally to embrace the Christian faith, a whole population is coming to understand, practice and cherish its underlying principles and ideals.

To some people this language of General MacArthur's may seem outmoded or antiquarian. The writings of the more publicized American theologians – darlings of leftist book-reviews – may indicate that the clear water of classical Christianity is drying up in a desert of experimental sociology, psychiatry, and institutionalized ethical culture. But such is not the case. The heart of America is still Christian in its felt need of redemption and salvation as well as in its fervent belief in the Resurrection.

Christianity in the historical, or classical, sense is closely allied with the founding and growth of America. It was the common adherence to some form of Christianity which made it "possible to develop some degree of national unity out of the heterogeneous nationalities represented among the colonists" of early America (*The Immigration and Naturalization Systems of the United States,* p. 231).

This acceptance of the tenets of Christianity as the basis of our American society gave our people a body of shared ideals – a universally accepted code of conduct. Firmly rooted in Christianity was our conception of honor, both personal and national. It was not until a dominant number of powerful preachers and church executives got tired of the church's foundation-stone, charity, and abandoned it to welfare agencies – it was not until these same leaders transferred their loyalty from the risen Christ to a new sort of leftist cult stemming from national councils and conferences – that public morality declined to its present state in America. But the people in the leftist-infiltrated churches have by no means strayed as far as their leaders from the mainstream of Christianity.

The really Christian people in all denominations wish to see restored in America the set of values, the pattern of conduct, the code of honor, which constitute and unify Western civilization and which once made ours a great and united country. It was precisely to this starved sense of spiritual unity, this desire to recover a lost spiritual heritage, that MacArthur the Christian made an unconscious appeal which burst forth into an enthusiasm never before seen in our country.

And so, when the Augean stables of our government are cleaned out, we must, in the words of George Washington, "put only Americans on guard." We must have as secretaries of State and Defense men who will go down through their list of assistant secretaries, counselors, division chiefs, and so on, and remove all persons under any suspicion of Communism whether by ideological expression, association, or what not. While danger stalks the world, we should entrust the destiny of our beloved country to those and only those who can say with no reservation:

"THIS IS MY OWN, MY *native* LAND!"

AMERICA CAN STILL BE FREE

In the closing speech of his play *King John*, Shakespeare makes a character say:

> This England never did, nor never shall
> Lie at the proud foot of a conqueror
> But when it first did help to wound itself.

In June, 1951, before the members of the Texas Legislature in Austin, General of the Army Douglas MacArthur made a speech of which the above quotation might have been the text. He said in part:

> I am concerned for the security of our great nation, not so much because of any potential threat from without, but because of the insidious forces working from within which, opposed to all of our great traditions, have gravely weakened the structure and tone of our American way of life.

The "insidious forces working from within" and "opposed to all our great traditions" are the first and most serious challenge that faces America. There are those who seek to corrupt our youth that they may rule them. There are those who seek to destroy our unity by stirring up antagonism among the various Christian denominations.

There are those who, in one way or another, intrude their stooges into many of our high military and executive offices. Effective in any evil purpose is the current menace of censorship, analyzed in Chapter V, and the even greater menace of a far more drastic censorship imposed not by those of alien origin and sympathy within our country, but by alien-dominated agencies of the United Nations.

Moreover, and even more significant, it must not be forgotten that an undigested mass in the "body politic," an ideologically hostile "nation within the nation," has through history proved the spearhead of conquerors. The alien dictators of Rumania, Hungary, Poland, and other Eastern European countries have been discussed in Chapter II. Throughout history members of an unassimilated minority have repeatedly been used as individual spies – as when the Parthians used Jews in Rome as spies while the Romans used Jews in Parthia for the same purpose. Recent instances of espionage – discussed above in Chapter II – involved the theft of atomic secrets from both Canada and the United States.

In addition to working individually for the enemies of his country, the unassimilated alien has often worked collectively.

According to *A History of Palestine from 135 A.D. to Modern Times*, by James Parkes (Oxford University Press, New York, 1909), Persians in 614 A.D. invaded Palestine, a part of the Christian Roman Empire of the East, and took Jerusalem. Here is Mr. Parkes's account:

> There is no doubt that the … Jews aided the Persians with all the men they could muster, and that the help they gave was considerable. Once Jerusalem was in Persian hands a terrible massacre of Christians took place, and the Jews are accused of having taken the lead in this massacre" (*op. cit.*, p. 81).

Mr. Parkes concludes that it "would not be surprising if the accusation were true."

Another famous betrayal of a country by its Jewish minority took place in Spain. In his *History of the Jews*, already referred to, Professor Graetz gives an account (Vol. III, p. 109) of the coming of alien conquerors into Spain, a country which had been organized by the Visigoths, a race closely akin in blood to the English, Swedes, Germans, and other peoples of the North Sea area:

> The Jews of Africa, who at various times had emigrated thither from Spain, and their unlucky co-religionists of the Peninsula, made common cause with the Mahometan conqueror, Tarik, who brought over from Africa into Andalusia an army eager for the fray. After the battle of Xeres (July, 711), and the death of Roderic, the last of the Visigothic kings, the victorious Arabs pushed onward, and were everywhere supported by the Jews. In every city that they conquered, the Moslem generals were able to leave but a small garrison of their own troops, as they had need of every man for the subjection of the country; they therefore confided them to the safekeeping of the Jews.
>
> In this manner the Jews, who but lately had been serfs, now became masters of the towns of Cordova, Granada, Malaga, and many others. When Tarik appeared before the capital, Toledo, he found it occupied by a small garrison only, the nobles and clergy having found safety in flight. While the Christians were in church, praying for the safety of their country and religion, the Jews flung open the gates to the victorious Arabs (Palm Sunday, 712), receiving them with acclamations, and thus avenged themselves for the many miseries which had befallen them in the course of a century since the time of Reccared and Sisebut. The capital also was entrusted by Tarik to the custody of the Jews, while he pushed on in pursuit of the cowardly Visigoths, who had sought safety in flight, for the purpose of recovering from them the treasure which they had carried off.
>
> Finally, when Musa Ibn-Nosair, the Governor of Africa, brought

a second army into Spain and conquered other cities, he also delivered them into the custody of the Jews.

The "miseries" which prompted the Jews of Spain to treason are explained by Professor Graetz. King Sisebut was annoyingly determined to convert them to Christianity, and among the "miseries" inflicted by King Reccared "the most oppressive of all was the restraint touching the possession of slaves. Henceforward the Jews were neither to purchase Christian slaves nor accept them as presents" (*History of the Jews,* Vol. III, p. 46). The newly Christianized East German Goths of Spain were noted for their chastity, piety, and tolerance (*Encyc. Brit.,* Vol. X, p. 551), but the latter quality apparently was not inclusive enough to allow the wealthy alien minority to own the coveted bodies of fair-haired girls and young men.

There is a lesson for America in the solicitude of the Visigoths for their young. Americans of native stock should rouse themselves from their half-century of lethargic indifference and should study the set-up which permits the enslavement of young people's minds by forces hostile to Western Christian civilization. Our boys and girls are propagandized constantly by books, periodicals, motion pictures, radio, television, and advertisements; and from some of the things that they read and see and hear they are influenced toward a degraded standard of personal conduct, an indifference to the traditional doctrines of Christianity, and a sympathy for Marxism or Communism. American parents must evolve and make successful a positive – not a negative – counter-movement in favor of the mores of Western civilization, or that civilization will fall. It is well known that *the Communists expend their greatest effort at capturing the young;* but in this most vital of all fields *those Americans who are presumably anti-Communistic have – at least up to the summer of 1952 – made so little effort that it may well be described as none at all.*

233

Since President Franklin Roosevelt's recognition of the Soviet masters of Russia (November 16, 1933), the United States has consistently helped to "wound itself" by catering to the "insidious forces working from within" (Chapter II and III), who are "opposed to all our great traditions" of Christian civilization. These powerful "forces" have been welcomed to our shores, have become rich and influential, and nothing has been expected of them beyond a pro-American patriotism rather than a hostile national separatism. In spite of all kindnesses, they have, however, stubbornly adhered to their purposes and have indeed "gravely weakened the structure and tone of our American way of life." But the wealth of our land and the vitality of our people are both so great that the trap has not yet been finally sprung; the noose has not yet been fatally drawn. Despite the hostile aliens who exert power in Washington; despite the aid and succor given them by uninformed, hired, or subverted persons of native stock; despite the work of the "romantics, bums, and enemy agents" (Captain Michael Fielding, speech before Public Affairs Luncheon Club, Dallas, Texas, March 19, 1951) who have directed our foreign policy in recent years, there is a chance for the survival of America. A great country can be conquered only if it is inwardly rotten. We can still be free, *if we wish*.

Basic moves, as indicated in preceding chapters, are three:

We must (i) lift the iron curtain of censorship (Chapter V) which, not satisfied with falsifying the news of the hour, has gone back into past centuries to mutilate the classics of our literature and to exclude from our school histories such vital and significant facts as those presented in Chapter I and II and above in this chapter. A start towards this goal can be made by exercising some of the Constitution-guaranteed rights discussed in Chapter VIII, and by subscribing to periodicals with a firm record of opposing Communism. The reading of periodicals and books friendly to the American tradition not only encourages and strengthens the publishers of such works but makes the reader of them a better informed and therefore a more effective instrument in the great cause of saving Western Christian civilization.

We must (ii) begin in the spirit of humane Christian civilization to evolve some method of preventing our inassimilable mass of aliens and alien-minded people from exercising in this country a power over our culture and our lives out of all proportion to the number of the minority, and to prevent this minority from shaping, against the general national interest, our policies on such vital matters as war and immigration. The American Legion seems to be working toward leadership in this vital matter. The movement should be supported by other veterans' organizations, women's clubs, luncheon clubs, and other groups favorable to the survival of America. In the great effort, no individual should fail; for there is no such thing as activity by a group, a club, or even a legion, except as a product of the devoted zeal of one or more individuals.

Our danger from internal sources hostile to our civilization was the subject of a warning by General MacArthur in his speech before the Massachusetts Legislature on July 25, 1951:

> This evil force, with neither spiritual base nor moral standard, rallies the abnormal and sub-normal elements among our citizenry and applies internal pressure against all things we hold decent and all things that we hold right – the type of pressure which has caused many Christian nations abroad to fall and their own cherished freedoms to languish in the shackles of complete suppression.
>
> As it has happened there it can happen here. Our need for patriotic fervor and religious devotion was never more impelling. There can be no compromise with atheistic communism – no half way in the preservation of freedom and religion. It must be all or nothing.
>
> We must unite in the high purpose that the liberties etched upon the design of our life by our forefathers be unimpaired and

that we maintain the moral courage and spiritual leadership to preserve inviolate that bulwark of all freedom, our Christian faith.

We must (iii) effect a genuine clean-up of our government (Chapter VIII) removing not only all those who can be proved to be traitors, but also all those whose policies have for stupidity or bad judgment been inimical to the interests of our country.

Following the removal of Acheson – and Marshall, who resigned in September 1951 – *and any successor appointees tarred by the same stick,* and following the removal of the cohorts of alien-minded, indifferent, or stupid people in their hierarchies and in other government agencies and departments, the chances of a third world-wide war will be materially lessened, because our most likely attacker relies on such people, directly or indirectly as the case may be, to perform or permit acts of espionage and sabotage. The chances of a world-wide war will be greatly lessened if four relatively inexpensive steps are taken by our government. Even if general war breaks out, a successful outcome will be more likely if the steps are taken – as far as possible under such circumstances as may then exist.

The word inexpensive is purposely used. *It is high time that our government counts cost, for, as Lenin himself said, a nation can spend itself into economic collapse as surely as it can ruin itself by a wrong foreign policy.*

The one horrible fact of World War II was the killing of 256,330 American men and seriously wounding of so many others. But the cost in money is also important to the safety of America. According to *Life* magazine's *History of World War II,* that war cost us $350,000,000,000 (*Christopher Notes,* No. 33, March, 1951). Also – and it is to be hoped that there is some duplication – the "Aid Extended to All Foreign Countries by the U.S." from July 1, 1940, to June 30, 1950, was $80,147,000,000 (Office of Foreign Transactions, Department of Commerce). This staggering figure is for money spent. The "costs from July 1, 1940, down to and including current proposals for such overseas assistance add up to $104 billions," according to Senator Hugh Butler of Nebraska, a member of the Finance Committee, in a speech in the Senate on June 1, 1951 (*Human Events,* June 6, 1951). See also "In Washington It's Waste As Usual" by Stanley High (*The Reader's Digest,* July, 1951). Thus Stalin's confidence in and reliance on America's collapse from orgastic spending as explicitly stated in his great March 10, 1939 address to the 18th Congress of the Communist Party could be prophetic.

Let us turn then to the four relatively inexpensive steps – in addition to the preservation, or restoration, of our financial integrity – for saving America. These steps – which can be taken only after the clean-up of our departments of State and Defense and our Executive agencies – are (a) the frustration of the plans of Communists actually in the United States; (b) the adoption of a foreign policy, diplomatically and defensively, which is based not on a political party's need of votes, but on the safety of America; (c) a study of the United Nations Organization and a decision that the American people can trust; and (d) a factual recognition of and exploitation of the cleavage between the Soviet government and the Russian people. A final sub-chapter (e) constitutes a brief conclusion to *The Iron Curtain Over America.*

(a)

For our reconstituted, or rededicated, government the first step, in both immediacy and importance, is to *act* against Communism not in Tierra del Fuego or Tristan da Cunha, but *in the United States.* Known Communists in this country must, under our laws, be at once apprehended and either put under surveillance or deported; and the independent Soviet secret police force, believed by some authorities to be in this country in the numbers estimated at 4,000, must be ferreted out. Unless these actions are taken, all *overseas* adventures against Communism are *worse than folly*, because our best troops *will be away from home when the Soviet give word* to the 43,217 Communists known to the F.B.I., to the 4,000, and incidentally to the 472,170 hangers-on (figures based on J. Edgar Hoover's estimated ten collaborators for each actual member) to destroy our transportation and communications systems and industrial potential. If the strike of a few railroad switchmen can virtually paralyze the country, what can be expected from a suddenly unmasked Red army of half a million, many of them slyly working among the labor unions engaged in strategic work, often unknown to the leaders of those unions? (See "100 Things You Should Know About Communism and Labor," 10¢, Government Printing Office, Washington, D.C.) The menace is not hypothetical. "Apparently there's no business like spy business in this country. For, according to the F.B.I. Director J. Edgar Hoover, the bureau shortly will investigate 90,000 separate instances of threats to America's internal security. Last year his agents probed into 74,799 such cases" (Victor Riesel's syndicated column, April 3, 1952).

Director Hoover of the F.B.I. is aware of the danger. In an interview (UP dispatch, March 18, 1951) he said: "The Communists are dedicated to the overthrow of the American system of government … the destruction of strategic industries – that is the Communist blueprint of violent attack." Secretary-Treasurer George Meany of the American Federation of Labor bears similar testimony ("The Last Five Years," by George Meany, A. F. of L. Bldg., Washington 1, D.C., 1951):

> … It is the Communists who have made the ranks of the labor their principal field of activity. It is the Communists who are hypocritically waging their entire unholy fight under the flag of world labor. It is the Communists whose strategy dictates that they must above all capture the trade unions before they can seize power in any country.

If anyone, after reading the above statements by the two men in America best situated to know, is still inclined to think our internal danger from the infiltration of Soviet Communism into labor a fantasy, he should read "Stalinists Still Seek Control of Labor in Strategic Industries" in the February 24, 1951, issue of the *Saturday Evening Post*. According to this source:

> ... The communist fifth column in the American labor movement has cut its losses and has completed its regrouping. It now claims to have 300,000 to 400,000 followers. Aside from Bridges' own International Longshoremen's and Warehousemen's Union, some of the working-alliance members are in such strategic spots as the United Electrical Workers; Mines, Mills and Smelter Workers; United Public Workers; and the American Communications Association.

For a full analysis of the strength, the methods, and the weapons of the Communists in a country they plan to capture, see *The Front is Everywhere: Militant Communism in Action*, by William R. Kintner (University of Oklahoma Press, Norman, Oklahoma, 1950, $3.75). A West Point graduate, a General Staff Corps colonel in the Military Intelligence Service in the later phase of World War II, and a Doctor of Philosophy in the field in which he writes, Colonel Kintner is rarely qualified for his effectively accomplished task. His bibliography is a good guide for speakers, writers, and others, who require fuller facts on Communism. Another essential background work is "Lenin, Trotsky, Stalin: Soviet Concepts of War" in *Makers of Modern Strategy*, edited by Edward Mead Earle (Princeton University Press, Princeton, New Jersey, 1943).

The ratios of actual Communists and other disgruntled elements of the total population in Russia of 1917 and the America of the middle of the twentieth century have often been compared and are strikingly similar. As of 1952, the American position is stronger than that of the Russian government of 1917 in that we have not just suffered a major military defeat. Our position is weaker, however, in the extent to which our administration is not only *tolerant of* but *infiltrated with* persons hostile to our traditions. Our actions against U.S. Communists must then include those in government. If inclined to doubt that communists are entrenched in government, do not forget that the C.I.O., *prior to the Tydings investigation*, expelled its United Public Workers Union (Abram Flaxer, president) for being Communist-dominated! And note the name "United Public Workers" in the *Post* list quoted above! Once more, let it be stressed that the removal of Communists from their strategic spots in the government must take precedence over everything else, for government Communists are not only able to steal secret papers and stand poised for sabotage; they are also often in positions where they prevent actions against Communists outside the government. For instance, Mr. Meany testified (*op. cit.*, p. 3) that some of the anti-Communist success of the American Federation of Labor has been accomplished "despite opposition even from some of our government agencies and departments!"

If any reader is still inclined to doubt the essential validity – irrespective of proof in a court of law with judge or judges likely to have been appointed by "We need those votes" Roosevelt or "Red Herring" Truman – of the charges of Senator Joseph McCarthy of Wisconsin, arch-enemy of Tydings whitewash, or is inclined to question the judgment of the C.I.O. in its expulsion of government Communists, he should ponder the test formulated by Christ in ancient Palestine: "Ye shall know them by their fruits" (*St. Matthew*, VII, 16). There have been large and poisonous harvests from our government-entrenched Communists. The most deadly, including atomic espionage and pro-Soviet foreign policy, have been analyzed above (Chapters II, IV, VI). More recent was the successful Communist *Daily Worker* campaign for the removal of General MacArthur – a campaign culminating in an across-the-page headline on April 9, 1951, just before General MacArthur was dismissed from his command in Korea, and from his responsibilities in Japan. The pressure of Communists was not the only pressure upon the President for the dismissal of General MacArthur. Stooges, fellow travelers, and dupes helped. The significance of the Communist pressure cannot be doubted, however, by anyone whose perusal of the *Daily Worker* has shown how many times Communist demands have foreshadowed Executive action (see "The Kremlin War on Douglas MacArthur," by Congressman Daniel A. Reed, of New York, *National Republic*, January, 1952).

Here follow some indications of recent fruitful Communist activity within our government – indications which should be studied in full by any who are still doubters. Late in 1948 an article by Constantine Brown was headlined in the Washington *Evening Star* as follows: "Top Secret Documents Known to Reds Often Before U.S. Officials Saw Them." "Army Still Busy Kicking Out Reds Who Got In During the War," the Washington *Times-Herald* headlined on February 11, 1950, the article by Willard Edwards, giving details on Communist-held positions in the "orientation of youthful American soldiers." "When Are We Going to Stop Helping Russia Arm?" was asked by O. K. Armstrong and Frederic Sondern, Jr., in December, 1950, *Reader's Digest*. "How U.S. Dollars Armed Russia" is the title of an article by Congressman Robert B. Chiperfield of Illinois, a member of the House Foreign Affairs Committee (*National Republic*, 511 Eleventh St., N.W., Washington 7, D.C., February, 1951). See the *Congressional Record,* or write to the senators concerned, for an account of the successful efforts of Senator Herbert F. O'Conor of Maryland and Senator John J. Williams of Delaware in breaking up the scandal of our officially permitting – and by our blockade actually aiding – the furnishing of supplies to Chinese Communists when their government troops were at the time killing our young men in Korea! See also the full "Text of House Un-American Activities Committee's Report on

Espionage in the Government" (*New York Times,* December 31, 1948; or, from your Congressman).

If existing laws against Communism – including the Internal Security law whose passage over the President's veto was discussed in Chapter VIII – are inadequate, appropriate new laws should be recommended by the Department of Justice for dealing with the Communist menace within the United States. They will surely be promptly passed by the Congress. Advance approval of the laws by the Department of Justice is desirable, so that no flaws in the laws' coverage can later be alleged by an enforcement official. If the Justice Department will not at once provide the text of a needed law, the judiciary committees of the two Houses are amply able to do so, and should proceed on their own. If any administration, present or future, flouts the anti-subversive laws passed by the Congress, the Congress should take the necessary action – including impeachment, if other efforts fail – to secure the enforcement of the laws.

Unless action is soon taken against U.S. Communists (despite any "We need those votes" considerations), our whole radar defense and our bomb shelters are wasted money and effort, for there is no way of surely preventing the importation of atom bombs or unassembled elements of them across some point on our 53,904-mile detailed tidal shoreline (exclusive of Alaska, whose detailed tidal shoreline furnishes another 33,904 miles) except to clean out possible recipients of the bombs whether operating in government agencies or elsewhere in the United States. We would by no means be the first country to take steps against Communists. Progress in this direction in Spain and Canada is elsewhere mentioned. Also, "the Communist Party has been outlawed in the Middle East countries," except in "Israel" (Alfred M. Lilienthal, *Human Events,* August 2, 1950).

As a conclusion to this section of the last chapter of *The Iron Curtain Over America*, let it be stressed that American people in every city block, in every rural village, and on every farm must be vigilant in the matter of opposing Communism and in persuading the government to take effective measures against it. "There has been a tremendous amount of false information disseminated in the world as to the alleged advantages of Communism," said General Wedemeyer to his summation of his recommendations to the MacArthur Committee of the Senate (*U.S. News and World Report,* June 22, 1951). "People all over the world are told that Communism is really the people's revolution and that anyone opposing it is a reactionary or a Fascist or imperialist." Because of the prominence of Jews in Communism from the Communist Manifesto (1848) to the atomic espionage trials (1950, 1951), anti-Communist activity is also frequently referred to erroneously as anti-Semitic (see Chapters II, III, and V). This propaganda-spread view that Communism is "all right" and that those who oppose it are anti-Semitic, or "reactionaries" of some sort, may be circulated in your community by an actual member of the Communist Party. More likely, it is voiced by a deluded teacher, preacher, or other person who has believed the subtle but lying propaganda that has been furnished him. Be careful not to hurt the ninety per cent or more of American-minded teachers (*Educational Guardian,* 1 Maiden Lane, New York 7, New York, July, 1951, p. 2) and a probably similar majority of preachers; but use our influence to frustrate the evil intent of the "two or five or ten percent of subverters." Draw your inspiration from Christ's words, "For this cause I came into the world" (*St. John* XVIII, 37) and let the adverse situation in your community inspire you to make counter efforts for Western Christian civilization. Never forget that the basic conflict in the world today is not between the Russian people and the American people but between Communism and Christianity. Work then, also, for the friendly cooperation of all Christian denominations in our great struggle for the survival of the Christian West. Divided we fall!

(b)

In the second place, our foreign military policy must be entirely separated from the question of minority votes in the United States and must be based on the facts of the world as known by our best military scholars and strategists. That such has not been the case since 1933 has been shown above (Chapter VI) in the analysis of our official attitudes toward China, Palestine, and Germany. Additional testimony of the utmost authority is furnished by General Bonner Fellers. In reviewing Admiral Ellis M. Zacharias's book *Behind Closed Doors* (Putnam's, New York, $3.75), the former intelligence officer General Fellers states: "*Behind Closed Doors* reveals that we have embarked upon a military program which our leaders know to be unsound, yet they are unwilling to tell the American people the truth!" (*The Freeman*, October 30, 1950.)

This statement prompts a mention of the fact that a colonelcy is the highest rank attainable in and from the United States Army (similarly, a captaincy in the Navy). By a regulation inherited from the days when the total number of general officers was about twenty-five, all appointments to general rank from the one-star Brigadier to the five-star General of the Army are made by the President of the United States (so also for the corresponding ranks in the Navy). It is obvious that merit is a factor in the choice of generals and admirals as field and fleet commanders. Merit is surely a factor also for many staff positions of star-wearing rank. Just as surely, however, the factor of "political dependability" *also* enters into the selection of those high-ranking staff officers who make policy and are allowed to express opinions. "The conclusion is inescapable that our top military Commanders today are muzzled. They do not dare to differ within the civilian side of military questions for fear of being removed or demoted" (from "Louis Johnson's Story is Startling," by David Lawrence, *The Evening Star*, Washington, June 18, 1951). In view of such testimony derived from a former Secretary of Defense, it must be concluded that it was to a large extent a waste of time for the Senate to summon generals and admirals close to the throne in Washington in the year 1951 for an analysis of Truman-Acheson policies. The following passage from the great speech of General MacArthur before the Massachusetts Legislature (July 25, 1951) is highly pertinent:

> Men of significant stature in the national affairs appear to cower before the threat of reprisal if the truth be expressed in criticism of those in higher public authority.
>
> For example, I find in existence a new and dangerous concept that the members of our armed forces owe primary allegiance and loyalty to those who temporarily exercise the authority of the executive branch of Government, rather than to the country and its Constitution which they are sworn to defend.

If the Congress wants to learn other aspects of a strategic or logistic situation besides the administration's viewpoint, it must summon not the agents and implementers of the administration's policy, but non-political generals, staff officers below star rank, and retired officers, Regular, National Guard, and Reserve. Competent officers in such categories are not hard to find. There are also a number of other patriotic Americans with diplomatic experience. In an address over three major networks (April 13, 1951) Representative Joseph W. Martin, Jr., Republican leader in the House, named seven generals including Krueger, Whitney, Chennault, and Wedemeyer; seven admirals including King, Halsey, Yarnell, and Denfeld; four Marine Corps generals, and ten diplomats including Hurley – all of the twenty-eight expert in one way or another on the Far East and none of them close to the Washington throne where Far East policy decisions have come from the plans and thinking of persons such as John Carter Vincent, John S. Service, Owen Lattimore, Philip C. Jessup, Lauchlin Currie, Dean G. Acheson, and their fellow travelers!

No attempt can be here made to analyze fully the complex structure of our foreign relations. Nowhere are any guesses made as to future national policy. No attempt is made to enter into details in the fields of logistics and manpower, and no suggestions will be made on the tactics or strategy of a particular operation, for such decisions are the responsibility of informed commanders on the scene.

A few words are indicated, however, in our choice of the two allied subjects of *gasoline* and *distance from a potential enemy* as factors in the defense of the West.

This matter of gasoline is most significant in our choice of areas for massing troops against a possible thrust from the Soviet. Of the world's supply, it was estimated in 1950 by petroleum experts that the U.S. and friendly nations controlled 93%, whereas the Soviet controlled 7%. The fighting of a war on the Soviet perimeter (Korea or Germany) would appear thus as an arrangement – whether so intended or not – to give the Soviet leaders a set-up in which their limited supply of gasoline and oil would not be an obstacle.

Beyond question, the Soviet maintains at all times sufficient gasoline reserves for a sudden thrust into close-at-hand West Germany. But the Soviet almost certainly does not have enough gasoline for conquering, for instance, a properly armed Spain which, because of its distance from Soviet supply sources and because of its water and mountain barriers, has in the age of guided missiles superseded Britain as the fortress of Europe.

This fact, inherent in the rise of the significance of the air arm, prompts an analysis of the Roosevelt and Truman attitudes towards Spain. Though Franklin Roosevelt tolerated benignly the bitter anti-Franco statements of his Communist and other leftist supporters, he maintained more or less under cover a friendly working arrangement by which during World War II we derived from Spain many advantages superior to those accorded by Spain to the Axis countries. Adequate details of Spain's help to America in World War II can be had in a convincing article, "Why Not a Sensible Policy Toward Spain?" by Congressman Dewey Short of Missouri (*Reader's Digest*, May, 1949). The reader interested in still further details should consult the book, *Wartime Mission in Spain* (The Macmillan Company, New York) by Professor Carlton J. H. Hayes, who served as our Ambassador to Spain from May, 1942, to March, 1945.

To one of the many ways in which Spain helped us, the author of *The Iron Curtain Over America* can bear personal testimony. When our aviators flew over France, they were instructed, if shot down, to make their way to Spain. If Franco had been pro-Hitler, he would have returned them to the Germans. If he had been neutral, he would have interned them. If friendly, he would have turned them over to the United States to give our leaders their priceless intelligence information and to fly again. That is precisely what Franco did; and it was to the office of this writer, then Chief of the Interview Section in the Military Intelligence Service, that a representative number of these fliers reported when flown to Washington via Lisbon from friendly Spain.

The principal trouble with Spain, from the point of view of our influential Leftists, seems to be that there are no visible Communists in that country and no Marxists imbedded in the Spanish government. Back in 1943 (February 21) Franco wrote as follows to Sir Samuel Hoare, British Ambassador to Spain: "Our alarm at Russian advances is common not only to neutral nations, but also to all those people in Europe who have not yet lost their sensibilities and their realization of the peril... Communism is an enormous menace to the whole world, and now that it is sustained by the victorious armies of a great country all those not blind must wake up." More on the subject can be found in Frank Waldrop's article, "What Fools We Mortals Be," in the Washington *Times-Herald* for April 17, 1948.

It is not surprising perhaps that, just as there are no visible

Communists in Spain, an anti-Spanish policy has long been one of the main above-board activities of U.S. Communists and fellow travelers. Solicitude for the leftist votes has, as a corollary, influenced our policy toward Spain. For America's unjustified tendency "to treat Spain as a leper," not from "any action on the part of Spain in the past or the present," but for the "winning of electoral votes," see "Britain and an American-Spanish Pact," by Cyril Falls, Chichele Professor of the History of War in Oxford University (*The Illustrated London News*, August 4, 1951).

The following anti-Franco organizations have been listed as Communist by the U.S. Attorney General (see the Senate report, *Communist Activities Among Aliens and National Groups*, Part III, p. A10):

> Abraham Lincoln Brigade
> Action Committee to Free Spain Now
> Comite Coordinator Pro Republica Espanola
> North American Committee to Aid Spanish Democracy
> North American Spanish Aid Committee
> United Spanish Aid Committee

Another cause of the anti-Spanish propaganda of American left-ists is the fact that Spain – aware of History's bloody record of the treason of ideologically unassimilated minorities – has not complicated its internal problems by admitting hordes of so-called "refugees" from Eastern Europe.

The same world forces which blocked our resumption of full diplomatic relations with Spain have prevented the UN from inviting Spain to be a member of that organization.

Whether Spain is in or out of that ill-begotten and seemingly expiring organization may matter very little, but Spain in any defense of the West matters decisively. "In allying itself with Spain the United States would exchange a militarily hopeless position on the continent of Europe for a very strong one" (Hoffman Nickerson: "Spain, the Indispensable Ally," *The Freeman*, November 19, 1951). The way for friendship with Spain was at last opened when the Senate, despite President Truman's bitter opposition, approved in August, 1950, a loan to that country, and was further cleared on November 4, 1950, when the UN, though refusing to lift the "ban against Spain's full entry into the United Nations," did vote to allow Spanish representation on certain "specialized agencies such as the world health and postal organizations" (AP dispatch, *Dallas Morning News*, November 5, 1950). As to the loan authorized by Congress in August, 1950, it was not until June 22, 1951, that the "White House and State Department authorized the Export-Import Bank to let Spain buy wheat and other consumer goods out of the $62,500,000 Spanish loan voted by Congress last year" (*Washington Post*, June 23, 1951).

In his testimony to the combined Armed Services and Foreign Relations Committees of the Senate on May 24, 1951 (AP dispatch from Washington) Chief of Staff General Omar Bradley admitted that "from a military point of view" the Joint Chiefs would like to have Spain on our side. Finally, the clamor of the public and the attitude of the military prevailed and in July, 1951, the United States, to the accompaniment of a chorus of abuse from the Socialist governments of Britain and France (*New York Times*, July 17, 1951), began official conversations with Spain on mutual defense. On August 20, 1951, a "military survey team," which was "composed of all three armed services," left Washington for Spain (*New York Times*, August 21, 1951). This move toward friendly relations for mutual advantage of the two countries not only has great potential value in the field of defense; it has, if possible, an even greater diplomatic value, for Spain is the Mother Country for all of Latin America from Rio Grande to Cape Horn with the sole exception of Brazil. Spain is, moreover, of all European countries the closest in sympathy with the Moslem world. Each year, for

instance, it welcomes to Cordoba and Toledo thousands of Moslem pilgrims. Peace between Moslem and Christian was a century-old fact until ended by the acts of the Truman administration on behalf of "Israel." It will be a great achievement if our resumption of relations with Spain leads to a renewal of friendly relations with the Moslem world. We must be sure, however, that our military men in Spain will not be accompanied by State Department and executive agencies vivandières, peddling the dirty wares of subversion and Communism (*Human Events*, August 8, 1951).

With the Atlantic Ocean, the Mediterranean, and the lofty Pyrenees Mountains as barriers; under the sheltering arm of distance; and above all with no visible internal Communists or Marxists to sabotage our efforts, we can – if our national defense so requires – safely equip Spain's eighteen well-disciplined divisions, can develop airfields unapproachable by hostile ground troops, and in the deep inlets and harbors of Spain can secure safe ports for our navy and our merchant fleet. Our strengthening of Spain, second only to our keeping financially solvent and curbing Communists in this country, would undoubtedly be a very great factor in the preventing the Soviet leaders from launching an all-out war. Knowing that with distant Pyrenees-guarded and American-armed Spain against them, they could not finally win, they almost certainly would not begin.

Our strengthening of Spain's army, potentially the best in Europe outside of Communist lands, would not only have *per se* a powerful military value; it would also give an electric feeling of safety to the really anti-Communist elements in other Western European countries. Such near-at-hand reassurance of visible strength is sorely needed in France, for that country since the close of World War II has suffered from the grave internal menace of approximately 5,000,000 known Communists. In the general election of members of the French National Assembly on June 17, 1951, the Soviet-sponsored *Communist Party polled more than a fourth of all votes cast* (*New York Times,* June 19, 1951), and remained the largest single political party in France. Moreover, Communist leaders dominate labor in crucial French industries. "In France, the Communists are still the dominate factor in the trade unions" ("The Last Five Years," by George Meany. American Federation of Labor, Washington, D.C., p. 11). See also the heavily documented article, "French Communism," by Andre La Guerre in *Life,* January 29, 1951. With Communists so powerful and so ready for sabotage or for actual rebellion, the France of 1952 must be regarded as of limited value as an ally. As said above, however, the dependability of France in the defense of the West would be enhanced by United States aid to the military forces of anti-Communist Spain.

With Spain armed, and with the Socialist government of Britain thrown out by Mr. Churchill's Conservative Party in the election of October 25, 1951, the spirit of Europe may revive. If not, it is too much to expect America to save Europe forever, for "if 250 million people in Western Europe, with industry far larger than that of Russia, cannot find a way to get together and to build a basis for defense on land, then something fundamental may be wrong with Western Europe" (*U.S. News and World Report,* June 22, 1951, p. 10). Perhaps the "wrong" is with our policy – at least largely. For instance, deep in our policy and irrespective of our official utterances, "Germany is written off as an ally" to avoid "political liability in New York" (Frank C. Hanighen in *Human Events,* February 7, 1951).

Spain, with its natural barriers and the strategic position of its territory astride the Strait of Gibraltar, could become one anchor of an oil-and-distance defense arc. By their location and by their anti-Communist ideology, the Moslem nations of the Middle East are the other end of this potential crescent of safety. Friendship with these nations would, like friendship with Spain, be a very great factor in preventing a third world-wide war.

Among nations on the Soviet periphery, Turkey, mountainous

and military-minded, is pre-eminently strong. Perhaps because it would be an effective ally, it long received the cold shoulder from our State Department. Suddenly, however, in the autumn of 1951, Turkey, along with Greece, was given a status similar to that of the nations of Western Europe (not, however, including Spain) in the proposed mutual defense against Communism. This apparently reluctant change of policy by our government toward Greece and Turkey seems – like the sending of a military mission to Spain – to have grown unquestionably from pubic clamor in America as shown in the newspapers, especially in letters from the people, as heard on radio from the patriotic commentators, and as reflected in polls of public opinion. This success of the people in changing national policy should hearten the average citizen to newer efforts in the guiding his country to sound policies. It is most essential for every individual to remember that every great achievement is the result of a multitude of small efforts.

Between Spain and Turkey, the Mediterranean islands – Majorca and Minorca, Corsica and Sardinia, Sicily and Malta, Crete and Cyprus – are well deployed and well fortified by nature. Perhaps the United States should make some of them into impregnable bases by friendly agreement with their authorities. The incontestable value of an island fortress is shown by Malta's surviving the ordeal of Axis bombing in World War II as well as by Hitler's capture of Crete, an operation so costly in time and matériel that it was a factor in the German failure before Moscow in the following December.

In the Eastern Mediterranean, the island of Cyprus (visited by the author) is potentially a very strong bastion. In relationship to the Dardanelles, the Soviet oil fields, and the strategic Aleppo-Baghdad-Cairo triangle, Cyprus's water-girt site is admirable. Since its mountain ranges reach a height of more than 6,000 feet, and are located like giant breastworks defending a broad interior plain, the island might well become the location of underground hangars and landing fields for a great air fortress. Others of the islands listed above offer advantages of one sort or another to air or other forces.

South of the Mediterranean's necklace of islands, lies Africa, the ultimate key to the success or failure of the Western World in preventing an aggressive move against Europe. It is air power in Africa, in the great stretch of hills and plains from Morocco to Egypt, that might well be the major deterrent of any hostile move in Europe or in the Middle East by the Soviet Union. "Air power offers the only effective counter-measure against Russian occupation of the Middle East. The deeper the Red Army moves into this priceless strategic area, the more its supply lines can be disrupted by air strikes" ("Africa and Our Security," by General Bonner Fellers, *The Freeman*, August 13, 1951). In his valuable article, General Fellers states further that a "small, highly trained and mobile ground force, *with adequate air protection and support*," can defend African air bases, which in turn could prevent the crossing of the Mediterranean by hostile forces in dangerous numbers.

The Moslem lands of the Middle East and North Africa (as sources of oil and as bases for long range bombers) should, by a proper diplomatic approach, be pulled *positively and quickly* into the United States defense picture. Barring new inventions not yet in sight, and barring disguised aid from our government (such as Truman and Acheson gave the Chinese Communists in the Strait of Formosa), the Soviet Union cannot win a world war without the oil of the Middle East. Soviet delay in making overt moves in that theater may well have been determined by gasoline reserves insufficient for the venture.

The Soviet squeeze upon Iran was initiated at the Tehran Conference, where Stalin, who is said to be unwilling to leave *his territory*, entertained our rapidly declining President *in the Soviet Embassy* in a grandiose gesture insulting alike to the Iranians and to our staff in that country. Stalin's alleged reason that his embassy was the only safe spot was in truth an astute face-raising gesture before

253

the peoples of Asia, for he displayed Roosevelt, the symbolic Man of the West, held in virtual protective custody or house arrest by the Man of the East.

Details of the dinner in the Soviet Embassy to which Stalin invited "Father and the P. M.," are given by General Elliott Roosevelt in *As He Saw It* (pp. 188, 189). Stalin proposed that Germany's "war criminals" be disposed of by firing squads "as fast as we capture them, all of them, and there must be at least fifty thousand of them."

According to General Roosevelt, the proposal shocked Prime Minister Churchill, who sprang quickly to his feet.

" 'Any such attitude,' he said, 'is wholly contrary to our British sense of justice! The British people will never stand for such mass murder ... no one, Nazi or no, shall be summarily dealt with before a firing squad, without a proper legal trial.,.!!!' "

The impasse was resolved by the U.S. President: " 'Clearly there must be some sort of compromise,'" he said, accordingly to his son. " 'Perhaps we could say that instead of summarily executing fifty thousand war criminals, we should settle on a smaller number. Shall we say forty-nine thousand five hundred?' "

It was in this way, prophetic of the crime of Nuremberg, that President Roosevelt, unquestionably very tired and probably already too ill to know the full import of his words and acts, threw away the last vestiges of our government's respect for law, and for the Western Christian tradition. In return, our President got nothing but flattering of the Leftists around him and the gratification of a whim of his decline which was to make Churchill scowl and Stalin smile! What a spectacle of surrender in the very capital of strategically important and historic Persia!

Over all Stalin's triumphs and Churchill's defeats at Tehran was the shadow of the derricks of the Iranian oil fields. "Should the Abadan refineries be shut down or their output flow in another direction, the results would be felt around the world. These refineries are the largest in the world, processing 550,000 barrels a day" (monthly *Newsletter* of Representative Frances Bolton of Ohio, June, 1951). And what a sorry figure America has played in this vital oil area from Tehran to 1951! "Our Government's Deplorable Performance in Iran Has Contributed to a Great Disaster," was the subtitle of a *Life* editorial, "How to Lose a World" (May 21, 1951), on Acheson's policy of doing nothing except "let the pieces settle" after the expected disaster in the world's greatest oil-producing area. In Iran or in an adjacent area, the Soviet may find it necessary to strike for her gasoline and lubricants before any major attempts can be surely successful elsewhere.

The well-known leftism in our State Department – as indicated in many ways, especially by the carefully documented testimony of Harold Stassen; and the C.I.O.'s expulsion of the United Public Workers Union – and the early predilection of Prime Minister Attlee (1945-1951) for Communism raise the inevitable fear that the oil crisis in Iran, while publicly deplored by Britain and America, may well have been engineered by the very American and British government officials who then shed crocodile tears at the oil's probable loss to the West!

A major world fact in the early 1950's was the fall of British prestige in the Middle East, and drawing of the Soviet into the resultant vacuum. The Attlee government's protest on Iranian oil nationalization commanded no respect anywhere, for the Iranians were copying the home program of the Socialist government of Britain! Britain's humiliation in Iran was made graver by the long threatened but never carried out dispatch of some 4,500 paratroopers to the oil fields – a gesture which was said to have stemmed from the Socialist Defense Minister at that time, the Jewish statesman, Mr. Emanuel Shinwell (UP dispatch from Tehran, May 25, 1951). Whether or not Mr. Churchill's government (October, 1951) can save the situation is for the future to show. There was no comfort for non-Communists in his speech before the two houses of the U.S. Congress on January 17, 1952 – a speech which called not for peace with justice to the Moslems of the Middle East but for U.S. troops!

The moral power of America as a mediator, like that of Britain, has moved toward zero. Nearly a million destitute Moslems refugees from Palestine — who have in their veins more of the blood of Biblical peoples than any other race in the world today – are straggling here and there in the Middle East or are in displaced persons' camps, and are not silent about the presence of American officers (Chapter VI, above) commanding the troops which drove them from their homes. For details on these hopeless refugees sent to wandering and starving by our policy, see Alfred M. Lilienthal's "Storm Clouds Over the Middle East," *Human Events*, August 2, 1950. The evil we did in Palestine may be our nemesis in Iran and in Egypt! The truth is that because of America's sponsoring of bloody little "Israel" – and Britain's falling in line – the Moslem Middle East resents the presence of the previously respected and admired Anglo-Saxon powers (Mr. Churchill's speech).

Moreover, the Zionists are not quiescent. The summer of 1951 saw clashes on the "Israeli" frontiers and the exposure of Zionist schemes in other parts of the Middle East. Here is a sample:

> Baghdad, Iraq, June 18 (AP)–Police said today they had discovered large quantities of weapons and explosives in Izra Daoud Synagogue. Military sources estimated it was enough to dynamite all Baghdad.)
>
> This was the latest discovery reported by police, who said yesterday they found a large store of machine guns, bombs, and ammunition in the former home of a prominent Jew.

After details of other discoveries the dispatch concludes, "Police said the ammunition was stored by the Baghdad Zionist Society, which was described as a branch of the World Zionist Organization" (*New York Times*, June 19, 1951).

In spite of our deserved low reputation in the Moslem world, American counter-moves of some sort to save Middle East oil and the Suez Canal are imperative. The proper approach is obvious, but *will our government make it?* "The Moslems, and those allied with them religiously and sympathetically, compose almost one-half of the world's people who control almost one-half of the world's land area. We infuriated them when we helped to drive a million Arabs from their native lands in the Middle East" (*Newsletter* of Congressman Ed Gossett of Texas February 1, 1951). "The recapture of the friendship of 400,000,000 Moslems by the United States, and its retention, may prove the deciding factor in preserving world peace" (statement of Congressman Ed Gossett of Texas in the House of Representatives, June 12, 1951, as recorded in the *Congressional Record*). In the Washington *Times-Herald* (Sept. 28, 1951), Senator Malone of Nevada also called attention to the sound sense and strategic advantage of having the Moslem world on our side.

The recapture of friendship with the Moslem is not only a question of acts of justice on our part but is tied to the question of absolutely vital oil reserves. The oil of the Middle East is essential to our preventing World War III or to our winning it. In World War II we had gasoline rationing *with* the oil of the Middle East on our side. What would we do in another war, far more dependent on gasoline, with the Middle East oil on the other side? And what would we do if the West should lose the Suez Canal?

The first move to prevent such a disaster – after cleaning out our State Department as the American Legion demanded by a vote of 2,881 to 131 at it's National Convention in Miami (October, 1951) – should be to send a complete new slate of American diplomats to the Moslem nations from Egypt and Yemen to Iraq and Iran. These new diplomats should be unsullied, square-shooting Americans and should have instructions to announce a changed policy which is long overdue. The present State Department, stained with past errors, could not succeed even if it should wish to succeed.

A changed policy implemented by new officials would almost certainly be received by the Moslem world with cordiality and gratitude, for until the Israel grab was furthered in this country America was throughout the Middle East the least disliked and least feared foreign power. "At the close of the Second World War the Near East was friendly to the United States and her allies," said Ambassador Kamil Bey Abdul Rahim of Egypt (*Congressional Record*, June 12, 1951) in an address delivered at Princeton University on June 2, 1951. By 1952, however, "a spirit of resentment and even revolt against the Western democracies" was sweeping through the Middle East. For the unfortunate fact of our having lost our friends the Ambassador finds the reason in the "policy of the West":

> The Palestine question is an outstanding example of this policy. Everyone knows that the serious injustice inflicted upon the Arabs in Palestine has alienated them and undermined the stability of the area.
>
> The West's continued political and financial support of the Zionists in Palestine is not helping the relations with the Near East, nor is it strengthening the forces which are fighting communism there.

By being again honorable in our dealing with the Moslem nations and by helping them, with a supply of long-range bombers or otherwise, to defend their oil, for which we are paying them good money, and will continue to pay them good money, we could quickly create a situation under which the Soviet cannot hope to conquer the Middle East. Thus lacking oil, the Soviet could not hope to conquer the world. It must not be forgotten, too, that apart from oil the Middle East has great strategic significance. "Israel" and the adjacent Moslem lands are a vestibule which leads to Europe, to Asia, and to Africa.

In addition to building, primarily by honorable conduct and

secondarily by thoughtfully planned assistance, a strength crescent from Spain through the Mediterranean and North Africa to the Middle East, other significant agenda involve a solution to our present problem in Korea and plans for the safety of Japan, Formosa, and the Philippines. But as Senator Jenner of Indiana has pointed out, "We cannot have peace in Asia if the negotiations are carried on by the men of Yalta" (*Human Events,* May 30, 1951). Then, there is Alaska, one of whose islands, Little Diomede, is only three miles from and in sight of an island, Big Diomede, belonging to Russia. Of the Soviet's two Far Eastern fronts, one is the hinterland of Vladivostok and the other is an armed quadrilateral opposite Nome, Alaska. Here, according to the military critic, Hanson Baldwin, is a garrison which "probably numbers more than 200,000 men" (see article and map, *New York Times,* March 15, 1949). No specific suggestions are here made, but it seems obvious that the defense of Alaska should receive priority over at least some of our more far-flung global ventures.

In conclusion of this section, a warning is in order – a warning that should be heeded in all of America's planning at home and abroad. In any efforts at helping the world, the primary help we can give is to remain solvent. A bankrupt America would be worse than useless to its allies. Foreign military aid should be granted, therefore, with two associated principles. We should cease mere political bureaucracy-building in this country and cut to a reasonable minimum our government's home spending. We should insist that foreign governments receiving our aid should also throw their energies and resources into the common cause.

There is no more dangerous fallacy than the general belief that America is excessively rich. Our natural resources are variously estimated at being six per cent to ten per cent of the world's total. These slender resources are being more rapidly depleted than those of any other power. Our national debt also is colossal beyond anything known in other parts of the world. Can a spendthrift who is heavily in debt be properly called a wealthy man? By what yardstick then are we a "rich" nation?

Fortunately a few Americans in high places are awake to the danger of a valueless American dollar. General MacArthur, for instance, in his speech before the Massachusetts Legislature gave the following warning:

> The free world's one great hope for survival now rests upon the maintaining and preserving of our own strength. Continue to dissipate it and that one hope is dead. If the American people would pass on the standard of life and the heritage of opportunity they themselves have enjoyed to their children and their children's children they should ask their representatives in government:
>
> "What is the plan for the easing of the tax burden upon us? What is the plan for bringing to a halt this inflationary movement which is progressively and inexorably decreasing the purchasing power of our currency, nullifying the protection of our insurance provisions, and reducing those of fixed income to hardship and despair?"

(c)

An early duty of a completely reconstituted Department of State will be to advise the Congress and the American people on the United Nations.

Launched in 1945, when our government's mania for giving everything to the Soviet was at its peak, the United Nations got off to an unfortunate start. Our most influential representative at San Francisco, "The Secretary-General of the United Nations Conference on International Organization," was none other than Alger Hiss. It is not surprising, then, that United States leftists, from pink to vermilion, found homes in the various cubicles of the new organization. According to a personal statement to the author by the late Robert Watt, American Federation of Labor leader and authority on international affairs, all members except the chairman of one twenty-one-member U.S. contingent to the permanent UN staff were known Communists or fellow travelers. These people and others of the same sort are for the most part still in UN harness.

Moreover, and as is to be expected, the work of our own delegation cannot be impartially assessed as being favorable to the interest, or even the survival, of the United States as a nation. Very dangerous to us, for instance, is our wanton meddling into the internal affairs of other nations by such a program as the one we call land reform. "The United States will make land reform in Asia, Africa, and Latin America a main plank in its platform for world economic development. At the appropriate time, the United States delegation [to the UN] will introduce a comprehensive resolution to the Economic and Social Council of the United Nations" (dispatch, August 1, by Michael L. Hoffman from Geneva to the *New York Times,* August 2, 1951). Can anyone with any sense think that our collection of leftists, etc., in the UN really know how to reform the economic and social structure of three continents? Is not the whole scheme an attack on the sovereignty of the nations whose land we mean to "reform"? Does the scheme not appear to have been concocted mainly if not solely to establish a precedent which will allow Communists and other Marxists to "reform" land ownership in the United States?

Meanwhile, certain international bodies have not delayed in making their plans for influencing the foreign and also the internal policies of the United States. For instance, at the World Jewish Conference which met in Geneva, Switzerland, on September 10, 1951, "far and away the most important matter" was said to be an opposition to "the resurgence of Germany as a leading independent power" (*New York Times,* September 10, 1951). The special dispatch to the *New York Times* continues as follows:

> "We are strongly and firmly opposed to the early emancipation of Germany from Allied control and to German rearmament,"

Dr. Maurice Perlzweig of New York, who represents Western Hemisphere Jewish communities, said today.

Leaders expect to formulate and send to the Foreign Ministers of Western powers the specific views of the world Jewish community on the German question. *; Palestine Question*

The above quotation shows an *international* effort to shape foreign policy. At the same "Congress," attention was also given to exerting influence *within America*:

> ... Dr. Goldman said non-Zionists must learn to contribute to some Zionist programs with which they did not agree.
>
> "Non-Zionists should not be unhappy if some money is used for Halutziuth [pioneering] training in the United States," he told a press conference. Zionists would be unable to accept any demand that no such training be undertaken, he added.

How would outside power force its will upon the United States? The day-by-day method is to exert economic pressure and to propagandize the people by the control of the media which shape public opinion (Chapter V, above). At least one other way, however, has actually been rehearsed. Full details are given by John Jay Daly in an article "UN Seizes, Rules American Cities" in the magazine, *National Republic* (September, 1951). As described by Mr. Daly, troops flying the United Nations flag – a blue rectangle similar to the blue rectangle of the State of "Israel" – took over Culver City, Huntington Park, Inglewood, Hawthorne, and Compton, California. The military "specialists" took over the government in a surprise move, "throwing the mayor of the city in jail and locking up the chief of police ..) and the chief of the fire department. ...The citizens, by a proclamation posted on the front of City Hall, were warned that the area had been taken over by the armed forces of the United Nations." If inclined to the view that this United Nations operation – even though performed by U.S. troops – is without significance, the reader should recall that the United States has only one-sixtieth of the voting power in the Assembly of the United Nations.

The present location of the UN headquarters not only within the United States but in our most alien-infested great city would make easy any outside interference intended to break down local sovereignty in this country – especially if large numbers of troops of native stock are overseas and if our own "specialist" contingents in the UN force should be composed of newcomers to the country. Such troops might conceivably be selected in quantity under future UN rule that its troops should speak more than one language. Such a rule, which on its face might appear reasonable, would limit American troops operating for the UN almost exclusively to those who are foreign-born or sons of foreign-born parents. This is true because few soldiers of old American stock speak any foreign languages, whereas refugees and other immigrants and their immediate descendants usually speak two – English, at least of a sort, and the language of the area from which they or their parents came.

As has been repeatedly stated on the floors of Congress, among others by Senator Pat McCarran on April 25, 1949 (see the government pamphlet, *Communist Activities Among Aliens and National Groups*, p. A1), the presence of the UN within the United States has the actual – not merely hypothetical – disadvantage of admitting to our borders under diplomatic immunity a continuing stream of new espionage personnel who are able to contact directly the members of their already established networks within the country. There are other signs that the UN organization is "useless," as John T. Flynn has described it in a Liberty network broadcast (November, 1951). The formulation of the North Atlantic Defense Treaty or Security Alliance in 1949 was a virtual admission that the UN was dead as an influence for preventing major aggression.

263

A Serious Question

American's strong-fisted forcing of unwilling nations to vote for the admission of "Israel" dealt the UN a blow as effective as Russia's vetoes. Another problem to give Americans pause is the dangerous wording and possibly even more dangerous interpretation of some articles in the UN Covenant. There is even a serious question of a complete destruction of our sovereignty over our own land, not only by interpretations of UN articles by UN officials (see *The United Nations – Action for Peace,* by Marie and Louis Zocca, p. 56), but by judicial decisions of the leftist-minded courts in this country. Thus in the case of Sei Fujii vs. the State of California, "Justice Emmet H. Wilson decided that an existing law of a state is unenforceable because of the United Nations Charter" ("These Days," by George Sokolsky, Washington *Times-Herald* and other papers, March 9, 1951).

Lastly, and of great importance, is the consistent UN tendency to let the United States, with one vote in 60, bear not merely the *principal* burden of the organization, but *almost all* of the burden. Thus in the UN-sponsored operation in Korea, America furnished "over 90% of the dead and injured" (broadcast by ex-President Herbert Hoover, December 20, 1950) among UN troops, South Koreans being excluded from the figures as South Korea is not a UN member. And as the months passed thereafter, the ratio of American causalities continued proportionately high. By the middle of the summer of 1951 more of our men had been killed and wounded in Korea than in the Revolutionary War, the War of 1812, the Mexican War, and the Spanish-American War, combined! It is thus seen that the United Nations organization has failed miserably in what should be its main function – namely, the prevention or stopping of war.

In view of the above entries on the loss side of the ledger, what has the United Nations accomplished? A United States representative, Mr. Harding Bancroft, furnished the answer in a spring of 1951 broadcast (NBC, "The United Nations Is My Beat"). The

Need New clean leadership @ Dept of state

leadership are UN Advisors to USA

three successes of the Security Council cited by Mr. Bancroft were achieved in Palestine, the Netherlands East Indies, and Kashmir. With what yardstick does Mr. Bancroft measure success? Details cannot be given here, but surely the aggregate of the results in the three areas cited cannot be regarded as *successful* by anyone sympathetic with either Western Christian civilization or Moslem civilization!

Patriotic Americans should be warned, finally, against spurious attempts to draw parallels between the United States Constitution and United Nations regulations. The Constitution, with its first ten amendments, was designed specifically to curb the power of the Federal government and to *safeguard the rights of states and individuals.*

On the other hand, the United Nations appears to have the goal of *destroying many of the sovereign rights of the member nations and of putting individuals in jeopardy everywhere* – particularly in the United States.

In view of all these matters, the American public is entitled to advise on the UN from a new clean leadership in the Department of State. The Augean stables of the UN are so foul that the removal of the filth from the present organization might be too difficult. Perhaps the best move would be to adjourn *sine die.* Then, like-minded nations on our side, including the Moslem bloc – which a clean State Department would surely treat honorably – might work out an agreement advantageous to the safety and sovereignty of each other. Cleared of the booby traps, barbed wire, poisonous potions, and bad companions of the present organization, the new international body might achieve work of great value on behalf of world peace. In the U.S. delegation to the new organization we should include Americans only – and no Achesonians or Hissites from the old. In any case *the Congress needs and the people deserve a full report on the United Nations from a State Department which they can trust.*

We must never forget, moreover, that the Russian people are at heart Christian. They were converted even as they emerged onto the stage of civilized modern statehood, and Christianity is in their tradition – as it is ours.

We must finally not forget that leaders in Russia since 1917 are not patriotic Russians but are a hated coalition of renegade Russians with the remnant of Russia's old territorial and ideological enemy, the Judaized Khazars, who for centuries refused to be assimilated either with the Russian people or with Western Christian civilization.

In view of the facts of history, from which this book has torn the curtain of censorship, it is reasonable to assume that the true Russian people are restive and bitter under the yoke and the goading of alien and Iscariot rule. To this almost axiomatic assumption there is much testimony. In his book *The Choice*, Boris Shub states that in Russia, "There is no true loyalty to Stalin-Beria-Malenkov in any significant segment of the party, the state, the army, the police, or the people." In *The Freeman* (November 13, 1950) Rodney Gilbert says in an article "Plan for Counter-Action": "Finally, there is a Soviet Russian home front, where we probably have a bigger force on our side than all the Western world could muster." According to the *Catholic World* (January, 1941): "The Russian mind being Christian bears no resemblance to the official mind of the Politburo." Likewise, David Lawrence (*U.S. News and World Report,* December 25, 1950) says: "We must first designate our real enemies. Our real enemies are not the peoples of Soviet Russia or the peoples of the so-called 'Iron Curtain Countries.'" In *Human Events* (March 28, 1951), the *Reader's Digest* Editor Eugene Lyons quotes the current *Saturday Evening Post* headline, "Our enemies are the Red Tyrants not their slaves," and with much documentation, as might be expected from one who was six years a foreign correspondent in the Soviet Union, reaches the conclusion that "the overwhelming majority of the Soviet peoples hate their rulers and dream of liberation from the Red yoke." So, finally, General Fellers testifies thus in his pamphlet "Thought War Against the Kremlin" (Henry Regnery Company, Chicago, 25 cents): "Russia, like the small nations under its heel, is in effect an occupied country." General Fellers recommended that our leaders should not "blame the Russian people for the peace-wrecking tactics of the Kremlin clique," but should make it clear that we "share the aspirations of the Russians for freedom." The general scoffs at the idea that such propaganda is ineffective: "From wartime results we know that effective broadcasts, though heard only by thousands, percolate to the millions. Countries denied freedom of press and speech tend to become huge whispering galleries; suppressed facts and ideas often carry farther than the official propaganda."

What an opportunity for all of our propaganda agencies, including the "Voice of America"! And yet there is testimony to the fact that our State Department has steadily refused suggestions that it broadcasts direct propaganda not against the Russian people but against their enslaving leaders. The "Voice," which is not heard in this country – at least not by the general public – is said to be in large part an unconvincing if not repelling air mosaic of American frivolities presented as an introduction to American "culture" – all to no purpose, except perhaps to preëmpt from service to this country a great potential propaganda weapon. The "Voice" appears also to have scant regard for the truth. For instance, a CTPS dispatch from Tokyo on April 13 (Washington *Times-Herald,* April 14, 1951) reported as follows:

> A distorted version of the world reaction to Gen. MacArthur's removal is being broadcast by the Voice of America, controlled by the State Department, a comparison with independent reports showed today.
>
> "Voice" listeners here got an impression of virtually unanimous approval of President Truman's action.

Sometimes the "Voice" is said actually to state to the enslaved Russian people that the United States has no interest in changing "the government or social structure of the Soviet Union." For carefully documented details, see the feature article, "Voice of America Makes Anti-Red Russians Distrust U.S., Serves Soviet Interests" in the *Williams Intelligence Summary* for June 1951 (P. O. Box 868, Santa Ana, California, 25¢ per copy, $3.00 per year [out of business. – *Ed., 1995*]).

Finally, it should be noted that in the summer of 1951, there was a secret testimony to the Senate Committees indicating "that Communist sympathizers have infiltrated the State Department's Voice of America programs" (AP dispatch in Richmond *Times-Dispatch*, July 10, 1951).

The apparently worse than useless "Voice of America" could, under a cleaned-up State Department, become quickly useful and powerful. We could use it to tell the Russian people that we know they were for centuries in the fold of Christian civilization and that we look forward to welcoming them back. We could say to the Russian people that we have nothing against them and have *under our laws* removed from our government leaders who for self-perpetuation in office or for other causes wanted a big foreign war. We could then invite Russian hearers of the broadcast to give thought to a similar step in their country. Such broadcasting, if it did not actually bring about the overthrow of the present rulers, would almost certainly give them enough concern to prevent their starting a war.

Such broadcasts also would pave the way to assistance from inside Russia in the tragic event that war should come. Broadcasts of the new type should begin quickly, for the Soviet leaders have a thought censorship, even as we have, and our task will be increasingly difficult as each month sees the death of older people who will know the truth of our broadcasts from personal pre-1917 experience.

(e)

The patriotic people of America should not lose hope. They should proceed with boldness, and joy in the outcome, for Right is on our side. Moreover, they are a great majority, and such a majority can make its will prevail any time it ceases to lick the boots of its captors.

One point of encouragement lies in the fact that things are not quite as bad as they were. Most patriotic people feel that their country is in the lowest depths in the early fifties.

Conditions were even worse, however, in 1944, and seems worse now only because the pro-American element in the country is prevailing to the extent, at least, of turning on a little light in dark places.

Unquestionably, 1944 was the most dangerous year for America. Our President and the civil and military coterie about him were busily tossing our victory to the Soviet Union. In November the dying President was elected by a frank and open coalition of the Democratic and Communist parties. The pilgrimage of homage and surrender to Stalin at Yalta (February, 1945) was being prepared. The darkest day was the black thirtieth of December when the Communists were paid off by the termination of regulations which kept them out of the Military Intelligence Service. The United States seemed dying of the world epidemic of Red fever.

But on January 3, 1945, our country rallied. The new Congress had barely assembled when Mr. Sabath of Illinois moved that the rules of the expiring Seventy-Eighth Congress be the rules of the Seventy-Ninth Congress. Thereupon, Congressman John Elliot Rankin, Democrat, of Mississippi, sprang to his feet and moved as an amendment that the expiring temporary Committee on Un-American Activities be made a permanent Committee of the House of Representatives.

Mr. Rankin explained the function of the proposed permanent committee as follows:

The Committee on Un-American Activities, as a whole or by subcommittee, is authorized to make from time to time investigations of (1) the extent, character, and objects of un-American propaganda activities in the United States, (2) the diffusion within the United States of subversive and un-American propaganda that is instigated from foreign countries or of a domestic origin and attacks the principle of the form of government as guaranteed by our Constitution, and (3) all other questions in relation thereto that would aid Congress in any necessary remedial legislation.

In support of his amendment to the Rules of the House, Mr. Rankin said:

The Dies Committee, or the Committee on Un-American Activities, was created in 1938. It has done a marvelous work in the face of all the criticism that has been hurled at its chairman and at its members. I submit that during these trying times the Committee on Un-American Activities has performed a duty second to none ever performed by any committee of this House.

Today, when our boys are fighting to preserve American institutions, I submit it is no time to destroy the records of that committee, it is no time to relax our vigilance. We should carry on in the regular way and keep this committee intact, and above all things, save those records.

Congressman Karl Mundt, Republican, of South Dakota, rose to voice his approval of the Rankin amendment. There was maneuvering against the proposal by Congressman Marcantonio of New York, Congressman Sabath of Illinois, and other congressmen of similar views, but Mr. Rankin, a skillful parliamentarian, forced a vote. By 208 to 186, with 40 not voting, the Rankin amendment was adopted and the Committee on Un-American Activities became a permanent Committee of the House of Representatives (all details

271

and quotations are from *Congressional Record*, House, January 3, 1945, pages 10-15 – pages which deserve framing in photostat, if the original is not available, for display in every school building and veterans' clubroom in America).

The American Communists and fellow-travelers were stunned. Apart from violence, however, there was nothing they could do. Moves made as "feelers" showed them they could get nowhere with their hoped-for uprising in the American South, almost all of whose people were patriotic Americans. Also, except for two widely separated and quickly dwindling incidents, they got nowhere with their plans for a revolt in the army. Despite its success at Yalta, and despite its continued influence with the American Administration, the Soviet moved more cautiously. The Rankin amendment gave the United States of America a chance to survive as a nation under its Constitution. Is it then to be wondered at that Mr. Rankin *has been subject to bitter reprisals ever since by Communists and fellow-travelers and their dupes?*

Though the Rankin amendment gave America its chance to live, the recovery has been slow and there have been many relapses. This book, *The Iron Curtain Over America*, has diagnosed our condition in the mid-century and has suggested remedies, the first of which must be a cleaning-out of the subversives in the executive departments and agencies in Washington. The degree of infestation by Communists, and those indifferent to or friendly to Communism, in our bureaucracy in Washington is staggering beyond belief. Details are increasingly available to those who study the publications of the congressional committees concerned with the problem.

"Communist Propaganda Activities in the United States," a report published early in 1952 by the Committee on the Judiciary, United States Senate, deals principally with *Communist propaganda carried on with the help of the Department of State and the Department of Justice of the United States!* The report (pp. v-ix) climaxes a stinging rebuke of the State Department's pro-Communist maneuvers with this statement:

> The policy of the Department of State is in effect an administrative nullification of an established law.

One result of the "nullification" of existing law was the dissemination in the United States in 1950 of more than 1,000,000 Communist books, magazines, and other printed documents, 2,275 Soviet films, and 25,080 phonograph records (pp. 24-25). By a special Department of Justice ruling these were dispatched individually "to state institutions, universities or colleges, or to professors or other individuals," with no statement required on or with any of the parcels that they were sent out for propaganda purposes or had emanated from the Soviet Union or other Communist government! Is this what the American people want? It is what they have been getting in Washington.

Following a removal of top leaders and their personal henchmen, there will be no reason for despair even for the departments of State and Defense. In the Department of State there are many whose records suggest treason, but there are also many workers of low and medium rank whose tenacious patriotism has in a number of instances prevented a sell-out of our country. These people will rally to a new leadership. The same is true in the Department of Defense. Except for a mere handful, committed to wrong-doing to cover their old sins of omission or commission, our generals and admirals, like all other ranks, have the good of their country at heart.

Disciplined by tradition to subordinate themselves to civilian authority, our General Staff officers pursue a hated policy from which there is for them no escape, for on one hand they do not wish to denounce the administration and on the other they see no end good for America in the strategically unsound moves they are ordered to make. Below the appointive ranks, the civilian personnel, both men and women, of such strategic agencies as Military Intelligence are with few exceptions devoted and loyal and competent Americans. With our top state and defense leadership changed, our policy shaped by patriots, our working level Department of Defense staff will be able to furnish a strategically sound program for the defense of this country, which *must stand* not only for us and our children but as the fortress of Western Christian civilization.

Meanwhile, patriotic State Department personnel face a ghastly dilemma. If they remain, they are likely to be thought of as endorsing the wrong policies of their superiors. If they resign, they are likely to see their positions filled by persons of subversive leanings. Fortunately for America, most of them have decided to stick to their posts and will be there to help their new patriotic superiors, after a clean-up has been effected.

A clean-up in our government will give a new life not only to patriotic Washington officials, civilian and military, but to our higher military and naval officers everywhere. Their new spirit will bring confidence to all ranks and to the American people. Once again, military service will be a privilege and an honor instead of, as at present to most people, a sentence to a period of slavery and possible death for a policy *that has never been stated* and cannot be stated, for it is at best vote-garnering, bureaucracy-building, control-establishing program of expediency.

A clean-out of our leftist-infected government will also have the great virtue of freeing our people from the haunting nightmare of fear. Fear will vanish with the Communists, the fellow-travelers, and the caterers to their votes. For America is essentially strong. In the words of General MacArthur in Austin:

> This great nation of ours was never more powerful ... it never had less reason for fear. It was never more able to meet the exacting

tests of leadership in peace or in war, spiritually, physically, or materially. As it is yet unconquered, so it is unconquerable.

The great general's words are true, *provided we do not destroy ourselves*.

Therefore, with their country's survival at heart, let all true Americans – fearing no political faction and no alien minority or ideology – work along the lines suggested in this book to the great end that all men with Tehran, Yalta, and Potsdam connections and all others of doubtful loyalty to our country and to our type of civilization be removed under law from policy-making and all other sensitive positions in our government. In that way only can a start be made toward throwing back the present tightly drawn iron curtain of censorship. In that way only can we avoid the continuing interment of our native boys beneath far-off white crosses, whether by inane blunderings or for sinister concealed purposes. In that way only can we save America.

ACKNOWLEDGMENTS

Since *The Iron Curtain Over America* developed out of many years of study, travel, and intelligence service, followed by a more recent period of intensive research and consultation with experts, the author is indebted in one way or another to hundreds of people.

First of all, there is a lasting obligation to his former teachers – particularly his tutors, instructors, and university professors of languages. The more exacting, and therefore the most gratefully remembered, are Sallie Jones, Leonidas R. Dingus, Oliver Holben, James S. McLemore, Thomas Fitz-Hugh, Richard Henry Wilson, C. Alphonso Smith, William Witherle Lawrence, George Philip Krapp, C. Pujadas, Joseph Delcourt, and Maurice Grammont. Some of these teachers required a knowledge of the history, the resources, the culture, and the ideals of the peoples whose language they were imparting. Their memories are green.

In the second place, the author is deeply obligated to M. Albert Kahn and to the six trustees of the American Albert Kahn Foundation – Edward Dean Adams, Nicholas Murray Butler, Charles D. Walcott, Abbott Lawrence Lowell, Henry Fairfield Osborn, and Henry Smith Pritchett – who chose him as their representative abroad for 1926-27. Without the accolade of these men, and the help of their distinguished Secretary, Dr. Frank D. Fackenthal, the author might not have found the way, a quarter of century later, to *The Iron Curtain Over America.*

In the third instance, the author owes, of course, a very great debt to the many men and women who were his fellow workers in the extensive field of strategic intelligence, and to those persons who came to his office for interview from all parts of the world. This obligation is not, however, for specific details, but for a general background of knowledge which became a guide to subsequent study.

To friends and helpers in several other categories, the author expresses here his deep obligation. A score or more of senators and congressmen gave him information, furthered his research, sent him needed government documents or photostats when originals were not available, introduced him to valuable contacts and otherwise rendered very important assistance. Certain friends who are university professors, eminent lawyers, and political analysts, have read and criticized constructively all or a part of the manuscript. The staffs of a number of libraries have helped, but the author has leant most heavily upon the Library of Congress, the Library of the University of Virginia, and above all the Library of Southern Methodist University, where assistance was always willing, speedy, and competent. Finally, four secretaries have been most patient and accurate in copying and recopying thousands of pages bristling with proper names, titles of books and articles, quotations, and dates.

For a special reason, however, the author will call the name of no one who has helped him since 1927. "Smears" and reprisals upon eminent persons become well known, but for one such notable victim, a thousand others in the government, in universities, and even in private citizenship, suffer indignities from arrogant minority wielders of the power of censorship and from their hirelings and dupes. Reluctantly, then, no personal thanks are here expressed. The author's friends know well his appreciation of their help, and will understand.

To all the works cited and to all the authorities quoted in *The Iron Curtain Over America*, the author owes a debt which he gratefully acknowledges. For the use of copyrighted excerpts over a few lines in length, he has received the specific permission of authors and publishers, and takes pleasure in extending thanks to the following: *The American Legion Magazine* and National Commander (1950-1951) Earle Cocke, Jr.; Professor Harry Elmer Barnes; Mr. Bruce Barton and the King Features Syndicate; The Christophers; the *Clover Business Letter;* Duell, Sloan, and Pearce, Inc.; *The Freeman;* The Embassy of Lebanon; *Human Events; The New York Times; The Tablet;* The Universal Jewish Encyclopedia Company, Inc.; The Washington *Daily News;* and the Washington *Times-Herald.* Further details including the titles and names of authors are given on the appropriate pages, in order that those interested may know how to locate the cited work, whether for purchase or perusal in a library.

Two newspapers and two magazines deserve especial thanks. Because of a full coverage of news and the verbatim reprinting of official documents, the current issues and the thoroughly indexed bound or on microfilmed back numbers of the *New York Times* were essential in the preparation of *The Iron Curtain Over America.* The Washington *Times-Herald* was obligatory reading, too, because of its coverage of the Washington scene, as well as the international scene, with fearless uncensored reporting. After careful checking for accuracy and viewpoint, both the *American Legion Magazine* and *Foreign Service,* the magazine of the Veterans of Foreign Wars, have published feature articles by the author in the general field of the United States-Soviet relations. Dedicated as it is to those veterans who gave their lives, *The Iron Curtain Over America* may be considered as a token of gratitude to our two great organizations of veterans for personal introductions to their five million patriotic readers.

To one and all, then – to publishers, to periodical, and to people who have helped – to the dead as well as to the living – to the few who have been named and to the many who must remain anonymous – and finally to his readers, most of whom he will never know except in the spiritual kinship of a great shared mission of spreading the Truth, the author says thank you, from the bottom of his heart!

John Owen Beaty
(1890–1961)

The author of *The Iron Curtain Over America* has written, or collaborated on, a dozen books. His texts have been used in more than seven hundred colleges and universities, and his historical novel, *Swords in the Dawn*, published originally in New York, had London and Australian editions, and was adopted for state-wide use in the public schools of Texas. His education (M.A., University of Virginia; Ph.D., Columbia University; post-graduate study, University of Montpellier, France), his travel in Europe and Asia, and his five years with the Military Intelligence Service in World War II rounded out the background for the reading and research (1946–1951), which resulted in *The Iron Curtain Over America*.

INDEX

Augean Statler of The Union Natic

<u>Department of State</u>

Representon / America / UN
relations / leadership
ps 265

Haiti

7
1
8 → 17 → 42
17
8
___

24

Arabesque

1̶5̶   32
1   20 → 55
2̶   3
1̶6̶   ___
1̶0̶
1